The Theory of Language Holog

Guanlian Qian

The Theory of Language Holography

Guanlian Qian
Guangdong University of Foreign Studies
Guangzhou, China

Translated by
Lin Zhang
College of Foreign Languages
Qufu Normal University
Qufu, Shandong, China

ISBN 978-981-16-2041-6 ISBN 978-981-16-2039-3 (eBook)
https://doi.org/10.1007/978-981-16-2039-3

Jointly published with Shanghai Translation Publishing House
The print edition is not for sale in China (Mainland). Customers from China (Mainland) please order the print book from: Shanghai Translation Publishing House.

Translation from the Chinese language edition: 语言全息论 by Guanlian Qian, and Lin Zhang, © Shanghai Translation Publishing House 2016. Published by The Commercial Press. All Rights Reserved.

This Springer imprint is published by the registered company Springer Nature Singapore Pte Ltd.
The registered company address is: 152 Beach Road, #21-01/04 Gateway East, Singapore 189721, Singapore

Preface

The considerations and explications of phonetic forms amount to phonetics, those of the relationship between linguistic signs (the signifier) and the objects to which they refer (the signified) to semantics, those of the syntagmatic relations between signs to syntax, and those of the relationship between language signs and their users (the explicators) to pragmatics.

What considerations and explications, then, amount to *The Theory of Language Holography* in front?

It is a consideration of the properties and theory of language by virtue of the law of biology holography, the law of cosmos holography and of the system theory. People might ask, since the properties and theory of language are already the products of considerations and explications, and are already thoughts, isn't the consideration of them the thought of thought, the consideration of consideration? The answer is Yes. The thought of thought, or the consideration of consideration, is a philosophy. This work can be read as a philosophical one. Taking language as the title notwithstanding, it however excavates world structure (the cosmos, reality, substance, Being, and the like), language and human beings, and the relations between them. It is on account of these that I decide that this book is philosophical. In the last chapter (The Conclusion), it is thus said: "Western philosophers are so devoted to language analysis merely because language (its structure, reference, meaning, etc.) enables them to see the world, and the structure of linguistic substances can reveal the structure of the reality, and hence the age-old philosophical problems left by ontology and epistemology can be settled, e.g., What is there?" Whereas Western philosophy performed linguistic turn and headed towards the philosophy of language after the two long, long road of ontology and epistemology, the theory of language holography comes into being directly from sciences (the law of biology holography, the law of cosmos holography, and the system theory), and hence it is also a sort of linguistic philosophy.

TheTheory of Language Holography considers about various properties and theories of language by means of the law of biology holography, the law of cosmos holography, and the system theory. It happens that a Modestae School in the Middle Ages believed that "When it can be demonstrated that there is a certain connection between the laws of nature and the inner laws of language, linguistic phenomena could be interpreted." I am doing this homework: to interpret linguistic phenomena by virtue of the laws of nature.

You the readers will find that this book is theoretically based on the law of biology holography, the theory of cosmic holographic unity, and the system theory. Some might ask: since the theory of language holography is based on the law of biology holography, the law of cosmos holography, and the system theory, if the former two were wrong, would not the whole theoretical construction of the theory of language holography collapse accordingly? It is not the first time that such a question is raised. Some once asked: When the first axiom on which the whole Euclidean geometry relies were wrong, would not all the following deductions get ruined? There might have been thousands and hundreds of people who thought about and raised this question, mathematics however has never been ruined by the several crises in its history; rather, it has been striding on the road for development. All the sciences develop and advance in challenges and, I think, there are mainly two causes.

In the first place, also the fundamental one, the top interest of sciences is not to maintain some conclusion to the end but to provoke wisdom and grasp other problems by analogy during the process of investigation. It is always an honor in the history of sciences to overthrow a determined conclusion accepted for long. It is my contention that theoretical discussion is per se an intellectual game. It is not that important whether or not the conclusions of some theory are correct (which can be examined by practices); rather, that which is more important is the process of exploration during which various unpredictable and indeterminable intellectual discoveries are more wonderful, important, and significant than the conclusions themselves. This has been demonstrated by innumerable processes of scientific research. If, in the future, there should be someone who can point out the flaws of this book, even deconstruct it, I would not feel ashamed, nor would I feel destroyed; but rather, wisdom at various levels (also unlimited theoretical joys) would surely be discovered during the process of subverting and being subverted between the two parties of the discussion which, ultimately, would promote the development of the discipline.

In the second place, the "presumption of innocence" is taken into consideration. In the sphere of law, you are not allowed to presume that a suspect is guilty. Anyone accused before legal investigations, public trial, court defense, and determination should be considered as innocent. Facts determine everything. In this connection, as to whether or not the law of biology holography is correct, we should make sure whether or not the relationships between organisms are de facto holographic. The same holds to the law of cosmos holography. So far, to my finite knowledge, I remain to find some materials telling that the relationships between organisms or those between things in the cosmos are not holographic. Mr. Wang Zongyan correctly said, "Those who are engaged in academic studies are supposed to be tolerant, and to permit different ideas to be published, and there is not the necessity to give any conclusion before the facts become clear."[1]

---

[1]Wang. Zongyan, My fifty years of working with chalks and oil lamp. In *Foreign Languages in Fujian*, 2001, 1.

Some of Wilhelm Humboldt's suggestions with respect to the methods of language research are a case in point. He believes that dynamic methods are supposed to be employed to study language. Therefore, I cite and comment on his ideas as such in section 3 of Chapter 2 of this book, namely "The methodology (of the theory of language holography)":

"To grasp the essence of language and make comparisons between many languages, our investigation into language must all the time set its sights on its lived functions....Any facet relevant to language can only be compared to the physiological process rather than the anatomical one; there is no static thing whatsoever in language, and it is dynamic (dynamisch) toto coelo."[2]I am delighted to find that the functional grammar prevailing around the world "sets its sights on" the "lived functions" of sentence components, pragmatics is nothing other than the dynamic study of language's functions, and "it is dynamic toto coelo". It can be seen how accurate Humboldt's prediction at his time was. This offers an inspiration to us: **the discoveries of language's methodology and the innovations of its research methods will provoke a revolutionary progress in linguistics**. To this connection, we may as well consider the theory of language holography as a methodology since it provides a brand new perspective to us on observing language. From this perspective, we can: (1) find or discover some new important properties of language, say, the holographibility of language, viz., the law of language holography, and hence it is not an illusion that the sense of sound appears in foregone generations, and the like; (2) find the source of the various inherent properties of language and various linguistic theories—the holographic and uniform relationship among things in the cosmos. Language is merely a subsystem of the cosmos. We have no reason to affirm that it is the "ultimate" source, but I believe that it has indeed found a satisfactory locus for the various language properties and linguistic theories.

I remain to know what the statements in this book would bring to the world. The net of the cosmos and that of language agree, coincide, and tally with each other in every aspect, weaving the lives, human life, and human body called "human" all together. This is an epic pertinent to the cosmos, human body, and language. The statement as such depicts a prospect of the unified and satisfactory location of them. It never arrives in sudden fashion. Elbert Einstein once said with amazement, "The world's most confusing thing is, it is understandable". He felt it amazing that his simple and pretty formulas were so perfectly coincident with the real world. So do the cosmic structure and the linguistic one. A scholar correctly notes, "The plurality in sciences and the universality of exploring the world are two different blades of the sword of cognition the lack of either of which will make us superficial and easily satisfiable. The thorough pluralism is itself supposed to tolerate those who are against it. The history shows, it seems, that virtually all the great progresses of human beings in the sphere of rational sciences are due to the fact that they have found: the interconnections between the seemingly independent aspects of the world; the fact

[2]Cf. Wilhelm von Humboldts,*Whihelm von Humboldts Gesammelte Schriften. Wilhelm Richter, Berlin;* photomechanischer Nachdruck Berlin, 1968.

that all the initial points of departure result from the dissatisfaction with the split established realities."[3]

Now I publish this purely interpretative work in which I employ the method of deduction not commonly used in Chinese linguistic sphere. A question then arises: what is the usage (we have been accustomed to asking what the usage is when we are faced with any theory) of it since it can neither bring any help to language teaching nor provide any benefit to the economic construction and market development? It happens that someone's (also on behalf of a government) solemn declaration can answer this question.

In the editorial (Chinese version according to the Xinhua News Agency, July 2, 2000) written by Jiang Zemin to *Science* the American journal, he thus says, "Chinese government supports scientists to perform fundamental researches on the premise of the combination of national needs and scientific frontiers, respects their particular sensitivity and creative spirit, and encourages them to make 'investigations driven by their curiosity'". It is the first time in the history of Chinese culture and thoughts that a government made so solemn a commitment on such an occasion. It can be said that this is the sciences' spring in the true sense of the word. When true words are given from above, there will surely be responses from below. The fact proved this: in the Fourth National Academic Seminar of China Association for Comparative Studies of English and Chinese (hosted by Xiamen University), Yang Zijian the then president thus said in the opening address: "True scientific studies are supposed not to completely take application as the ultimate goal but to follow the principle of 'truth for truth's sake, and knowledge for knowledge's sake'. That is to say, human beings should recognize and interpret this world by dint of their own reason." If possible, this book of mine can really be labeled as "a study driven by the curiosity". In effect, it is this epoch—the steady development of the economic and cultural construction over two decades after "the Cultural Revolution", notably the situation of developing the country through science and education and technological innovation upheld in the past couple of years—that provoked the birth of such theoretical works with philosophical properties.

Presumably, this book has merely finished a homework. As was presented by Saussure, "The second task of linguistics is to discover a force functioning eternally and universally in all the languages, and to analyze the universal law, namely the law that can generalize all the specific historical phenomena."[4]The title is offered by Saussure, and I merely finish a homework. I even dare not expect that it can pass the test.

Those professors who have read parts of the book and offered me constructive amendments are: Xu Shenghuan, Zhou Haizhong, Wu Tieping, Zhang Jin, Zhang Houchen, and Wang Mingchu. Prof. Li Xiyin answered my questions in time; Zhou

[3]Zhao. Nanyuan, Cognitive Sciences and General Evolution Theory. Tsinghua University Press, 1994. p.150.

[4]Ferdinand de Saussure, 1857-1913, *Cours de linguistique générale. Course in General Linguistics* (1916), Eds. C. Bally and A.. Sechehaye, Revised English Edition, Collins (1974). Also cf. Liu. Runqing (ed.), *Schools of Linguistics*, Beijing: Foreign Language Teaching and Research Press, 1997. p.94.

Huanqin an assistant professor of Beijing Language and Culture University collected materials for me; despite the risk in market, the Commercial Press supported the publication of such a work that can bring no profit; Dr. Feng Huaying the editor-in-charge of this book did so much specific work for its publication; the National Key Research Base of Liberal Arts and the research office of our university funded this book; some doctor candidates helped to find problems of the book on my request; and, at last, Prof. Gui Shichun who was so busy with his own studies and the direction of the construction of our Base spared his time to read my book before writing a preface to it (in addition, my student Huo Yongshou helped to check the whole book). For all of them, I have deep respect.

To be sure, scientific study is a course accomplishable via the individual's efforts, it is all the more a course of society and nation. I give these remarks at the moment when our airspace is invaded by the United States (their bombardment of our Embassy in Yugoslavia is still fresh in my memory) not without the hope that it can provoke the awareness of self-improvement, self-alertness, and self-propulsion of our Chinese scientists and humanists as well as our nation.

First draft completed in November 3, 1999; the third revision completed in April 8, 2001.

Guangzhou, China Guanlian Qian

Prelude

There is the web of the cosmos over our heads which we saw, and of which we thought.
There is, also, the web of language over ours which none saw, and of which none thought.
The two webs are de facto harmonious, coincident, and fused with one another everywhere.
Both weave our lives and our lifetime.
And both weave human body named "human".

—This is an epic pertaining to the cosmos, human body, and language.

—The author

Along with the advancement of modern sciences, scientists begin to observe language from various perspectives such as sociology, psychology, computer science, and the like, which has greatly enlarged people's horizon. In this vein, linguistics should not be wedded to the conventional bonds. Qian Guanlian implemented this idea. He is industrious on thinking, courageous on studying, and brave on presenting new ideas. *The Theory of Language Holography* is a book deserving recommendation in that clichés are seldom read in it; but rather, this book is characterized by academic explorations after the author's contemplations. Presumably, not every reader would appreciate all the viewpoints in this book, but no one can easily ignore them. Instead, the questions raised by the author merit everyone's meticulous consideration and pondering, and down-to-earth exploration and investigation.

—Gui Shichun

Contents

Part I
Introduction

Chapter 1
Introduction: The Harmony of the Cosmos, Human Body, and Language

Abstract Readers of *Aesthetic Linguistics* will find that the content in the first three sections of this chapter are familiar. Why, then, do I repeat them? This is because I raised a question in that book but remained to offer the answer—there is a sort of seemingly mysterious harmony between language structure and the cosmos. This book is the answer as such. On this account, to tell the original progress is the readers' demand (or else there would not be the possibility for the present discussions to come into force), it is also my responsibility and, all the more, it accords with the academic norms (since in the academic history, one's thought forever comes down in one continuous line). This apart, I could not introduce the new conclusion of the present book without giving the aforementioned facts first. Just as was said by Hu Shi, "Insofar as one writes books and sets up one's own philosophy, there is always a system with which his thought and theories accord, and there cannot be great conflicts in it" (Hu Shi, Outline of the history of Chinese philosophy. Shanghai Classics Publishing House, Shanghai, 2000, p. 15). To readers remaining to read *Aesthetic Linguistics*, whereas, this chapter might be fairly interesting.

Keywords The theory of language holography · The cosmos · Human body · Language · Holography · Dynamic balance-structure · Harmony

1 The Questions Unanswered in *Aesthetic Linguistics*

What is the relationship between the theory of language holography and aesthetic linguistics? Why is aesthetic linguistics concerned here? The answer is, I remain to give the answers to the core questions raised by the author when he was engaged in constructing aesthetic linguistics, namely, "Why does language run in rhyme as does the natural macro cosmos?", and "Why is the cosmos' beauty manifested in the same way as language's?" Now I can see that the ultimate answer lies in the theory of language holography. In this connection, to find the whole trajectory of the theory of language holography discovered by the author, this book needs to start from the gestation of aesthetic linguistics.

When I was immersed in reading Xu Jimin's *The History of Scientific Aesthetics* (hereafter referred to as *Aesthetic History*), my heart palpated with excitement. At the

G. Qian, *The Theory of Language Holography*,
https://doi.org/10.1007/978-981-16-2039-3_1

moment when my consciousness wandered in the air and my thought soared freely, I intuited, by virtue of the frame of senses of my native language and a couple of foreign languages deposited in my mind, that all the laws and rules of the cosmos's beauty described in that book can be mirrored in language structure. The gestation of this thought can be traced back to 1988.

It was an intuition, a hazy one. Fortunately, intuition is tolerable at the initial stage of scientific creation. As a rule, that which is initially provoked before many scientists make creations and inventions is also nothing but a little intuition. With regard to the history of scientific aesthetics, *Aesthetic History* performs systematic elucidations the coverage of which runs from the periods of ancient Greece, ancient Rome, ancient China, the Middle Ages of Europe, and the middle ages of China, via those of modern renaissance, Newton, Kant-Laplace, Darwin-Maxwell, and modern times of China, to those of the thoughts of modern scientific aesthetics, say, the periods of Einstein, DNA, modern China (Yang Zhenning, Li Zhengdao, and Wu Jianxiong's researches on the symmetric beauty of the cosmos), and so forth. Albeit these cases of the development of scientific aesthetics cannot be immediately connected with language, the fundamental properties of scientific aesthetics' thoughts they follow tally with and correspond to, in an intermittent or vague fashion (the connection with ordinary speeches remains to be sensed at the beginning), the levels of language structure. The rather indefinite coincidence and correspondence as such was finally figured out into the fundamental properties of the thought of scientific aesthetics: the cosmos' beauty is accepted; the manifestation of the cosmos' beauty is order and harmony; the unity of rational cognition and intuition of aesthetic perception is stressed; the unity of the macro and the micro cosmoses is stressed, and so on and so forth.

Apparently, not each one of the above fundamental properties can get embodied in language structure, some fundamental concepts of scientific aesthetics however undoubtedly guided me to figure out a new discipline resulting from the overlapping of aesthetics and linguistics—a monograph entitled *Aesthetic Linguistics*. To be frank, the initial exploration is nothing but analogy. We can hardly evade from this initial stage. The analogy as such is by no means a slavish imitation. Its benefit is enabling us to enter deeply into two facts, namely, the two stages of $1 + 1$. The stage of $1 + 1 = 2$ is merely one whence analogy is performed and facts are added but no new thing is generated. As to whether or not an abstract or a creation can be developed afterwards, it is the business of a higher stage, viz., the stage of $1 + 1 = 3$.

Nonetheless, what is used to perform the analogy? What can act as the reagent? Some fundamental concepts of scientific aesthetics need to be selected, say, unity, multiplicity, simplicity, complexity, order and harmony and integration, symmetry, beauties of form and content and conservation, and so on and so forth. The fundamental aesthetic laws and regularities surely have their projections in the whole material and spiritual worlds. Well, since we have vaguely sensed from the materials of the several languages in our mind the embodiment of the fundamental aesthetic concepts, why can't we unfold language structure layer by layer hence make an exhaustive investigation? As was expected, in virtue of this investigation, we discovered the aesthetic selections at each structure and level of language (see Chapter 3 of that book). They are: sign—communicative channel—language variety—type of writing—type of communication—speech act—speech sounds—word—sentence—discourse. At each level, we identify one by one some fundamental rules and laws of scientific aesthetics. Sometimes, symmetry is sensed amidst detailed classifications, conservation amidst thorough analyses; sometimes, the levels are harmonious with one another and keep self-perfection and self-sufficiency, which brings pleasant surprise to people who might then even forget themselves.

Analogy is merely a half of the work. The more important half is abstraction, namely, the generalization of the universal law from among the facts. The general laws obtained after ten layers of analogy are language aesthetic selections. "**Language aesthetic selection**" is of two implications: (1) In all the speech events and speech acts, people will always select the speech form catering for the dynamic balance of their own lives and arousing pleasant senses of beauty. This refers to the speech qua the uttered individual "parole"; (2) All the structures and layers of language are constructed by people according to the aesthetic laws and intents. This appertains to language, the "language" existing qua a system, namely, the ten layers mentioned afore. It should be said that language's aesthetic selection is one of the polar theories of aesthetic linguistics, the other being the properties and laws (mainly the strategy to pursue beauty) of the beauty of speech.

After we settle the question, or differently put, whether or not language structure and layers are coincident with aesthetic laws, we are faced with the biggest question: how can the ordinary language and individual speech acts become the aesthetic objects? This whip of bafflement was all the time hung there during the whole process of my writing *Aesthetic Linguistics.* Apparently, this is a primary question concerned with whether or not aesthetic linguistics can become a "theory." As is noted in *Aesthetic History*, "The growing point at the level of the combination of aesthetics and natural sciences is supposed to be the objective beauty in natural phenomena." In language system, the beauty as such can be reified into two specific seeking processes: first, can the objective beauty be sensed in all the structures and each level of language? Secondly, can the objective beauty also be sensed in ordinary language? The first process has ended with the finding, via analogy, of aesthetic selection in terms of language structure and levels. That which is currently at stake is the second process.

How can ordinary language become an aesthetic object? We need start from relevant phenomena.

The first phenomenon is, one is supposed to say pleasant words. "Say pleasant words" has gone far beyond—albeit also embraced—the utilitarian purpose of pleasing the hearer by virtue of pleasant words. "The pleasant," viz., "pleasant words," is de facto that which expresses the fundamental properties of **the beauty of speech**, and that which expresses the various strategies of speech's law of seeking beauty (see Chapter 5). The fundamental properties of the beauty of speech are as follows: (1) the utterer selects appropriate utterances in an appropriate context, namely, the arrangement of the utterances are coincident with both social and discourse backgrounds (contexts); (2) the utterer selects exquisite rhymes and proper rhythms in terms of language form, namely, he/she selects the utterances coincident with the law of the beauty of form to express the matters. In the strict sense, "pleasant words" conforms to these two meanings. As was recalled by Xin Fengxia[1] a famous Pingju Opera actress, a speech event once happened to Laoshe: when he visited the actors at the backstage of the theatre, he said, "The Beijingers are accustomed to taking a morning wander (*liuzao* 遛早), saying hello to one another (*wenhao* 问好), filling the stomach (*chibao* 吃饱), and then enjoying being a *Tianqiao*[2] stroller (*guangguang-Tianqiao* 逛逛天桥)." Yang Xingxing replied, "*Tianqiao* is a wonder (*hǎo* 好)! You can listen to the storytelling, watch the Beijing Opera, and look on the conjuring tricks, and there are also circuses and innumerable foreign drummers and trumpeters (*yangguyanghào* 洋鼓洋号); you can enjoy the *Quyi* 曲艺,[3] *Dagu* 大鼓[4] and ancient *Lianhualào* 莲花落[5]; you can also choose your meal from among quick-scalded tripe, hotpot, braised pork, pot meat, braised mutton, etc., which will cost you no more than two *máo* 毛.[6]" Needless to say, the two persons' utterances are the selected proper ones in proper contexts. I myself also experienced such a speech event: a professor of Hunan Normal University generalized his attitude toward seeking a quota of people for professor as follows: first, I don't expect much; secondly, I won't make trouble; thirdly, I want the professional title." These utterances are not that rhymed, they however are sonorous and forceful at the level of rhythm. Since they are uttered in privacy, the proper context is no more a problem. In addition, the utterances are not without the flavor of satire, which shows that the aesthetic choice was made naturally and at will. "Saying pleasant words" is one of man's pursuits of meaning, also a pursuit of aesthetic taste. It is aimed at harmonious interpersonal relations, but it is also a psychological remedy for "inappropriate" topics. Moreover, one cannot but say pleasant words. May I ask: outside the context in which one is faced with one's rivals, is there any one who speaks for the sake of tormenting others?

The second phenomenon is, there is a musical inclination in one's speech activities. "People are all the time trying every means to 'make into music' the vocal language sequences. Even when they fail to make music, they will try to make the voices pleasant to the ear, and their rhythms harmonious. This phenomenon can be called 'the musical inclination of speech sounds.'"[7] What is the rationale for the inclination as such? Calling, one of the early means of commodity advertisement, sings the words of sale—it is of weak as well as strong beats, being mild and continuous like flowing clouds, which is qualified for an important "fossil-like" evidence that language can be an aesthetic object, and that the most primary and most natural speech activities are inclined to music. There are other evidences: singing what you

[1]Cf. "Laose treated friends to malt sugar ball". In *Tuanjie Dao*, 1990, 01, 24.

[2]A marketplace-like place where Beijing's traditional culture is properly displayed.

[3]Chinese folk art forms including ballad singing, story telling, comic dialogues, clapper talks, cross talks, etc.

[4]A sort of storytelling with drum accompaniment.

[5]A popular folk song sung to the accompaniment of the castanets. Its name is usually about lotus.

[6]Two *jiao* 角, equal to 0.2 *yuan* 元 RMB.

[7]Qian (1993. p. 42).

want to say (I once encountered such an old man in a village of the Tujia nationality of western Hubei), singing in antiphonal style, substituting songs for orders (which were originally used to unify people's paces and to organize their productive processes), accompanying actions with songs (e.g., crying for being married, beating funeral drums, holding beam-raising ceremony, hunting, picking tea-leaves, pulling out weeds, laboring, billing and cooing, or the like), boatmen's work songs, heavy work songs, declaring war with a song (In Southern Africa, there is an aboriginal race called Zulu. When the Zulu people declare war on the enemy, they sing the declaring words sonorously and orderly at the front, one hand holding the long spear, the other the shield, before making war and shedding blood.), matching the rowing of dragon boat with ballads, Chinese monks chanting the scriptures, Western churches singing hymns, the impromptu poetry antiphonal reciting, the monkey juggler directing the monkey by singing, the master of the wedding ceremony singing aloud various orders, the converting of breathe into singing in India Yoga (According to the report of *Yangcheng Evening News* of August 8, 1991, in the headquarter of India Yoga, accompanied by the orchestra, the songs reverberated deeply with a male and a female singing alternatively. Singing is a part of the Yoga practices, a musicalized "exhale-inhale skill."), performing (singing de facto) the drinkers' wager game, and the fact that the spacecraft "Voyager II" went to call the extraterrestrial beings with greetings in 60 languages and 27 musical compositions[8] (The natural alliance of utterance and music has become a bridge connecting human beings and the cosmos). Still more evidences can be given.

The third phenomenon is, beauty-seeking strategies are constantly employed. Language's law (strategy) of beauty-seeking is: to correspond to the utterer at the level of rhyme and rhythm in accordance with the aesthetic melody, and converge with him/her. This is an intentional act of beauty-seeking, and the strategy employed during the process is the beauty-seeking law. Many an example for this law can be found: When Mao Zedong led his army to fight in northern Shaanxi, they once settled in Tianjiawan village at night. The landlady said once and again nervously, "The cave dwelling is too small, the place is too small, so I am sorry for you the chief." Mao Zedong murmured along with the landlady's rhythm, "Our troops are too many, our people are too many, so I am sorry for you the sister."[9] This dialogue is an excerpt from a true record (rather than from a novel), and the answerer said so as a result of being driven by the law of beauty-seeking. The law as such can be divided into two levels. The first level is the law of formal beauty. The law of formal beauty defines that sentence patterns are in good order, the rhythms are adjusted and the utterances are rhymed. It is sometimes manifested in the law of deviation (temporary deviation from beauty), which is a sort of variation of the normal language form, being wonderful and interesting. The second level is the offering of images (and the change-seeking of meaning, speaking vernacular, speaking with implied meanings, mobilizing the good vibrations of the sense organs, antiphrasis collision, and so on). For instance, in *Nanfang Daily* (1991), a reporter thus depicted the situation

---

[8]Etd. and Trans. Yu (1989).

[9]Quan (1989).

of low work efficiency at that time: "At present, when some matter is handled, it is like many crabs are put in one basket where they claw one another as a result of which no one can move." The beauty shown by this vivid picture is the beauty of image rather than that of language form. A big question then arises: when "image" is introduced into aesthetic linguistics, we go back to general aesthetics. Language then becomes an aesthetic media rather than an object. What is to be done? If we abandon this part, it means that we deny an evident linguistic fact: in human life, there are such utterances that can evoke the image of beauty but remain to have the properties of formal beauty. When creating images, they as an aesthetic media coincide naturally with the language in literary works without previous consultation. Literary aesthetics nevertheless is incapable of covering such utterances since they are not the dialogues between the characters in literary works but the true ones in authentic daily life. Therefore, we cannot study the beauty as such in the sphere of literary aesthetics. Our way out is to separate the beauty of such utterances from the first level of linguistic beauty and call it the second level of the beauty of speech, but keep the study of it within aesthetic linguistics. This separation never means that we are asking for trouble since it is really a truth that language can be both an object and a media of aesthetics. It is my contention that this separation well classifies aesthetic linguistics and literary aesthetics (particularly literature), but it also well encompasses the beauty in ordinary speech acts.

Is there beauty in "middling" utterances? Is there beauty in abusive language? To be frank, these two "bombs" can virtually destroy the proposition of "Individual speech acts can be an aesthetic object." Take the middling utterances as the first example. In early years, there were such warning labels in Guangzhou's buses: "Three *jiao* for aboard ticket, three *yuan* for no ticket." Originally, "three *jiao* for one ticket" is already clear on meaning, and hence "aboard" (*shangche* 上车) is redundant information, but what caused the addition of the two syllables of "aboard"? Apparently, it was intentionally done so for the sake of keeping identical with the following six syllables, namely, "three yuan for no ticket" (This is the ultimate aim of making this label: to remind the passengers that they would be fined for buying no ticket), so as to obtain the effect of ordered rhythms. Such cases are innumerable in oral activities. The problem would be simplified if we said that there is no beauty in abusive language. Needless to say, abusive language hurts, so the whole society is obligated to reproach such behaviors. Be that as it may, when the linguist deals with linguistic problems, he is not supposed to be concerned with ethic or moral factors. In the eyes of the linguist, even abusive language might have aesthetic values. The crux is whether or not the language as such is coincident with the context (time, place, humane environment, or something). Even bandits and gangsters pay attention to smooth reading and rhymes when speaking. On October 1, 1949, when the national flag was raised at Tian'anmen Square in Beijing, there were two gentlemen in Guangzhou quarreling with each other. It turned out to be that Jiang Jieshi and Li Zongren were settling the old grudges. Jiang persuaded Li to escape by crossing the Taiwan Strait. Mr. Li stroke the table and said, "The bastard would go to Taiwan!"[10]

[10]Cf. the TV documentary "Centurial Trip".

This might be an oath: Were I to go to Taiwan, I would be a bastard. It might also be a curse: If you were to go there, you would be a bastard. In terms of the latter condition, it becomes a curse from the deputy to the head. "Bastard" is the harshest curse among the rich and wealthy people. When Mr. Li spoke, the table was also stroke (striking the table is attributable to "accompanying symbol ray interfering the utterances"), which is an "accompany." Just imagine: when [ba2-s-tard4] ([*wang*2-*ba-dan*4] [王 2-八-蛋 4]) is accompanied by the noise of the palm striking the table, the situation and scene, the sound and rhyme, and the noise and voice, and the like, can be said composing a historic melody. Are there utterances containing no beauty, even scandals? Of course yes, and there are not a few. Pure beauty only exists in recognition, and the beauty in real life is forever mixed, containing both positive and negative factors. The beauty of speech is no exception, being the mixture of positive and negative factors. Scandal is also a research object of aesthetic linguistics, and it will not hinder ordinary speech from becoming an aesthetic object.

2 Human Body: The Conditions Ready for the Status of the Inner Language Holography vs the Outer Language Holography

Then, what is human in essence? Only when this question is investigated in detail and a proper answer is given, can we know why human makes aesthetic choices as regards language, why he/she intends to say pleasant words, why musical tendency is produced in speech acts, and why beauty-seeking strategies are constantly employed.

Presumably, we are supposed to start from dissipative structure (presented by Belgian scholar I. Prigogine). This structure is particularly characterized by acting as a counterweight to the second law of thermodynamics dominating all the physical and chemical facts. According to this law, in any isolated system, there is a tendency that kinetic energy is always decreasing. This is an irreversible process which will ultimately lead the cosmos to dead silence. This notwithstanding, the dissipative structure is of the property of resisting the overall death. Where does the resisting energy come from? First, it is constantly absorbed from outside; secondly, the structure itself constantly exhales the old and inhales the new, and, as a result, the process of exchanging energy with the outside world is accomplished. Meanwhile, this structure keeps a steady and ordered state. It always keeps a state of non-equilibrium, an always circulating and moving state.

Human is a dissipative structure, and that is why he/she can effectively resist death by means of the life's non-equilibrium. This conclusion is already jointly corroborated by human anatomy, physiology, and life science.

Can human be transferred from corporeal dynamic balance to a higher level, viz., mental dynamic balance? The answer is yes. Large quantities of facts prove that human's ever-changing mental life is de facto also a dynamically balancing structure. It seems that the constituents of human's mental life is of two aspects: one is characterized by struggles, conflicts, and sufferings, and the other by perfection, harmony, and tranquility when a limited goal is attained. When is human's happiness produced? The moment when a limited goal is attained, happiness is indeed produced. Nevertheless, the more important part of happiness is connected with the whole process of dynamic balance. The process wherein human pursues pleasure and happiness is endless.

The fact exactly expected by aesthetic linguistics encompasses mental dynamic balance and speech's creation for novelty and beauty. Modern language studies show that human speech act (doing things by means of language) is also a mental process, and the property of resisting death and keeping far away from absolute balance is necessarily reflected in it. This reflection is the endless pursuit of the creative happiness and aesthetic enjoyment in speech acts. To pursue beauty, one will endlessly make choices in speech acts. As a natural result of the choices, he/she obtains the articulatory system, lexical system, sentence structure, and discourse composition that can meet the aesthetic requirements relatively and to a certain extent. The individual also makes endless choices in his/her speech acts and, as a natural result, he/she obtains the linguistic habit in terms of pronunciation, vocabulary, sentence, and discourse that inherits his/her mother tongue system and has its particular style as well, and meets his/her own aesthetic requirements. This creative tendency seeking novelty and beauty—the award for creation is the aesthetic enjoyment—is nothing else than the lived manifest of the mental dynamic balance. People's new styles of wording when speaking, their repetition of the new variation of some word, and the like, are all creations. As it were, creation is both the development of old capacities and the generation of the new ones. The fundamental capacity of any sort of life is to seek an opportunity to manifest itself. Manifestation is life insomuch as the manifestation of life capacity is all the time accompanied by vitality and happiness. The bits and pieces of new attempt and new creation of one's usage of language are a part of his/her life. When the individual is using language, the life's expressive desire is manifested in his/her constantly creating acts.

The base sequence inside human body requires phonetic harmony. When inputting the genetic code of a sort of coliform into the computer terminal, Japanese scholars Takesi Hayasi and Nobuo Munakata designated each base letter with a musical note:

G for "2" (re), C for "3" (mi), T for "5" (so)...

When the melody made according to this base sequence was played, a beautiful tune was obtained. After the first tune of genetic code in the world came into being, a cell biologist of the US cooperated with musicians before transcribing a "suite of genetic code." The British scientists composed a "concerto of genetic code" the public performance of which achieved great success. Dr. Susumu Ohno, a candidate for Nobel Prize, and an invited fellow of the City of Hope National Medical Center of the U. S., reported at the conference of Nobel Prize for Chemistry his research topic "Genetic music," which astounded the scientists present. All these indicate that genetic codes embrace beauty melodies. Can we, then, conjecture reversely, namely, can beautiful music be converted to genetic codes? Some scientists translated the compositions of the world-class virtuosoes into genetic codes and compared them with the base sequence, and they ultimately found that the music of a base sequence in synthetic insulin was virtually identical with the note arrangement of the middle part of the third movement in Chopin's "*Funeral March*"! Doesn't this mean that human is himself a concretionary music embracing unlimited information, and music is the decoding of some genetic codes of human body? Yes, the beautiful melody embraced inside human body resonates with the external music. More experiments prove that human demands, if possible, that all the external sounds be converted to music so as to resonate with the "music" of base sequences inside his/her body. This is where the drive for the musicalization of speech sounds comes from (please see Sect. 3 of Chapter 4 of this book). In addition, since human's own figure (the arrangement of his/her organs) is harmoniously symmetric, he/she will feel pleased when he/she sees symmetric things in the outside world and feels the asymmetric disagreeable. Moreover, the symmetric visual beauty can be naturally transferred into auditory beauty as a result of which human will feel pleasant at symmetric and harmonious rhymes and rhythms and become fidgeted at the asymmetric, inharmonious, and disproportionate ones. This is also the origin of human's drive for all the aesthetic reforms of language. From dissipative structure to the drive for the aesthetic reform of language, all these are in a cause-and-effect relationship, and I would like to recite Qian Zhongshu's words here, namely, "All sequence is consequence."[11]

After reading the whole book, we will see that human body's dynamic balance and harmonious and symmetric figure create the conditions and lay the foundation for the outer as well as inner holographic states of language. The outer language holography refers to the holographic state between language system and the world (cosmic structure) outside it: language structure is isomorphic and similar to and embedded in the cosmic one. Specifically speaking, it means: language joins in the cosmic chorus (see this chapter), the cosmic-holography-law origin of language's various properties (see Chapter 5), the cosmic-holography-law of some language theories (see Chapter 6), the corroboration of the law of cosmic holography at the level of language (see Chapter 7), the holographic relationship between language and culture (see Chapter 8). **The Inner language holography means that of the layers of language, to wit., morpheme—word—phrase—(clause)—sentence—discourse, the parts are holographic with the whole; the parts share the same information with one another; each holographic node (subsystem) in language system has its counterpart or similar information, respectively, in the whole and other nodes. That is to say, each holographic node of the system becomes, to a different extent, a microcosm of the whole.**

3 Language: A Dynamically Balanced System

What is language? Only when this question is well answered, can we see why it does not refuse people's aesthetic choices pertinent to it but offers conditions to people

[11] Qian (1997).

to say pleasant words, helps them produce musical tendency, and facilitates them to employ various beauty-seeking strategies.

Originally, language is a structure "imitating" life's dynamic balance, being a dynamically balanced system. "According to whether or not human interferes in the formation and function of the system, the system can be classified into the natural and the artificial ones respectively" (Qian Xuesen), thus, language is an artificial system, which needs no more demonstration. "According to whether or not there are exchanges of matter, energy, and information between the system and its surroundings, the system can be classified into the open and the closed ones respectively" (ibid.), thus, language is an open system, which is provable: the changes in the surroundings will constantly add new words and expressions into language system which hence constantly weeds out the old ones. This indicates that language system has performed information exchange with the surroundings. By virtue of human interference (human qua a lived media is necessarily included), vivid and overall information exchange occurs between linguistic and social systems. "According to whether or not the system's state changes chronologically, the system can be classified into the dynamic and the static ones respectively" (ibid.), thus, language is a dynamic system, which has early been proved by facts: "change" is embodied from ancient Chinese to the modern one. This exactly indicates that language system has its own "anti-entropy" tendency, that resisting death. Aren't these the cases of language system's imitation of life's dynamically balanced system? We are not supposed to think that there is no dynamic balance in language system merely because language is non-lived. Qian Xuesen correctly says, "Without violating the second law of thermodynamics, the theory of dissipative structure makes possible the interconnections between two systems (i.e., life system and non-life system), which indicates that there is no truly rigorous boundary between the two systems, and that the expressional gap between them is de facto dominated by the same systematic law."[12]

Language's self-organizing process is another proof of its dynamic balance. "The process of language deviation is that of the self-organization of language system."[13] The process of the system's evolution is a self-organizing one. This process might be provoked by the changes in the surroundings outside the system, or by the changes of the factors inside it, including those of the factors' quantity, quality, and ordering. Some changes inside as well as outside the system sway its original structure. The evolution of the system is aimed at a reasonable self-organization, and the result of the deviation is to realize the reasonable reorganization of the structure. It is my contention that insofar as language deviates, the outer causes are first (at least it cannot be excluded) manifested in human's needs and intention. Andre Martinet the French linguist believes that the aim of the system's evolution is to keep some tense between human's needs and the structure's perfection. Moreover, we are supposed to be definitely aware that language's reasonable self-organization and reorganization will never exclude those conforming to aesthetic laws. If the understanding as such holds water, when it comes to the structure of language system, the whole process

[12]Qian et al. (1990, pp. 3–10).

[13]Xu (1991, p. 2).

from its swaying reorganization to the production of a new static structure is saying nothing but this: the balance of language system is dynamic and, a fortiori, it tallies and intermingles with human aesthetic consciousness.

There is a circumstantial evidence for the idea that language is a dynamically balanced structure, that is, **the speech's life consciousness**. It is a life phenomenon closely related to but different from language's physical and physiological attributes. The speech's life consciousness can be sensed at visual as well as auditory levels. Its auditory expression refers to the sound, breath, and pant (the latter two remain to be described by phonetics) rising over the simple and mechanic pronunciation but corresponding to or synchronizing with the life's rhythm and emotional variations. It expresses some peculiar life state and life phenomenon of the single utterer. Some sort of sound, breath, and pant can only be produced in some particular life state, and only they can express the state as such. The sound, breath, and pant synchronizing with life state vary along with the individuals and hence are manifested multifariously. The visual expression of the speech's life consciousness refers to the face and body gestures of the utterer harmoniously cooperating with the utterances. It also expresses the life state of the utterer. The sound, breath, and pant have five properties one of which is: the two expressions of the speech's life consciousness (auditory + visual) can constitute an inseparable three-item cooperation together with the utterances. The three cooperating items start and proceed in synchrony and cooperate with one another in a harmonious and compatible fashion. For instance, when one says "I love you," one's sound, breath, and pant naturally cooperate with it softly, followed by affectionate eyes and body gestures showing no self-constraint. In the normal situation, the following oddity would never occur: say, albeit one says "I love you" (one item, i.e., utterance), one complements it with a raucous and loud voice (another item, i.e., sound, breath, and pant) and cold and straight face and body gestures (the third item).

After reading this book, you will see that language's presentation of a dynamically balanced structure also lays a foundation for the outer as well as inner holographic states of language.

4 From the Harmony of the Three to the Theory of Language Holography

When human is in such a case, he/she has the inner aesthetic determination; when language is in such a case, it has the inner aesthetic determination also. The two inner determinations correspond to and tally with each other at the level of structure, being mutually reciprocal, which amounts to the production of the beauty of speech and that of language. In the final analysis, the efficiency of the beauty of speech and the structure of the beauty of language are supposed to be one part of the harmonious state of human life. It seems that only when we recognize the problems in such a way, can we really found the demonstration of the beauty of language and that of speech on the basis of sciences. As a consequence, our primary senses can become a science positively demonstrable.

We thus transfer from the beauty of the cosmos to that of language and speech. Insofar as the cosmos, human body, and his language are concerned, they are never incompatible with one another but can aesthetically communicate with each other inside. On surface, they show considerable differences; inside, they share the wonder of harmony.

In the first section of Chapter 7, "The micro-cosmos of language and the macro-cosmos of nature," of my *Aesthetic Linguistics*, I write this:

> The micro-cosmos of language harmoniously and uniformly communicates and is identical with the macro-cosmos of nature.[14]

"Language is similar to any form of social behavior at the level of structure and organization" (*Semiotic Aesthetics* by Roland Barthes), whereas I dare not infer thereby that language is similar to the natural macrocosmos at the level of structure and organization as it is a topic going beyond my capacity. As regards the structure and organization of the natural macrocosmos, I know little, not to mention comparing language's structure and organization to them. Be that as it may, I believe that they share the following ideas:

1. Sound is one of the substances of nature. Language is sonic, being a masterpiece of the sound in nature, a beautiful sound merely inferior to music.
2. The motion of the natural macrocosmos is rhythmic, and so is that of language.
3. In terms of the form of manifestation, the beauty of the natural cosmos is identical with that of language.[15]

Seen at present, this conclusion is not without encouragement. After all, at the end of the 1980s (When I began to construct the frame of my *Aesthetic Linguistics*) before the emergence of cosmic holography, **I saw the similarities between the natural macrocosmos and the linguistic micro one, which composed a proper preclude for the theory of language holography**. Alas, nonetheless, I failed to probe further into this primal discovery. Why is "The motion of the natural macro cosmos is rhythmic, and so is that of language"? Why is "In terms of the form of manifestation, the beauty of the natural cosmos is identical with that of language"? *Aesthetic Linguistics* remains to answer them. Today's proceeding, whereas, exactly starts from the conclusion as such: language is similar to the natural macrocosmos at the level of structure and organization.

More than being similar, they are also holographically isomorphic. The case is so not merely between language system and the natural macrocosmos, but also between the natural macrocosmos, human beings, and their language.

Let us go further. The three's holographic isomorphism draws forth the law and the theory of language holography. When either of them is mentioned in this book, I am all the time designating the states of the inner or the outer language holography.

---

[14]Qian (1993, p. 381).

[15]Qian (1993).

That is to say, the law of language holography includes two parts: first, the state of the outer language holography (the holographic relationships between language system and the outer world): language structure is isomorphic and similar to and embedded in the cosmic one. Second, the state of the inner language holography (the holographic relationships inside language system).

The change from the harmony to the holographic isomorphism of the three and to the law and the theory of language holography is qualitative. This notwithstanding, they come down in a continuous line.

It is time for us to try to turn a new page.

References

Hu. Shi, *Outline of the history of Chinese philosophy*. Shanghai: Shanghai Classics Publishing House, 2000.

Qian. Guanlian, *Aesthetic linguistics*. Shenzhen: Haitian Press, 1993.

Qian. Zhongshu, Preface to the *Brief History of Chinese Literature*. In *Essays of Qian Zhongshu*. Hangzhou: Zhejiang Literature & Art Publishing House, 1997.

Qian. Xuesen, Yu. Jingyuan & Dai. Ruwei, A new scientific sphere—The open complex giant system and its methodology. In *Chinese Journal of Nature*, 1990, 1. pp. 3–10.

Quan. Yanchi, "The bodyguard's answer to the author". In October, 1989, 3

Xu. Shenghuan, Language deviation and language system. In *Linguistics and Applied Linguistics*, 1991, 1, p. 2

Yu. Fei, Gramophone records fly in the cosmos, seeking soulmates in the outer space. *The People's Daily*, December 17, 1989.

Chapter 2
The Overall Frame of the Theory of Language Holography

Abstract This chapter contains two sections pertinent to the theoretical foundation of the whole book: one is Sect. 4, "The law of cosmos holography," the other being Sect. 5, "The system theory." The failure to understand them will immediately block the understanding of the whole book. The overall conception of the theory of language holography consists of two parts: one is the inner holographic state of language, the other being the outer holographic state of language.

Keywords The law of cosmos holography · The system theory · The outer language holography · The inner language holography · Chinese embedded box · The principle of dragon lantern

1 The Configuration of Language and the Theory of Language Holography

What is the overall state of language? Where is language? This is a big question fairly interesting and profound but remaining to be determined in one word. As a rule, people might ignore quotidian things. A case in point is "forgetting the trap as soon as the fish is caught," living in the air without knowing that there is air. Only when you ask earnestly "What is language? Where is it?" and try to seek the answers, will you feel it rather thorny, and you might even have no idea handling it. Some think that language is situated in the dictionary. De facto, the dictionary is merely a second-class symbolic record of language cells, being a product abstracted by human beings from the practical speeches but never being language itself. Some others believe that language is situated in grammar. Grammar is nothing but the law presenting the sentences' horizontal syntagme and longitudinal selection, which is also a sort of abstraction, being not language itself, either. The possible answer is: **language is inherited and reserved in the mind of generation after generation in a three-dimensional mode, namely, pitch impression plus the law of selection plus concept, and it turns into the states of sound, breath, and pant when synthetically pronounced**. We need to note that, albeit the synthetic pronunciation of the three dimensions is finished in a split second, the acquisition of them is not the case. The overall state of language can be described thus: **that which is spoken is speech,**

G. Qian, *The Theory of Language Holography*,
https://doi.org/10.1007/978-981-16-2039-3_2

being the first-class symbol (the written symbol is the second-class) in the states of sound, breath, and pant; that which is inherited and reserved in human mind is language system, to wit., the three-dimensional mode of pitch impression plus the law of selection plus concept. Synthetically seen from the two aspects, language is never separable from human life state. To this connection, the state of the language manager's life information is closely linked with language system. The overall state of language as such, a fortiori, carries the biological and cosmic information, giving a scientific introduction and prologue to the production of the theory of language holography.

I started the investigation of the theory of language holography under the guidance of such a view of the overall state of language.

The theory of language holography is a language theory interpreting the states of the outer as well as the inner language holography by means of the law of biology holography, the law of cosmos holography, and the system theory. In general, the theory of language holography studies two big problems: one is the inner holographic state of language, the other being the outer one. **This is the overall configuration of the theory of language holography**. Insofar as the essence of language holography is concerned, the theory is one and the same with **the law and the property of it**, all referring to the states of the outer as well as the inner language holography. The differences between them are: "the theory of language holography" qua a terminology refers specially to such a theory of language, being the name of the latter; "the law of language holography" is on a par with another terminology of "the law of biology holography"; "the property of language holography," whereas, is employed to make prominent an essential quality parallel to other ones of language.

The theoretical foundation of the theory and the law of language holography is: the system theory, the law of biology holography, and the law of cosmos holography (holographics).

It can be said that the theory of language holography is accomplishing a task presented by Saussure, a task supposed to be accomplished by linguistics. Saussure contends, the second task of linguistics is: "To find out the force eternally and universally functioning in all the languages, and to analyze the universal laws, namely, the laws capable of generalizing all the specific historical phenomena." As regards this, Liu Runqing thus comments, "The second task can exactly tell Saussure's foresight. To be sure, prescriptive grammar is of great limits, descriptive grammar is never the ultimate aim, either; to find out the eternal force and to analyze the universal laws are the authentic goal of a science." In this connection, to make macro descriptions of language by means of the law of cosmos holography is nothing else than the "to find out" expected by Saussure, namely, "to find out the force eternally and universally functioning in all the languages."[1] The assiduously seeking as such will necessarily lead linguistics to the depth of the cosmos. My construction of the theory of language holography is supposed to be a response to Saussure. I hope that the following discussions can amount to the hand-mind synchronous tracing and the correct contour-sketching.

[1]Saussure (1916, 1974). Qtd. Liu Runqing (1997).

2 The Object

The object of the theory of language holography is neither the form nor the application of language but the sources of various language properties. The theory of language holography is the consideration as regards the language properties which are themselves abstract and, consequently, this theory is the consideration of abstractness, the consideration of considerations. In the study here, albeit I put stress on language form, I employ it for the sake of transferring, as soon as possible, to the properties' sources behind the form.

In the milieu of the theory of language holography, the state of the inner language holography is the most fundamental topic. I approach it from the substance of language (According to Britain linguist M. A. K. Halliday, substance, i.e., the original materials of language, refers to the sound in uttering and the symbol in writing), but do not analyze its form as in grammatical operations or discuss the application of these forms as in pragmatic analyses. My interests of study focus on this: to describe the holographic situation inside the substance of language. My purpose of study is to conclude the state of the inner language holography: in each level of language's morpheme-word-phrase-clause-sentence-discourse, the part is holographic with the whole; one part contains the same information as the others; each holographic node (subsystem) has its counterpart or similar information in the whole and other nodes, respectively, namely, each holographic node in the system becomes, to a different extent, a microcosm of the whole (as to the detailed demonstration, please see Sect. 4 of Chapter 3). The conclusion thus reached appertains to the properties of language: the essential property of language lies in the fact that language is holographic with and isomorphic to the cosmos. This essential property is exactly the object of the theory of language holography.

As to the "sources of various language properties," I have studied them before. I have also elucidated the sources of language's linearity and fuzziness. This notwithstanding, it is my contention that without relying on the theory of cosmic holographic unity, to wit., the law of language holography and the system theory, the elucidations of the sources of language properties will not be the most drastic, and hence will not be sufficiently reliable albeit they can indeed settle not a few problems.

Since the theory of language holography takes various language properties and their sources as the object of study, all the disciplinary categories capable of expressing language properties belong in the sphere of it. This sphere encompasses, in addition to language form, various linguistic theories and disciplines, and the like.

In general, the overall macro descriptions of language from the perspectives of the law of cosmos holography and the system theory are performed in accordance with the overall configuration of the theory of language holography—the states of the outer as well as the inner language holography. Specifically, they are thus:

to observe language structure is to demonstrate the state of the inner language holography;

to study the holographic relationship between language and cognition is also to demonstrate the state of the inner language holography;

to analyze various language properties (particularly the holographability) is to seek outward for their sources, namely, the sources of the law of cosmos holography and the system theory;
to review some linguistic theories is to seek outward for the origin of elucidations around them; to observe some language facts is to corroborate the law of cosmos holography and the system theory;
to observe the relationship between language and culture is also to find out the state of the outer language holography;
and, to present some language conjectures is to prepare for the future scientific verifications with regard to the theory of language holography since all the sciences are predictable. That which cannot be predicted thereby is not scientific.

3 The Methodology

The theory of language holography is a linguistic theory deduced from the law of biology holography, the law of cosmos holography, and the system theory. That is to say, the method of this topic is mainly deductive reasoning.

This method requires that the law of cosmos holography (and the system theory) is first and foremost confirmed before it is employed to examine various language properties. With deductive reasoning, comparison is the first choice, namely, the law of cosmos holography (and the system theory) is compared horizontally and vertically with language structure and various language properties. In this book, the study of the sources of various language properties at the level of the law of cosmos holography in Chapter 4, the holographic observations as regards linguistic theories in Chapter 5, and the corroboration of the law of cosmos holography from the perspective of language in Chapter 6 are all performed by virtue of comparisons.

The following specific methods can all be applied to deductive reasoning:

1. The systematic method. "Even the local dialect of the most uncivilized nation is one of the valuable masterpieces of nature, so we must never divide them into pieces before describing them piecemeal. The local dialect as such is also an organic organization, and we must treat it as an organism."[2] My interpretations with regard to this are: the malady of "dividing them into pieces before describing them piecemeal" lies in it destroying the holographic relationships between the levels of the structure of a language (even a local dialect). That which I would like to note is, the "systematic method" mentioned by Humboldt is not equivalent to the thought of "the system theory" in modern sense, and what I want to stress is exactly this: we must employ the thought of system and the system theory in modern sense. The system theory is one of the fundamental theories (as to the details, please see Sect. 5 of Chapter 2) of the theory of language holography. **The cosmos is a big Chinese embedded box, embracing the smaller one of language**.

---

[2]Qtd. Yao (1998) (4).

2. The dynamic method. "To grasp the essence of language and make comparisons between many languages, our investigation into language must all the time set its sights on its lived functions….Any facet relevant to language can only be compared to the physiological process rather than the anatomical one; there is no static thing whatsoever in language, and it is dynamic (dynamisch) toto coelo."[3] I am delighted to find that the functional grammar prevailing around the world "sets its sights on" the "lived functions" of sentence components, pragmatics is nothing other than the dynamic study of language's functions, and that "it is dynamic toto coelo." It can be seen how accurate Humboldt's prediction at his time was. This offers an inspiration to us: **the discoveries of language's methodology and the innovations of its research methods will provoke a revolutionary progress in linguistics**. To this connection, we may as well consider the theory of language holography as a methodology as it provides a brand new perspective to us on observing language. From this perspective, we can: (1) find or discover some new important properties of language, say, the holographibility of language, viz., the law of language holography, thus, it is not an illusion that the sense of sound appears in skipped generations (and hence provokes some revolution in terms of foreign language learning), and the like. (2) Find the source of the various inherent properties of language and various linguistic theories—the holographic and uniform relationship in the cosmos. Language is merely a subsystem of the cosmos. We have no reason to affirm that it is the "ultimate" source, but I believe that it has indeed found a satisfactory locus for the various language properties and linguistic theories.
3. The comparative method. "The investigations into language organism require that we should make, as broadly as possible, comparisons [between the languages]"; through comparison, the difference on the structure of human languages can be revealed, and "such an important question can be answered in essence: whether or not the languages can be classified according to their internal structures as is done in botany taxonomy."[4] As a matter of fact, the various language systems are discovered in this way, which indeed realizes "The languages are classified according to their internal structures as is done in botany taxonomy."
4. The historical method. Like any organism whatsoever, "Language is manifested in a specific and historical fact as to which we cannot but make specific and historical interpretations."[5] Since historical interpretations must be based on empirical observations, historical method is empirical.
5. The empirical method. Language is an object in experiences. The concept of language can only be established via empirical approaches.

The inner holographic state of language in Chapter 3 is the result of the comparative demonstrations between the law of biology holography, the law of cosmos

[3]Cf. Wilhelm (1968).

[4]Wilhelm (1968, pp. 7. 9).

[5]Cf. Yao (1998) (4).

holography (Sect. 4), and the system theory (Sect. 5) on the one hand and language structure on the other.

Just like a good game player can make all his wishes come true, the crux here lies in the fact that the research methods should start from reality.

4 The Law of Cosmos Holography: The First Theory Foundation-Stone

The theory of language holography is founded on the law of cosmos holography.

In January, 1984, Wang Cunzhen and Yan Chunyou presented a new concept of "the law of cosmos holography"[6] under the inspirations from Zhang Yingqing's "the law of biology holography" (1980, 1985) and the Eastern classic philosophical thoughts. Its fundamental idea is to unite nature, human society, and human mental world, or, in a word, the whole cosmos, into an organic whole for recognition, namely, to unite the different levels and processes in the cosmos. As regards the law of cosmos holography, Wang Cunzhen and Yan Chunyou presented a generally identical concept in two places in *The Theory of Cosmic Holographic Unity*. In one place, it is thus said:

> **The law of cosmos holography** means that all the things, including the cosmos, are of four-dimensional holographability, and everything is a holographic node of the cosmos," and then, "The law of cosmos holography includes the following contents: all the things are of four-dimensional holographability; mutual holographic relationship exists everywhere, between the parts and the whole of the same individual, things at the same level, things at different levels and in different systems, the beginning and the result of a matter, the macro and the micro progressions of a thing, and between time and space; each part embraces, and is simultaneously embraced by, other parts; materials generally have memory, and things are always trying to copy new ones according to the existent mode in their memories; holography is manifested in different fashions.[7]

In the other place, it is thus said:

> "The law of cosmos holography means that the cosmos is an n-dimensional holographic unity. Any constituent of it is a condensed information cosmos. The cosmos is the complex of innumerable information cosmoses. In brief, any system whatsoever embraces all the information of the cosmos as a whole."[8]

The statements in these two places are fundamentally identical, it's just that as to the dimension of the cosmos, there is a difference, namely, one is four, the other being n. Nonetheless, the two places both contain the meaning of "Any system whatsoever embraces all the information of the cosmos as a whole." The "multum in parvo" of "the theory of holography" is exactly clear and definite.

---

[6]Wang and Yan (1985) (2).

[7]Wang and Yan (1995, pp. 45–46).

[8]Wang and Yan (1995, p. 306).

According to "In brief, any system whatsoever embraces all the information of the cosmos as a whole," it can be generalized thus: the law of cosmos holography is: one is all, and all is one.

Following the statements afore, the authors discussed the ten major principles of the theory of cosmos holography. Since the ten principles are of great benefit to the elucidations of language's various properties, I compile them as follows:

"The ten major principles of **the theory of cosmos holography** are:

First, the parts is holographic with the whole. This is the cornerstone of the edifice of the theory of cosmos holography, and hence it is the most fundamental and important principle.

Secondly, all the systems are holographic. This principle indicates that every material state, from the lowest to the top one (the brain and the mind), is the microcosm of the cosmos. Therefore, all the holographic systems are mutually equivalent.

The third one is the conservation law of cosmic information....Like all the materials and energy in the cosmos, none of the information can be created or destroyed....The cosmos will not generate things it never conceives....When a system dies, the information turns into a latent state in the form of holographic quantum, being situated in a new system or spacial locus in a new way....The common information created by human beings is nothing but the manifestation of the latent one. This is because even human beings themselves are a manifestation of the higher information state of material hidden in the lower one. 'Creation' is nothing else than a visualization.

The fourth one is the latent/manifest law of cosmic information. ...In brief, the process is a result of the mutual conversions of latent and manifest information states. Consequently, any system whatsoever is a manifestation of the synthetic effect of latent and manifest informations. This principle is of critical importance....Holography cannot be seen simply from the manifest state; but rather, it can only be seen from the sum of latent and manifest informations, or else we would not reach the conclusion of cosmos holography....When we look into cosmos holography, we must proceed from the perspective of the sum as such, and from the hight of deformation resemblance and deformation holography (Different from the conformation holography, it refers to the state in which things are different on form but have the sum of information in common. A case in point is the holography of the leaves with the root of a tree)....

Fifthly, homogeneity necessarily means isomorphism, isomorphism holography, holography isomorphism, and isomorphism homogeneity. The three are equivalent and absolutely identical.

The sixth one is the infinite holographic recursive structure....Any material system whatsoever embraces infinite information layers each of which is the microcosm of all the other ones, namely, each information layer embraces infinite other information layers and vice versa: it is also embraced by all the other layers. In this way, the information layers reflect one another, recurring layer by layer, ad infinitum.

The seventh one is the integral transmitting law of information. The information of any holographic system is transmitted in an integral fashion, and any holographic wave's band or locus carries the integral information, to wit., the whole and complete information. We call the 'integral information' as such 'full quantum'. The storage and extraction of information are both integral, namely, they are both manifested in the mode of holographic quantum. Thus is formed the information circulating ring.

The eighth one is the law of system evolution. All the material systems embrace the identical evolution information and follow the identical evolution law, emerging, developing, and dying in accordance with the essentially identical law.

The ninth one is the law of holistic identity. Parts are whole, whole parts, being absolutely identical with one another.

The tenth one is the unified field of cosmic information. The information is material, and the cosmos is unified in information. Cosmic information exists in an infinitely dense fashion, i.e., in the state of infinitely approaching absolute or infinite continuity. The sum of the state as such is the unified field of cosmic information."

To be sure, by means of my intellectual structure alone, I cannot affirm that the theory of the law of cosmic holography is invulnerable, I however confirm that the law of biology holography (there are citations and discussions of it in Sect. 2 of Chapter 3, "The inner language holography") is cogent. What's more, I was already deeply convinced by the harmony and unity of the cosmos before I knew this law.

As regards the harmony and unity of the cosmos, natural scientists' work have verified it millions of times, so much so that any minor demonstration here would seem non-essential. Be that as it may, I cannot help citing a small case[9]: the "Butterfly Effect," namely, a butterfly flapping its wings in Brazil might provoke, via a series of chain reactions, a hurricane in the "Cape Fear." To be sure, the phenomenon of a small act bringing about a big result can be interpreted by means of the chaos theory, yet it can all the more be interpreted by means of the theory of cosmos holography. On March 24, 1997, a butterfly named Alan Greenspan merely flapped his wings once, but the interest rates were raised by 1/4 percent point, equal to 5% of the then interest rate, and thus begun the global financial turmoil. In this way, the material worlds are mutually interconnected, and all the activities in human society pull each other.

On this account, the migration from the law of biology holography to the law of cosmos holography is convincible and logical. Moreover, we will find, in the following inquiries into language properties, the inimitably rounded interpretative power of the law of cosmos holography, and the considerable aesthetic charm of the harmony and unity of them (i.e., the holographic node of language and the holographic body of the cosmos). Let me note in passing, please permit me to remind the readers not familiar with the law of biology holography and that of cosmos holography that they are supposed to figure them out first, or else they would feel it out of place when they read the following explications of language properties and the predictions about language.

The aim of my study of the law of cosmos holography is to transfer to the explications as regards the holographic relationship between the cosmic world and language. Understanding the law of cosmos holography is never my immediate purpose, which will be comprehensively explained in Chapter 3 and Sect. 4 of it.

[9]Zhang (1999, p. 9).

5 The System Theory: The Second Theory Foundation-Stone

The system theory is the second fundamental-stone of the theory of language holography. In this section, I will merely introduce the system theory at the level of principle. As to how to demonstrate the inner holographic state of language by means of the system theory, I will perform it in the last section (Sect. 5) of Chapter 3.

After Saussure, many linguistic scholars are saying that "Language is a system." Nonetheless, many facts indicate that the system in their mind's eye merely refers to a set of language structures and rules composed of phonetics, vocabulary, and grammar, which is of its reason. Nonetheless, if our recognition stops here, it remains to be the language view of the system theory. **Without wholeness, mutual connection, or dynamicity, the combination of rules revealing non-orderliness and non-purposefulness is not a system**. Just like the child plays tricks in a game, when the rule is unfavorable to him, he would set a new one and force the other partners to follow it. Such rules are unchecked and irregular, and the combination of them has no vitality at all hence will collapse at any time. A country with an undeveloped and imperfect market system is, as a rule, the victim of such irregular rules facing collapse at any time.

We all strongly feel that language is a system, but feeling can never replace scientific demonstration. Without the scientific demonstration, we could not affirm that language is a system merely from the fact that it has structures and rules. Only when we can see that the systematic properties of the system theory and systematic thoughts in the sense of modern science run in language, can we affirm that language is a system. As a matter of fact, Saussure at his time could not demonstrate his assertion ahead of time by virtue of modern system theory.

Apparently, before the formal demonstration (Sect. 5 of Chapter 3, "The argument for the state of the inner language holography in terms of the system theory"), my work in this section of this chapter is to expound the systematic properties and thoughts duly belonging to the system theory.

5.1 What Is System?

"System" is a concept as ancient as cultivation itself. Aristotle's statement of this concept is "**The whole is more than the sum of its parts.**"[10] *Merriam-Webster's Collegiate Dictionary* thus defines "system": a collection of objects united by some form of interaction or interdependence. On this account, a system can be considered as a set of interrelated constituents. The properties of the constituents and the various relationships among them are naturally determined by the mode of system with which they are faced. The fact that a system can be considered as a set is rather useful in

[10]Cf. Vemuri (1978, p. 25).

that we can thus have free access to the edifice of knowledge of set theory, topology, and the theory of function.

As to system, Qian Xuesen thus defines it: "**We call the considerably complicated object of research a system, to wit., an organic whole having certain functions and being composed of many constituents interacting with and relying on one another. The system is itself a constituent of a bigger one to which it belongs.**"[11] It is my contention that a brilliant point of this definition lies in it noting this: "The system is itself a constituent of a bigger one to which it belongs." The reason why I contend that this replenishment is important and brilliant is, it coincides with the fact that the cosmos is an infinitely recursive structure.

The definition of system presented by Ludwig Von Bertalanffy (1973, 1955, 1962. The original name will be used hereafter.) is widely employed. It is: **a system is a whole constituted by the parts interrelated to one another and exchanging matter with their environment**.

The system is classified into natural and artificial ones, respectively. The natural system refers to the one existing originally and being composed of natural things. That is to say, it is the system produced in nature prior to the emergence of human beings or without artificial interferences, such as environmental system (not the one planned and built in a large scale by human beings, e.g., planted forest belt, greenbelt, sewage treatment plant, etc., but the original environmental system of the earth), water system (not the artificial one like China's Dujiangyan Project, the Three Gorges Project, etc.), cosmic system, mountain system, animal system, plant system, and the like.

The artificial system refers to the one constructed by virtue of human intentional practical activities. Such systems that can be sensed in our ordinary experiences are: mechanical system like clocks and watches, electronic system like wireless devices, industrial system like factories, educational system like colleges and universities, information processing system like the Internet, medical system like hospitals, and organizational system, environmental system, cybernetic system, and so on and so forth.

The system can be further classified into material (like the industrial, educational, mechanical, information processing systems, etc., listed above) and conceptual (various scientific theories) ones, respectively. The various language theories, say, the theory of language holography I am demonstrating, belong in the conceptual system.

[11]Qian et al. (1978).

5.2 *Modern System Theory: The Most Prominent Property of the System*

5.2.1 The Wholeness of the System

The idea that the system's properties or qualities are the simple sum (algebraic sum, the sum of sum) of those of its constituents is wrong (This is the system view of mechanism). Aristotle once noted: the whole is more than the sum of its isolated parts. Bertalanffy's wholeness is exactly based on this. It is from the perspective of theoretical biology that Bertalanffy presents this conclusion. A most typical experiment he cites is the famous experiment of sea urchin made by Hans Driesch an embryologist. The experiment thus goes: after the gastrula stage of embryonic development, the sea urchin's fertilized egg usually develops normally into a larva. He cut the egg in gastrula stage into two halves, having thought that only half of a larva could be born. To his great surprise, the half gastrula developed into a smaller but complete embryo, and eventually into a small but complete larva! Some biologists once interpreted this experiment by virtue of vitalism or epistemology. Insofar as the experiment itself is concerned, it indeed shows the property of wholeness, namely, the system is not the simple sum of its parts. If the system is merely the algebraic sum of its parts, the smaller half gastrula would only develop into a bigger one. The result however is a complete embryo. I would like to ask, where does the other half come from? Bertalanffy interprets this phenomenon with "different causes, same result" and equivalence, noting, "To understand a whole or a system, we need to understand each part, but we also need to understand their relationships (say, the interactions between enzymes in the cell, the various mutual influences between conscious and unconscious processes in one's personality, the structure and movement of social system, and so on)....To look for the general aspects, the uniformity, and the homomorphism of a system belongs in the scope of the general system theory." He takes Aristotle's famous proposition of "The whole is more than the sum of its parts" as the most fundamental property of the system.

5.2.2 The Organic Relevance of the System

The system's wholeness is guaranteed by its organicity. General system theory focuses on the interrelations and interactions between various factors of the system. In any system with wholeness, the connection between its internal factors is organic. These factors appertain to and interact with one another, co-constituting the whole system. The principle of organic relevance refers to the organic connection between the internal factors of the system on the one hand, and to that between the system and the external environment on the other. The relevance to the external environment is the open system in common sense, namely, there are exchanges between the external world and it at the level of material, energy, and information, and there are corresponding inputs and outputs, quantitative increases and decreases. This property is of critical importance for us to understand the gist of general system theory. In the second law of thermodynamics, the system is considered as an isolated one, namely, there is no exchange at the level of material, energy, and information between the system and the external world, which ultimately brings about the system's dead silence. Contrariwise, given that there are exchanges between an open system and the external world at the level of material, energy, and information, it has the inclination to resist dead silence.

5.2.3 The Dynamicity of the System

The system's organic connection is dynamic rather than static, being pertinent to time. Bertalanffy (1973) holds that the system changes over time. Seen from biological perspective, the dynamic state of the system is the premise of keeping the static one. For instance, one of the foundations on which the living organism keeps the internal balance is the existence of metabolism. Whereas that which organic connection stresses is the spacial distribution of all the factors, the principle of dynamicity puts stress on their temporal changes. On the one hand, the distributing places of the system's internal structure change over time rather than keeping fixed; on the other hand, as to the openness of the system, organic connection stresses the connection and exchange between the system and the external world at the level of material, energy, and information, whereas dynamicity puts stress on the existing state of the material, energy, and information which manifest themselves in a relatively steady state in the system. Nonetheless, steady state is by no means equal to static state. Steady state is a sort of moving state embracing the dynamic one. For instance, the concept of "development" embraces the meaning of "move" which refers to the streams of material, energy, and information, stressing the constant continuity.

Vemuri. V (1978) also notes that the complicated system changes over time rather than being static. Given that the environment in which the system runs is not always controlled by the observer, during the process it evolves over time, the influences on it from the environment are not that obvious at the initial stage. The design of any system is supposed to take it into consideration that the lesion currently showing no sign in the system might occur in the future. Therefore, the controlling system per se must also be capable of evolving so as to effectively handle the coming tumult.

5.2.4 The Orderliness of the System

The structure and levels manifested by the system's organic connectedness and the directionality of the progressive segregation manifested by the system's dynamicity are both the causes to the property of orderliness of the system. Bertalanffy contends that the system's evolution from disorder to order marks the increase of its organizedness or the degree of being organized which appertains, furthermore, to both the organic connectedness of the system's internal factors and the dynamic process of the system.

5.2.5 The Finality of the System

Bertalanffy holds that the system is ordered not for the order's sake but as a result of following a certain direction, nay, this direction is dominated by a certain finality. He notes that the direction of a system's development is determined by its finality. A system is decided by actual conditions, but it is also constrained by its final state. In this connection, finality is considered to be determined by the future. That is to say, a system's developing direction is determined not merely by its actual state (i.e., necessity) but also by its prediction of the future (i.e., contingency), and the unity of the two is finality. He contends that be it in the mechanic system or in other types of system, finality objectively exists. Nevertheless, as is noted by him, the finality of general system theory is purposiveness rather than teleology. In a narrow sense, **finality can be merely limited to the prediction and directedness of the "final state" that the system will reach**.

In the sphere of science, teleology is criticized, and hence there is the necessity to say something more with regard to this view of Bertalanffy's. He says that the biological world is a product of occasional events, and an accumulation of the meaningless functions of random variation and selection; the mental world is an odd, somewhat listless phenomenon of materials events. …Be that as it may, without considering the adaptability, finality, homing-ness (purpose-seeking) by various names, we could not understand creatures, let alone understanding behaviors and human society. …That which however deserves stress is, the teleological behaviors directed upon the characteristic final state or goal remain to transgress the boundary of natural sciences. Bertalanffy (1973, p. 25) and V. Vemuri (1978) also note that behavioral factors like the political, social, psychological, and aesthetic ones play a not minor role on the overall quality of the system's manifestation. On this account, the problems in many major systems are determined in terms of nature by the conflicts between the goals they seek. That which is meaningful is, those "political, social, psychological, and aesthetic behavioral factors" as such carry out human purposes, being the external interferences in the system.

5.3 Problems Relevant to the System Theory

5.3.1 The System's Lesion and External Disturbances

The acts of the system are not always exemplary or reassuring. The economic system is vulnerable to inflation, recession, and depression; the biological system might easily suffer lesion and decline; the educational system might be easily neglected; the ecological system is often disturbed by harmful substances and pollutions; and the aquatic system often suffers flood or drought disasters. On the whole, each system as a rule shows **external lesions and disturbances**. There are more relevant examples: the lesion of the mountain is manifested in the volcano injecting magma, human body system often suffers virus infections, and so on. To this connection, in the decision of artificial systems (say, the economic system, the educational system, etc.), supervision is particularly necessary. The coverage of lesion and disturbance being broad notwithstanding, the remedial methods and controlling means of them are as many. For instance, feedback control is a quite effective remedial method of lesions, and a person's faeces will tell whether or not there is a disease in his/her body and what it is.

Methods can be found to improve the lesion of a system. You can rebuild a new system and abandon the old one—substituting a new one for the old one. The alteration of political systems (the alternation of dynasties, or a government being replaced by another) and the change of simple institutional system are common phenomena. In some systems, whereas, alteration is never a feasible solution. Human body, the environment, and the like, are all irreplaceable systems. An attemptable alteration is to **perform "engineering transformation" of the original system, namely, to guide the system in "proper" direction of development, say, to change its structure or to modify its input, or both**. On achieving this, one of the methods is to observe the system's output and to perform the aforementioned alteration for the sake of enabling it, as far as possible, to see an ideal output.

5.3.2 The System's Structure or Configuration Cannot Be Self-evident

A system has a great many attributes needing description or identification. The trouble lies in the fact that not all attributes are observable. "The system's structure or configuration can seldom be self-evident" (Vemuri 1978, p. 2). This is a property of vital importance. Vemuri's further explication of it is: "In the major system concerned with the systems like human body, plant, computer, traffic line, etc., there are many configuration scopes of possibility the choice of merely one of which might exert far-reaching influences on the system."

I draw another conclusion therefrom: **the system's structure or configuration cannot verify itself**. When the assertion of "The system's structure and configuration can seldom be self-evident" goes one step further, it becomes: the system's structure or configuration cannot verify or assess itself. Thousands and thousands of facts have justified that the system cannot perform self-assessment. For minor examples: the doctor cannot diagnose himself/herself or give prescriptions, the machine cannot assess its own performance (and its obstacles also need excluding by man), human body cannot maintain the life by itself (but requires the external world to offer oxygen and food), the administrator cannot perform the administration unless under the earnest supervisions of other administrators or institutions (say, the board of directors, the parties not in office, the parliament, the People's congress Council, the Chinese People's Political Consultative Conference, workers' congress, and the like), the student cannot assess his/her own performance, the author of an academic essay cannot write appraisals of his own writings, it should be the Chinese who are entitled to evaluate the foreigner's grasping of Chinese, and the orbit of a planet in the space is ultimately determined by the attraction and exclusion amidst innumerable other astral bodies, and so on and so forth. This is because **a running system cannot doubt or make a value judgment about itself**.

5.4 The Principle of Dragon Lantern

A vivid metaphor of the system theory can be the principle of dragon lantern. First of all, I declare this: given that I watched every year in my childhood the adults' training of dragon lantern game, I am supposed to be qualified for generalizing the rules of the game, and my relevant senses approach the true situation.

The several typical properties of the system can all be embodied in dragon lantern game. The lantern's structure thus goes: the three major parts, namely, the dragon's head, body (it is composed of many segments), and tail are connected by fabrics (usually high-quality cloth even silk). The three parts are separately controlled, lifted, or waved, the rules of the game being formed in tacit understanding (accepted through common practice): when waved (the game begins), the dragon's head moves first, followed by the second segment of the body in accordance with the moving tendency of the head, and so does each following segment in a successive fashion, till the tail starts, which accomplish the whole dragon dance.

The structure and rules of dragon lantern game are virtually identical to those of language. In this connection, this book shows the convenience of being vivid and easy to understand when I elucidate language system by means of the principle of dragon lantern.

Sect. 5 of Chapter 3, namely, "The argument for the state of the inner language holography in terms of the system theory," will verify that the principle of dragon lantern will be given one by one in language structure and language game (language use).

The wholeness of dragon lantern game: albeit the movement of each segment is of different causes but same effect, insofar as the waving is concerned, all the segments pursue equivalence, uniformity, and isomorphism. The simple addition (algebraic sum) of the body's segments can only result in the whole motionless dragon lantern being laid there (as the mechanic sum of the parts), merely as a thing composed of cloth rather than the dragon lantern game that people like to appreciate. The impression and conception that the whole dragon lantern waved by people according to rules give to the appreciator is a waving dragon chasing the ball, far beyond the simple addition of each segments.

The organic connection of dragon lantern game: each segment of the dragon lantern is interrelated and interacts with any other segment before or after it. The dragon lantern is an open system the connecting mode of which with the external environment is mainly embodied by the player's lifting and waving the dragon. That is to say, the subject of the game is the player. Without the players' participation, the dragon lantern is a dead thing. The player's waving is the material and energy exchange with the dragon lantern system itself.

The dynamicity of dragon lantern game: each segment of the dragon lantern must wave, which is dynamic; moreover, the waving of each segment must decide its position and tendency according to those of the segment before it. This is the dynamic connection of the dragon lantern system. In addition, the connection of the whole game from starting via waving heatedly to the end is related to time. The dragon lantern without waving is of no value at all and cannot be called a game but merely a stage prop. When some player faints with tiredness, he will be replaced by another one, and the replacement is a result of training. This process of replacement manifests the metabolism of dragon lantern game.

The orderliness of dragon lantern game: when the game is played by the beginners, it is immediately expressed as the intermittence between the segments and the inharmony of the waving direction and strength, which is an disordered state of the dragon lantern; when the seniors play the game, the segments are harmonious on waving direction and strength, and thus is accomplished the dragon lantern game, which is the orderliness of this system. This is to say that the dragon lantern system's structure, levels, and dynamicity show a progressive segregating direction hence give the game its orderliness. Dragon lantern game's development from disordered to ordered marks the increase of its system's organized-ness and the degree of being organized, and the organized-ness is embodied by the organization of the players. Of course, the organized-ness of dragon lantern game is related to both its organic connection and its dynamic process.

The finality of dragon lantern game: each player of the game has a definite aim: "I must let the segment in my hand coordinate with the whole group and wave in harmony." This finality is approved by every player, or else he would not take his part, nor would others let him do so. As a consequence, the direction according to which dragon lantern game becomes ordered is determined by its finality. This is because the final state—to wave—people need to reach constrains every player.

The lesion and disturbance of dragon lantern game: the systematic behavior of dragon lantern game is not always reassuring. Its external lesion and disturbances might occur at any time. For instance, if one player faints with tiredness and suddenly falls, the whole game will be forced to stop. Dragon lantern game as an artificial system also needs supervision. There are also remedial and controlling means with respect to its lesion and disturbances, and a case in point is there are many substitute players in training. According to my knowledge, the time cost in training the substitutes to take the stage occupies more than a half of the whole training time. This is because the substitution is of great difficulty the source of which is: the substitution occurs in waving and cannot be done in a standstill state (for the audience would laugh at this and make catcalls). The game players of dragon lantern often change. In my hometown, Shahu town of Xiantao City of Hubei province, before 1952, the game players almost changed thoroughly every two years (the instructors however were relatively steady as they must be the experienced middle-aged or old people), and this is the reconstruction of the system—substituting the new one for the old one.

Be that as it may, when it comes to why language is a system, and why the system theory supports the theory of language holography, the demonstrating process is implemented in Sect. 5 of Chapter 3: "The argument for the state of the inner language holography in terms of the system theory." We will see therein that all the properties of the system (and the principle of dragon lantern) can be expressed most completely in language.

References

Liu Runqing, *Schools of lingusitics*, p. 94. Beijing: Foreign Language Teaching and Research Press, 1997.

Qian. Xuesen, Xu. Guozhi & Wang. Shouyun, The techniques of organizational management—Systems engineering. In *Wen Wei Po Daily*, September 27, 1978.

Saussure, Ferdinand de, *Cours de linguistique générale, Course in General Linguistics*, Collins, 1916, 1974.

Vemuri, V., *Modeling of complex systems: An introduction.* New York: Academic Press, 1978, p. 25.

Wang. Cunzhen &Yan. Chunyou, The theory of cosmos holography. In *Natural Information*, 1985 (2).

Wang. Cunzhen &Yan. Chunyou, *The theory of cosmic holographic unity.* Jinan: Shandong People's Publishing House, 1995, pp. 45–46.

Wilhelm von Humboldts, *Whihelm von Humboldts Gesammelte Schriften. Wilhelm Richter, Berlin;* photomechanischer Nachdruck Berlin, 1968.

Yao. Xiaoping, The historical relationship between linguistics and sciences. In *Foreign Languages in Fujian*, 1998 (4).

Zhang. Fan, Reflections on the global financial crisis. In *Du Shu*, 1999, 9.

Part II
The Inner Language Holography

Chapter 3
The Inner Language Holography

Abstract Chapter 3 is the core of the whole book. If this chapter could not hold water, nor would the whole book. In particular, Sect. 4 (the argument for the state of the inner language holography in terms of the law of cosmos holography) and Sect. 5 (the argument again in terms of the system theory) are the most critical. When the state of the inner language holography attains the support of the law of cosmos holography and the system theory, the "eye" of Chapter 3 would be lived; when Chapter 3 is lived, the whole book would be so. This notwithstanding, to understand the demonstrating process of the state of the inner language holography, we must know about the several key terms of the law of cosmos holography, the law of biology holography, the law of biology repetition, and the law of material-spiritual holography.

Keywords Information · Holographability · Holography · The law of holography · Holographic node · Holographic body · The law of biology holography · The law of material-spiritual holography

To see a world in a grain of sand,

And a heaven in a wild flower,

Hold infinity in the palm of your hand,

And eternity in an hour.

——W. Blake (1757 ~ 1827)[1]

After reading this chapter, the readers will naturally find that this poem is in extremely close relation to the law of language holography, so the citation here is by no means out of fancy ideas.

The theory of language holography is a language theory explicating the states of the outer as well as the inner language holographies by virtue of the law of biology holography, the law of cosmos holography, and the system

[1]Qtd. Yang. Zhenning (1998, 1, p. 212).

G. Qian, *The Theory of Language Holography*,
https://doi.org/10.1007/978-981-16-2039-3_3

theory. In the milieu of the theory of language holography, the state of the inner language holography is the first point of "the holographic observation of the various language properties," also a most fundamental topic of the theory of language holography. By approaching the state of the inner language holography from the familiar language structure, I will discuss the latter before entering into the theory of language holography, namely, I will unfold the discussions from the micro to the macro levels.

The descriptions as regards the holographic conditions in language substance can be attributed to the state of the inner language holography: at each of language's morpheme—word—phrase—clause—sentence—discourse levels, the part is holographic with the whole; the parts embrace identical information; each holographic node (subsystem) in language system has its counterpart or similar information, respectively, in the whole and other nodes, namely, that each holographic node of the system is, to a certain extent, a microcosm of the whole. In brief, as regards the relationship between the levels (layers) of language, one is all, all one.

Given that the theory and the law of language holography are developed on the basis of the law of cosmos holography—the law of biology holography—the law of spirit holography and the system theory, before the explications of the law of language holography are unfolded, the law of cosmos holography, the law of biology holography, and the law of spirit holography (the system theory has been introduced in Sect. 5 of Chapter 2) must be considered as a transitional period. I hope that you will not feel it verbose.

1 Some key-terms of the law of cosmos holography

"The law of cosmos holography means that all things, even the cosmos, are of the four-dimensional holographibility, and everything is a holographic node of the cosmos."[2]

How to understand the "four-dimensional" in the fundamental content of the law of cosmos holography? That to which man has been accustomed, and has accepted as well, is the three-dimensional space. We are all accustomed to saying that we live without doubt in a three-dimensional space, and hence people have merely developed the observation and thinking habit suitable for three-dimensional space but have no idea what a four-dimensional world looks like. This however never means that a four-dimensional world does not exist, just like the ant with merely two-dimensional observation and thinking habit is not supposed to deny the existence of a three-dimensional space. As to problems relevant to a four-dimensional world, the most cautious approach is: do not hastily deny it. Let us suspend the "four-dimensional holographability" tentatively before we make clear what "four-dimensional" is.

To better understand the law of cosmos holography, I will introduce the repetition law of the cosmos presented by Wang Cunzhen and Yan Chunyou: according to the repetition law of the cosmos, the developing process of any subsystem whatsoever is a microcosm, or a brief and rapid repetition, of the system's history even the cosmos' history of evolution, and the subsystem's mode of construction is the duplication of

---

[2]Wang. Cunzhen & Yan. Chunyou (1985 p. 2).

that of the system, even of the cosmos. Given that in the repetition as such, the former includes all the information of the latter, we also call this law the repetition law of cosmos holography. It contains three main laws: (1) the repetition law of the mode of construction; (2) the repetition law of cycle; and (3) the repetition law of process.

Apparently, to understand the law of holography, we must make clear the following key terms in the theory of holography: information, holographability, holography, law of holography, holographic node, holographic body.

"**Information.**" Information is an attribute or existing mode of material, energy, and spirit, the spatio-temporal order of them. Information also has another meaning: it is a mode of universal relation of things.

"**Holographability.**" Holographability is supposed to be the most essential quality of information. This concept originated from holography. Zhang Yingqing a Chinese holo-biologist later transplanted it into the field of biology in which the law of biology holography came into fruition.

"**Holography.**" **The fundamental meaning of "Holography" is: a part (subsystem) contains the same information as other parts, a part contains the same information as the whole, or a part contains all the information of the whole. This is the fundamental proposition and principle of the theory of cosmos holography. Holography also means full-scale mutual telepathy**.

"The law of holography." The law of holography is the law dominating the holographic phenomena.

"Holographic node" and "holographic body." Seen at the level of explicit information, the cosmos is a body of universal relations where all things are in full-scale interconnections, interactions, and inter-constraints, which enables everything or every locus of the cosmos to have all the interacting, interconnecting, and inter-constraining information from any locus whatsoever of the cosmos, and, as a result, any locus becomes an information microcosm of the cosmos. To this connection, each subsystem becomes a set of full-scale scattering relations, scattering in all directions its own information, acting upon all the other subsystems and the system; each subsystem is both an agglomeration interrelated with all the other subsystems and the system as a whole, and a set of relations agglomerated inward. **As to such a set of agglomerated relations, a subsystem, we call it a holographic node; as to the system as a whole, we call it the holographic body**.

That is to say, given that the holographic node is a set of relations, a subsystem, it is nothing other than a unit of the system as a whole.

Someone contends, "The area of the human pupil is no more than several square millimeters, but it can see things as far as the sun, the planets, the stars, and the nebulas. According to the new ideas of relevant experts, by means of a particular astronomical telescope, people can see the light information transmitted from another side of the cosmos. That is to say, what it seen is the whole cosmos."[3] Being a considerably small part, human pupil can embrace the information of another considerably big part, which can be taken as a paragon of the theory of cosmos holography. We will meet more examples in what follows.

[3] Li. Zhichao (1985).

What is the inner source of cosmos holography? Wang Cunzhen and Yan Chunyou thus interpret: the inner source of cosmos holography lies in the homology of all things in the world. All things share one origin, coming from the cosmos' "singularity"—also called "the primitive super-information cell," and hence each part also contains all the information in the "singularity," just like the organism originates from the seed hence owns all the information therein.

The law and the repetition law of cosmos holography are the extension of those of biology holography, so the latter that I will introduce next becomes the most important foundation for us to understand the former.

2 The law of biology holography

As is said in "**the law of biology holography**" discovered by Zhang Yingqing (1980, 1985), "Each part of a holographic node of the organism has its own respective correspondents in the whole and other holographic nodes; compared with the non-counterparts of a holographic node in the whole or some other holographic node, its counterparts always have more similarity at the level of biological property; in terms of the law of distribution, that of each part in one holographic node is identical to that of each counterpart in the whole and other holographic nodes. In this way, the results of distribution of each part with not exactly the same biological properties turn the holographic nodes into the microcosms of the whole to varying extents, and each holographic node is similar to others also to a different extent. We call this the law of biology holography."[4]

How to understand the holographically mutual embracement? Wang Cunzhen and Yan Chunyou note, "Biology holography will not be tenable unless it is understood from information, from the sum of implicit and explicit information. **The essence of the law of biology holography is information holography**. That is to say, any part of a biological organism embraces all the information of the whole. Seen in this regard, the part is absolutely holographic with the whole. **If understood merely from the morphological structure rather than information, a tiny part could by no means embrace the gigantic whole, and it would never be understandable that the part embraces the whole.**"[5]

There are a great many examples of the law of biology holography and it is impossible to give all of them in detail. To date, the cloned sheep that once shocked the world is not in the least mysterious any longer, and the cloned calf has come out.[6] The cloning of the organism is a case of making any part of it into a new whole under certain conditions, which is the most convincing evidence of the law of

[4]Zhang. Yingqing (1980, p. 2, 1985, p. 5).

[5]Wang. Cunzhen & Yan. Chunyou (1995, p. 90).

[6]According to the dispatch from the Xinhua News Agency on February 25, 1998: British PPL Therapeutics, the company once cooperated with the British Roslin Institute on creating Dolly the sheep, announced yesterday in London that they had cloned a calf by means of the technology

biology holography. Since the organism can perform asexual reproduction, human can also achieve this. The emergence of a cloned human being is only a matter of time, and some scientists have proclaimed their plan to clone human beings. Should cloned human beings emerge, the world would cease to be in a mess. As to this, Sun Wukong[7] has early "accomplished it" under the instruction of Wu Chengen—Wukong cloned himself (which again proves that the ancient people are never lower than modern people on intelligence). Before, this event was merely a myth, the change of the whole world however is a process of the actualization of myths. On the afternoon of August 11, 1999, CCTV4 (China Reports) reported the speech of Yang Xiangzhong the head of the Biotechnology Center's Transgenic Animal Facility in the University of Connecticut. He said, "Sun Wukong cloned himself. A cell of an organism embraces all the information of the latter." The five parts of the human eye correspond to the five human viscera, respectively: the eyelid corresponds to the spleen, the two corners to the heart, the sclera to the lung, the iris to the lever, and the pupil to the bone (The *Lingshu·Wulongjinyebiepian* 灵枢·五癃津液别篇 in the *Inner Canon of the Yellow Emperor* 黄帝·内经 records the reason: all the body fluids of the viscera diffuse upward into the eyes). The ear is like an upside-down baby, being a figure in miniature (As is said in *Lingshu·Kouwen* 灵枢·口问, the ear is where all the veins assemble); the face is holographic with the body (As is said in *Lingshu·Xieqizangfubingxing* 灵枢·邪气脏腑病形篇, the blood and *qi* 气 of the 12 arteries and 365 veins are all reflected by the empty holes on the face); man's limbs and joints are relatively independent parts, but they are also the different microcosms of the body. Any branch of a plant is identical to the whole in terms of shape and property. When an earth worm is cut into several pieces, each piece will develop into a new worm. On March 3, 1999, GDTV reported in the program of "Huaxia in 300s" a piece of news: a pig gave birth to a piglet with long ears and a long nose like an elephant. The piglet died two hours after its birth. This indicates that hybridization may occur between animals of different categories, and the rationale of this is: they share similar information. These are not the only cases.

Wang Cunzhen and Yan Chunyou hold that the law of biological time holography in the broad sense constitutes holography from three aspects, namely, time-time, individual-whole, and individual-individual holographies. Let us have a look at time-time holography first: seen at the cellular level, the trunk, leaves, and root of the bean embrace identical information with its seed, that is, they are absolutely holographic with one another. Then we turn to individual-whole holography: the progression of the individual is the microcosm of that of the whole. For instance, the evolution of human beings need as long as several billions of years whereas the human conception of the embryo only lasts ten months which however briefly and succinctly recapitulate in holographic fashion the process of the several billions of years. The third aspect

similar to that creating Dolly. The calf named "Mr. Jefferson" was created by them on 16th, last February in their subsidiary in Virginia, U.S.

[7]The monkey-king, also the first disciple of Xuanzang Master in the Chinese myth, *Journey to the West* 西游记 (Records of Xuanzang's going on a pilgrimage for Buddhist scriptures) authored by Wu Chengen.

is individual-individual holography: the difference of level at which the individual is located leads to the difference of extent to which the individual recapitulates the whole. This is merely the difference in the explicit state and there is no difference in the implicit one, say, plants of the same category must share the same properties, or we could not distinguish them.

Wang Cunzhen and Yan Chunyou note that the essential cause of biology holography is the self-duplication of DNA (deoxyribonucleic acid). The DNA molecules embrace all the genetic information passed on from the ancestors. At the split second when a single sperm fuses with an egg, a new genetic system comes into being. This new DNA system contains the whole set of genes of the future holistic information, namely, DNA is the storage depot of the holistic information from which the later progressions constantly extract the deposited information. The extraction as such is not scattered but is done generously and holistically in the form of the holistic information of DNA, which hence allocates each duplicated cell a complete copy of the meta-cell (The seed is also a meta-cell). As a result, when each group of cells constitute a higher-level holographic node, they also duplicate it according to this mode. In this way, each part of the organism embraces all the information of the DNA system, which hence amounts to the holographic correspondence among the holographic nodes.

To discuss such a proposition of "Human (physical as well as mental) is a minor cosmos" is a best starting point to recognize in depth the laws of cosmos holography and biology holography. What's more, **given that language is peculiar to human, it makes greatly convenient our transition to the theory of language holography after we are clear about the holography between human and the cosmos**.

In terms of the proposition about human body being the microcosm of the whole cosmos, it is never a new topic in Eastern and Western philosophies. Traditional Chinese medicine, *Yijing* 易经 (*I-Ching*), *Daodejing* 道德经 (*Laozi*) and the Buddhist Scriptures have all provided fairly abundant materials for demonstration. The parlance of "the integration of heaven and human" is one of them. Daoism School stresses the correspondence of nature of all things in the world and the identity between human and the cosmos. It believes that the happiness obtained via this identity is the absolute one in the true sense of the word, and the *Xiaoyaoyou* 逍遥游 (wander at random) in *Zhuangzi* 庄子 explicates the happiness as such. The first person presenting the thought of human-cosmos holography in the history of Western philosophy is Alcmaeon (Pythagorean) who believed that human and the whole cosmos were created in the same design, human being the microcosm of the whole macro world. "When you know the origin of thunder, wind and rain, and windstorm, you will know how the stomachache and artery spasm come about."[8] This is a corresponding relationship between human and heaven on movement. Seen at the level of time, human's whole life is the microcosm of that of the cosmos. German philosopher Friedrich Wilhelm Joseph Schelling (1775–1854) and scientist Loronz Oken (1779–1851) believed that human was the most perfect microcosmos and the ultimate product of the cosmic development, so he/she alone generalized the contents

[8]Mason. Stephen (1977, p. 215).

of all the previous developing stages. Oken contended, "Man is the summit of the development of nature, so he necessarily encompasses all the previous fruits, just like the fruit encompasses all the stages of development of the tree. In a word, man is necessarily the microcosm representing the whole cosmos. Since self-consciousness or spirit is embodied in man, 'natural philosophy' will necessarily prove that the spiritual law is of no difference from the natural one, and they describe one another and are similar to one another."[9] He also held that the more capable a thing is of conceiving the diversity of the cosmos inside itself, the more it approached eternity.

It is my contention that "conceiving the cosmos inside oneself" is not an ideal or a wish of all things but a fact naturally coming without being expected. If human is embedded in such an infinitely recursive structure of the cosmos, a fortiori, the cosmos will penetrate through human body. This is undoubtedly a theoretical topic, but all the more the admission of the fact. All the images and attributes of human (physically as well as mentally) correspond to those of the cosmos. In nature, there are surging rivers and babbling streams, whereas inside human body, there are pulsing arteries and seepage-flowing capillaries; it is not a distorted conclusion that the high mountain corresponds to the rounded breast; the water, sclerotin, and minerals in human body all exist in nature. Wang Cunzhen and Yan Chunyou believe that human brain is a result of the cosmos' highly developed memory properties, a highly specialized memory organ of the cosmos; human visual sense is a proof of the existence of the visible light; human auditory sense is a remained ancient sound and will not exist without continual sound stimulations; human and other creatures are also constantly exchanging information with the cosmos, and hence the changes of the earth, even of the cosmos, can all be reflected on human body, organisms, even man's mood.

As regards human repeating the evolution of the cosmos, Wang Cunzhen and Yan Chunyou thus say in the essay of "The repetition law of cosmos holography": "Human body is an extremely diversified universe, encompassing innumerable minor ones, from the most beautiful spiritual flower in the cosmos to the kingdom of cells, the atom world, the molecular models... All the information in the cosmos is conceived in human body. It is not hard to infer therefrom: all the future information latent in the cosmos also hides in human body. In this connection, we can clearly see from the hight of information that human is a microcosm of the cosmos. Human body conceives all the past, present, and future information of the cosmos, and so do other things." This indicates that there is a profound holographic relation between human and the cosmos. Zha Ruqiang who holds the same idea says, "The ascending transitional order of the levels of human structure is: elementary particle, atom, molecule, biomacromolecule, the system of biomacromolecule, cell and cell body; during the development of nature, the upward branching phases can be thus divided: the state of elementary particle in the very early stage of the Big Bang (Of course, this is merely a scientific hypothesis at present), and the successive productions of elements, molecular compounds, biomacromolecules on the earth—nucleic acids and proteins, and multicellular organisms. The transitional order mentioned afore is exactly the repetition of the branching phases of nature's development process,

[9]Mason. Stephen (1977, p. 332).

which resembles the fact that the growth of the individual organism is the repetition of that of the system, viz., the biological evolution."[10]

3 The law of material-spiritual holography

Language is a spiritual phenomenon, so we must discuss the holographic phenomenon at material and spiritual levels before carrying out the transition from the holography of the material world to the holographic relationship between language structure and the cosmic one.

Wang Cunzhen and Yan Chunyou contend that the subject (human) encompasses all the information of the object (human's practical or cognitive objects) and vice versa. This is the fundamental connotation of the law of subject-object holography. Since human capable of thinking is produced in the material world, it means that the subject in the narrow sense, to wit., human, already hides in the object. Recognition is the self-aware information of the object, the rebuilding of the object's world, and the self-aware world of the object. Every artificial thing is nothing but a material sign manifesting the spirit. The subject is capable of recognizing the object merely due to the fact that he/she already contains inside him/herself the same information as the object, just like the adult can conjecture children's psyche insomuch as he/she has experienced his/her own childhood. Only identical information can recognize other identical information and mutually resonate with it. **The subject is holographic with the object primarily due to their homology. They are different developing forms of the same thing, and develop from the same thing. The homology as such essentially determines their holographability**. In terms of evolution, the spirit and the material are holographically isomorphic and parallel with each other. The spirit is the highly specialized material memory, and the latter is the primary form of the former. The fact that the spirit is capable of recognizing the material world justifies for its own sake the identity between the spirit and the material, namely, they are isomorphic and homogeneous, i.e., holographic, with one another.

This question I raise here is very significant. Language is both a spiritual phenomenon or product and a material phenomenon (sound). If there were no identity between the material and the spirit, namely, if they were not isomorphic, that will mean that there would be something irreconcilable with the cosmos! De facto, this irreconcilability does not exist. We will ultimately find that language structure is holographically isomorphic with the cosmic one. This also provides the rationale that language can recognize and describe the material world.

Language properties reflect such traits like social background, social group, career, age, sex, and the like. Everyone's idiolect and social dialect are determined by his/her social circumstances. Conversely, language is the social marker of every one. This fact shows the spiritual communication between language qua a material form and

[10]Zha. Ruqiang (1985, p. 5).

man. This idea is greatly favored by Humboldt who says, "Language is simultaneously an explicit phenomenon of a nation's spirit; a nation's language is their spirit, and a nation's spirit is their language."[11] Why is language a nation's spirit? According to the theory of holography, how a nation speaks or uses its language is **one of its spirit-generation modes**. Here, the material language and human spirit are isomorphic and homogeneous with each other. Just imagine, if there were no holographic relationship between the material language and the user's spirit, how could a nation's spirit be sensed from its language? A similar parlance is: "And speech is the distinctive mark of the personality, for good and ill, the distinctive mark of home and of nation, mankind's patent of nobility. So inextricably has language grown inside personality, home, nation, mankind, and life itself that we may sometimes be tempted to ask whether language is a mere reflexion of, or simply is not all those things—the very seed leaf of their growth."[12]

4 The argument for the status of the inner language holography in terms of the law of cosmos holography

4.1 The Introduction to the State of the Inner Language Holography

After the introduction of the theory of cosmos holography, the law of biology holography, and the material-spiritual holography, we have the conditions for the transition to the state of the inner language holography.

When discussing "the law of sense-by-intuition holography," Wang Cunzhen and Yan Chunyou mention the law of language holography:

"People's emotional communications are expressed by language. ...The holographability of language is obvious, say, people of the same language can very easily understand each other's 'meanings' whereas those of different languages have difficulty in understanding one another. ...People knowing the same language will necessarily produce the holographic resonance on language, and understand each other's meanings. This is the law of language holography."

"During the long evolution process, human language has been integrated with 'meaning' and has formed concepts in human mind. When people hear someone's utterances, that which they hear is not a single word but the 'meaning' qua a whole. Nevertheless, the holographic degree of language per se is not that high, and under many circumstances it cannot properly express our intended meanings; furthermore, due to the fact that different people have different intellectual backgrounds, different levels of understandings might be given as to the same word."

---

[11]Qtd. Zhao. Shikai (1990, p. 197).

[12]Hjelmslev (1969, p. 3).

"De facto, the holographic connection between the minds completely relies on sense-by-intuition, a state or act in which one knows clearly about the meaning but cannot tell what it is or cannot express it by means of language. It can also be called an intuition. Sense-by-intuition is a holographic resonance effect in the relatively deep thinking level, namely, so long as you send some information, the other party will immediately produce thinking resonance and understand the significance therein. …As a matter of fact, language communication is itself also realized via sense-by-intuition. …People are not restricted to language itself but know the implications it embraces. Albeit many things relying on sense-by-intuition cannot be uttered, the sense-by-intuition still relies on language's aid, say, we can immediately sense by intuition all the meanings merely via several utterances, words, or an action, mood, etc. This is attributed to the holographability of the information provided by language. The cognitive structure of sense-by-intuition in our mind might also be a holographic structure in that a little bit of information input from outside will produce holographic resonance hence holographic sense-by-intuition."[13]

The law of language holography they expound can be summarized as follows:

(1) "People knowing the same language will necessarily produce the holographic resonance on language, and understand the each other's meanings."
(2) "The holographic degree of language per se is not that high, and under many circumstances it cannot properly express our intended meanings." In this vein, when language can properly express our intended meanings, its holographic degree is high.

In fact, this is not the law of language holography.

The first point can be merely regarded as the "holographic connection in mind between the utterer and the hearer." Their "holographic resonance effect in the relatively deep thinking level" and "thinking resonance" are the "law of sense-by-intuition holography" in Wang and Yan's terminology, being entirely different from the law of language holography. Equating them results from wrongly determining the subject of holography. The subject of the law of language holography is supposed to be the part and the whole, the part and other parts, this level and that level, or the like, within language substance. What is astonishing is, how can the authors leave their definition of the law of cosmos holography and Zhang Yingqing's law of biology holography when discussing the law of language holography? How come the law of language holography becomes the interpersonal mental communication "relying on the aid of language" but sets aside the relationships between the subsystem and other subsystems (i.e., the holographic node and other holographic nodes) of language system, and between the part and the whole? **The law of language holography means: (1) the state of the inner language holography (Inside the language system, the part is holographic with the whole; one part contains the same information as other parts; each holographic node of a system becomes to a different extent an microcosm of the whole). (2) The state of the outer language holography (the holographic state between language system and the**

[13]Wang. Cunzhen & Yan. Chunyou (1995, pp. 148–150).

external world; language structure is isomorphic and similar to and embedded in the cosmic one).

In one word, the law of language holography is supposed to include the holographic conditions inside the language substance and the state of the outer language holography, being entirely different from the mental communication between the utterer and the hearer. As has been noted, insofar as the essence is concerned, the theory of language holography, **the law of language holography, and language holographability** are one and the same, referring to the states of the inner as well as the outer language holography. Be that as it may, "the theory of language holography" particularly designates a language theory; "the law of language holography" is parallel with another term, "the law of biology holography"; and "language holographability" refers to an essential property of language.

Then, does the second point mentioned above ("The holographic degree of language per se is not that high, and under many circumstances it cannot properly express our intended meanings") designate the holographic isomorphism between language system and human? The meaning of the first half of the word is not clear; as to the second half, it might mean that the imperfection of language's function is irrelevant to the hight of holographic degree of language itself. Language's function is never perfect. As to this, please cf. my *Pragmatics in Chinese Culture.*[14] Furthermore, the hight of the holographic degree of language itself is not determined by whether or not it properly expresses one's intended meanings but by the holographic conditions between the holographic nodes and between the part and the whole within language system, and by the isomorphic conditions between language system and human. In addition, even in terms of the isomorphism between language system and human, the case is not what is said by the authors, namely, whether or not language can properly express one's intended meanings.

Of course, the hight of the holographic degree of language itself deserves discussion, but the authors' rationale of the judgment, i.e., "The holographic degree of language per se is not that high," is out of place. I will not repeat the interpretations here.

What is the state of the inner language holography?

The state of the inner language holography is: of the layers of language, to wit., morpheme—word—phrase—(clause)—sentence—discourse, the parts are holographic with the whole; the parts share the same information with one another; each holographic node (subsystem) in language system has its counterpart or similar information, respectively, in the whole and other nodes. That is to say, each holographic node of the system becomes, to a different extent, a microcosm of the whole. The last judgment, namely, "Each holographic node of the system becomes, to a different extent, a microcosm of the whole," is taking "one" (a holographic node) for "the whole" (the microcosm of the whole," viz., the state of the inner language holography).

[14]Qian. Guanlian (1997, pp. 83–89).

That which merits particular stress is, it is only in the sense of holography that the mutual embracement and conversion of language's holographic nodes is understandable. Just imagine, if it is in the sense of phonetic form, how can the single syllable or word embrace the whole language system? That which is mutually embraced among the holographic nodes is the other party's information rather than its substance itself, and the infinite information can be compressed into a very tiny space (Please see the demonstrations in the following two cases of the English "vicissitude" and the Chinese "*leizhui*累赘"). That the holographic nodes are capable of converting into each other is exactly due to their holographability, and the fact itself exactly indicates that each holographic node embraces the others' information.

The present investigation as regards the state of the inner language holography is limited to the substantial holographic nodes—syllable, word, phrase, sentence, and discourse, among others.

4.2 Demonstrations of the State of the Inner Language Holography

If the organism can be roughly divided into three levels, namely cell, cell group, and the complex (the organ) of cell groups, we have two methods to divide language. In the first place, we can divide it by information unit: morpheme, word, phrase, sentence, and discourse. In the second place, we can do so by the pattern of things (i.e., sound): phoneme, syllable, the combination of syllables, and language flow.

We now examine the relationships among the holographic nodes of language to see whether or not these are true: "The same information is shared by the part (subsystem) and other parts or by the part and the whole; the part embraces all the information of the whole; and, any holographic node (subsystem) is a microcosm of the whole."

The first demonstration: the part embraces all the information of the whole.

Let us take the first word of the inaugural address of George Washington the first president of the United States as a case: Among the vicissitudes incident to life, no event could have filled me with greater anxieties than that of which the notification was transmitted by your order, and received on the 14th day of the present month.[15]

With "vicissitude" as an example, let us have a look at whether or not it embraces all the information of English. As is known, the meaning of any word in a language cannot interpret itself but can only be determined or interpreted by some other words. The interesting thing is, these other words cannot interpret themselves either and cannot but be determined or interpreted by still other words, ad infinitum. … What might be the result? Let us have a look at the process first:

[15] *Famous Inaugural Addresses of the The Presidents of The United States*. Beijing: World Publishing Cooperation, 1996.

The first level of information:
Vicissitude embraces this information:
change, especially in somebody's fortunes[16] (Irrelevant information is omitted, similarly hereinafter).
The second level of information (where all the words on the first level are deduced respectively):
change embraces this information:
changed or different conditions; something used in place of another or others;
especially embraces this information:
to an exceptional degree; in particular;
in embraces this information:
indicating physical surroundings, circumstances, etc.
somebody embraces this information:
some person; replaced by anybody in interrogative or negative, etc. sentences;
fortune embraces this information:
chance; chance looked upon as a power deciding or influencing somebody or something; fate; good or bad luck coming to a person or undertaking.
So far, the deduction of all the words on the first level of information is finished.
The third level of information (where the words on the second level are deduced respectively):
changed embraces this information: …
or embraces this information: …
different embraces this information: …
conditions embraces this information: …
…
undertaking embraces this information: …
So far, the deduction of all the words on the second level of information is finished.
…
Until the nth and (n + 1)th levels embrace this information: …?

What might be the result of the deduction as such? That is, a word can be deduced into a complex with an astoundingly vast number of words, including almost all the words in the lexicon. What's more, the information embracement is performed rigorously in accordance with the lexical definitions and, on the premise that the grammar is guaranteed as regards correctness, it can be continuously described, prescribed, fulfilled, and replenished. This is to say that new branches can grow out by means of various subordinate clauses, and independent clauses of participle, adjective, noun, etc., ad infinitum. Differently put, each word (In Chinese, it is "character (*zi*字)") contains latently all the other words (characters) of this language. Before the computer was invented, this sort of deduction sounded like a myth. Today when the computer stores English and Chinese lexicons, this checking work becomes far more

[16] All the following information from this piece on is excepted from *Oxford Advanced Learner's Dictionary of Current English*. Longdon, 1974, A. S. Hornby.

easy. I have a metaphor: the function of each piece (say, rook, knight, cannon, etc.) of the Chinese chess is determined by all the other pieces and their interrelations. It is impossible for us to genuinely understand the function of every piece unless we are clear about the functions of all the other pieces and their interrelations. There are 16 pieces in either party of the chess, which means that one piece embraces the information of all the 16 ones, namely, the part is holographic with the whole.

Let us take Chinese "*leizhui* 累赘 (encumbrance) as another example and see how it embraces all the words in the whole Chinese lexicon.

The first level: 累赘;

the second level: (deduced from 累赘) (about things) *duoyu* 多余 (more than what is due), *mafan* 麻烦 (trouble);

the third level: (deduced from 多余) *chaoguo xuyao shuliang de* 超过需要数量的 (more than the due number); *bu biyao de* 不必要的 (unnecessary);

(deduced from 麻烦) *fansuo*烦琐 (tedious); *feishi* 费事 (troublesome) *shi ren feishi huo zengjia fudan* 使人费事或增加负担 (trouble someone or increase someone's burden);

the fourth level: *chaoguo* 超过 (more than)—— …

xuyao 需要 (due)—— …

shuliang 数量 (number)—— …

de 的 (-'s)—— …

bu 不 (un-)—— …

biyao 必要 (necessary)—— …

fansuo 烦琐 (tedious)—— …

feishi 费事 (troublesome)—— …

shi 使 (make)—— …

ren 人 (someone)—— …

huo 或 (or)—— …

zengjia 增加 (increase)—— …

fudan 负担 (burden)—— …

…

till the nth and (n + 1)th levels: …?

The fourth level is deduced to the fifth one with a larger number, and the fifth to the sixth one with a far larger number… The deduction continues till the nth and (n + 1)th levels. The result is necessarily this: a Chinese word (character) can be interpreted by all the other words in the system of Chinese, namely, each Chinese word de facto embraces all the words (characters) in the system of Chinese.

The necessary conclusion of the previous demonstration is: in language system, the part is holographic with the whole.

Presumably, some may think: to be sure, it has been successfully demonstrated that one word embraces the information of all the other words of a language, but how about the morpheme, the syllable, or even the phoneme? Can it be said that a phoneme or a syllable embraces the information of the whole language system?

Sounding fantastic notwithstanding, this question is not hard to demonstrate. Any existent morpheme or phoneme (or syllable) in a language will appear more than ten thousands of times in its lexicon, and, without it, the whole language system would be left thousands of vacancies, just like the condition of one thousand boils and a hundred holes or ten thousand boils and ten hundred holes, and thorough disintegration is the necessary sequel. If an existent morpheme or phoneme (syllable) were omitted, it would disappear from hundreds or thousands of places, which is equal to the omission of hundreds and thousands of existent words. This is the so-to-speak "cut the ground from under one's foot." **When the omission of an existent morpheme or phoneme (syllable) can disintegrate the whole language system, doesn't it follow that a morpheme or phoneme (syllable) embraces the information of the whole language**?

The second demonstration: the part embraces the same information as all the other parts.

When we are clear about the aforementioned deductions of "vicissitude" and "累赘," we can be said having acknowledged that the part embraces the same information as all the other parts. For instance, merely out of intuition, we can acknowledge that "vicissitude" shares something in common with "change" and "fortune" in its second level of information, but we cannot imagine something in common between "vicissitude" and "exceptional." What is interesting is, in its third level of information, "vicissitude" encounters "exceptional" and is interpreted by the latter, namely, they embrace one another. Additionally, in the same level, it encounters with "look upon (look on as or consider)" seemingly more irrelevant to it like an apple and an oyster, and is interpreted by it, namely, they embrace one another. This means **the possible mutual embracement between "vicissitude" and some word in English lexicon at a rather far information level of the former, namely, they are holographic with each other**. In the same vein, it is understandable that "累赘" and "多余," "麻烦" in its next level of information embrace one another, but it is not that easy to imagine that "累赘" embraces the same information as "数量" or "必要" on the fourth level. This is a fact, though. To this connection, it is even harder to imagine that it embraces the same information as the words in further levels. That is also a factual embracement of information. This is to say that all possibly, "累赘" can embrace the same information as some word in Chinese lexicon at a very far level, as is the case of "vicissitude," namely, **each part embraces other parts, and is simultaneously embraced by the latter. This is the repetition of the law of cosmos holography in language, but it is also the property of any system whatsoever.**

The definition of each word also embraces that of any other one in a dictionary. This fact can obtain its circumstantial evidence from the proposition of "The cosmos of implicate order is a super-dictionary." Someone notes when commenting on the theory of implicate order—its founder is David Bohm (the professor of theoretical physics at London's Birkbeck College), one of the most outstanding contemporary physicists, "The meticulous research of any single element can in principle reveal the detailed information of any other element in the cosmos. In some sense, Bohm's cosmos of implicate order constitutes a super-dictionary in which the definition of every word embraces that of any other one in the dictionary."[17] The world is quite

[17]The original essay was in Science Abstracts, 1983. Qtd. Wang. Cunzhen & Yan. Chunyou (1995, p. 39).

amazing: "Any single element can in principle reveal the detailed information of any other element in the cosmos" parallels the fact that a word embraces all the information of its language!

Previously, I mentioned that "In its third level of information, 'vicissitude (change, especially in somebody's fortunes)' embraces 'look upon (look on as or consider)' seemingly more irrelevant to it like an apple and an oyster, and is embraced by the latter." Properly speaking, **in the law of cosmos holography, an apple and an oyster can be interrelated**. **If they were really irrelevant to one another, the whole edifice of the theory of cosmos holography would collapse**. "Human and heaven are integral, and all things in the world are of the same origin",[18] that is, not merely an apple and an oyster can be interrelated, the same also holds to all things in the world! **Being interrelated is being holographic. Being interrelated means mutually embracing each other's information**.

In language system, any part is holographic with any other one, which can be demonstrated by a simpler formal logic program: when "In language system, the part is holographic with the whole" (please recall the case that "累赘" embraces all the Chinese words) is a fact, a fortiori, any part of a whole is holographic with any other part, that is (the ~ is "holographic with" in the following formulae):

Hypothesis: the lexicon of any language is a holographic set Q; the element (each word) is n, so there is a holographic set (infinite set): Q = (n1, n2, n3, n4, n5 … nX).

Cause: n1 ~ Q or n2 ~ Q, or nX ~ Q, or nX + 1 ~ Q, …

Effect: n1 ~ n2 ~ nX ~ nX + 1.

This is a problem solvable by formal logic. For instance, "vicissitude" is holographic with "change" in its second level of information, or with "changed, or, different, conditions, something, used, in, place, of, another or others, …," till "undertaking," on the third level, a fortiori, any word above is holographic with any other one. In the same way, 累赘 is holographic with 多余 or 麻烦 in its second level of information or with 超过, 需要, 数量, 不, 必要, 烦琐, 费事, 使, 人, 或, 增加, 负担 on the third level, a fortiori, any single item above is holographic with any other one.

The third demonstration: each holographic node in language system has its counterpart or similar information, respectively, in the whole and other nodes.

The corresponding phenomenon as such is embodied to the extreme in biological sphere. How is it embodied in language system which is non-biological but imitates its dynamic balance?

Let us first examine the correspondence namely holographability between sentence (a holographic node) and phrase (a holographic node at the lower level) of Chinese on structure.

The relationships between the several sentence components of Chinese can be manifested in the form as follows:

[18]Ren. Jiyu, the inscription in *The Theory of Cosmic Holographic Unity*.

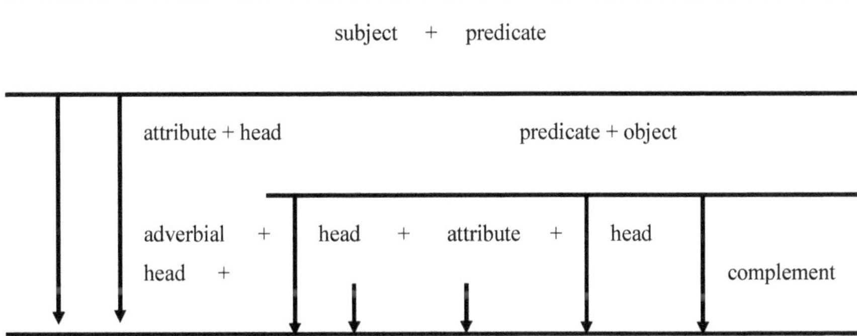

The head director has taken away this year's outlay.

Next, let us have a look at whether or not the subject-predicate, predicate-object, endocentric, complementary, and coordinate phrases have their respective counterparts or similar information in the above sentence.

The subject-predicate phrase, e.g., *fanying minjie* 反应敏捷 (react quickly), can correspond to the subject (The head director) + predicate (has taken away this year's outlay) sentence.

The predicate-object phrase, e.g., *qiaoji jianpan* 敲击键盘 (strike the keyboard), can correspond to the predicate + object (taken away this year's outlay).

The endocentric phrase, e.g., *caise pingmu* 彩色屏幕 (color screen), can correspond to the subject (the head director) or the object (this year's outlay) in the sentence (where the subject and the object are both manifested in the attribute + head structure).

The complementary phrase, e.g., *chu de kuai* 出得快 (be produced fast), can correspond to the head + complement structure (taken away) in the predicate of the sentence.

The coordinate phrase, e.g., *yingjian (yu) ruanjian* 硬件(与)软件 (hardware (and) software) in which the two parts are parallel to each other. Nevertheless, since neither the subject nor the object in the sentence above is a coordinate phrase, there is no correspondence. If the sentence were changed into "The head and the associate directors have taken away this year's outlay and equipments," there would be correspondence.

There is no corresponding point of prepositional phrase in the sentence above. Nonetheless, we could soon find some if the sentence were changed into one including a prepositional phrase.

This is to say that each sort of phrase can find its counterpart or **similar information** in the sentence as a whole. **This is holography per se. Of language levels, phrase and sentence are the two parts of the highest and the most obvious holographic degree in terms of correspondence and holography**.

The holographic degree with the same hight is also manifested in the holography between sentence and discourse one level higher than it. Various sentence structures—the "subject + predicate + object" and non-subject-predicate structures, the coordinate, subordinate, multiple and tight complex sentences, among others—show considerably amazing correspondence in the discourse. This is because the overall text structure is constructed by means of the recursive embedment (the repetition of identical structures) of the sentence structures above.

Then, does the word in a lower level have its counterpart in the sentence? Of course yes. The noun corresponds, respectively, to the subject and the object heads in the sentence, the verb to the predicate head, the adjective to the attribute of the subject and the object, the numeral plus the measure word to the attribute (no need of examples here), the adverbial (e.g., be in place [all at once]) or the complement (e.g., be tested [twice]), and the adverb to the predicate's adverbial (e.g., omit them [all]) and complement (e.g., [rather] amazing). Like the content word it replaces or demonstrates, the pronoun can also find its counterpart in the sentence. That which merits heed is, the interjection expresses joy, surprise, disillusionment, a call or a response, etc., usually being monosyllabic and independent, so it hardly has a corresponding point in the sentence structure. This indicates that the holographic degree between the interjection and the sentence is not high. This is the phenomenon of "non-holo-ness in holography," which will be discussed later. This notwithstanding, the interjection can find its counterpart in a higher level of the discourse. In the sphere of function words, the preposition cannot independently act as a sentence element but can only compose a prepositional phrase with other words, so the holographic degree between the sentence and it is not high; on the other hand, it is considerably highly holographic with the prepositional phrase (one level lower than sentence and one level higher than word). The conjunction is a function word joining words, phrases, clauses, or sentences, and its correspondence to the clause is implicit and latent. The auxiliary is a function word adhered to other language units to express the grammatical meanings of dynamicity, etc. It is characterized by strong adhesiveness. Structural auxiliary and dynamic auxiliary cannot find their respective corresponding points in the sentence. The modal particle can be placed at the pausing point at the end or in the middle of the sentence to express various moods, being fundamentally monosyllabic (e.g., *de* 的, *le* 了, *ma* 吗, *ba* 吧, *ne* 呢, *a* 啊), so it has no corresponding structural point in the clause. The situations of having no corresponding structural point all belong in the phenomenon of "non-holo-ness in holography," which will be expounded later.

Does the morpheme (also a holographic node) one level lower than word have its counterpart or similar information in the sentence? Theoretically, the mutual embracing relationship between it and the sentence is already demonstrated and is undoubtedly holographic, the structural correspondence between them however shows that their holographic degree is low. This is also a phenomenon of "non-holo-ness in holography," which will be expounded later, too.

From the discussions above as regards Chinese language materials, we can draw the following conclusion:

Each holographic node in language system has its counterpart or similar information, respectively, in the whole and other nodes; each holographic node becomes an microcosm of the whole to a different extent, namely, any part whatsoever of language system embraces all the information of the whole, and the part is absolutely holographic with the whole.

Next, let us take English as the language material to see whether or not we can draw the same conclusion.

The basic sentence pattern[19] of English being various as it is, it cannot go beyond the five types as follows. I would like to note in passing that the following generalization is a little questionable: in the so-called SVC, SV, SVO, SVOO, and SVOC, the S, O, and C (subject, object, and complement) are terms for the division of syntactic function whereas the only V (verb) is a term for that of lexical function, so P (predicate) is supposed to be substituted for V. As to this confused parlance, nevertheless, I will not change it here and now.

SVC structure (e.g., The man is a teacher; She looks fine; The tape recorder is on the table);

SV structure (e.g., Iron rusts);

SVO structure (e.g., Liverpool won the game);

SVOO structure (e.g., Mary lent me her car);

SVOC structure (e.g., They elected him president).

The closest level to the clause is the phrase.

Noun phrase: determiner + premodifier + noun + postmodifier

the tall boy sitting in the corner

Verbal phrase: simple verbal phrase

complex verbal phrase

finite verbal phrase

infinite verbal phrase (infinitive, gerund, and participle phrase)

Adjective phrase: modifier + adjective + postmodifier/ complement

too difficult for that child

too hot to be enjoyable

Adverb phrase: modifier + adverb + postmodifier

very clearly indeed

Prepositional phrase: modifier + preposition + complement

directly above my head

As a holographic node, the phrase is the closest to its counterpart in the clause as the holographic node one level higher, namely, their holographibility is the highest. Noun phrase corresponds, respectively to the subject, object, and complement in the clause. The mutual correspondence between verbal phrase and the V (supposed to be the predicate) in the clause is the most typical, and another relevant correspondence is that between infinite verbal phrase on the one hand and the subject, complement (or predicative), object, attribute, and adverbial in the clause on the other hand. Adjective phrase corresponds to the compliment (or predicative) and attribute in the clause. Adverb phrase corresponds to the adverbial in the clause. Prepositional phrase corresponds, respectively, to the attribute, adverbial, and complement (or predicative) in the clause.

Does the word one level lower than the phrase have its counterpart in the English sentence? Of course yes. Since the analysis of it resembles that in Chinese, I will not

[19]The grammatical materials in this book are mainly excerpted from Quirk et al. (1985, 1996).

give a detailed list of the self-evident holographibility (say, the mutual correspondences between the noun, pronoun, numeral, adjective, adverb, verb, preposition on the one hand and the structure of the clause on the other hand) but put more stress on the non-corresponding conditions mainly manifested in the article, the conjunction, and the interjection. Given that the article is always put before a noun and is not independent, it is usually not the object of stress, and hence its counterpart in the clause is implicit and latent; the conjunction is also a function word pronounced with no stress, and cannot act as an independent element in the clause, and hence its correspondence to the latter is also implicit and latent; the interjection is often treated as an independent element, and it has no counterpart in the clause, either. Nevertheless, in the discourse one level higher, it has its counterpart.

Does the morpheme (also a holographic node) one level lower than the word have its counterpart or similar information in the English sentence? Theoretically, the mutual embracing relationship between it and the sentence is already demonstrated, which is undoubted, in that the sentence is divided and formed on the basis of morphemes. Seen from the corresponding relationship between the morpheme and the clause, the holographic degree is low. This is also a phenomenon of non-holoness in holography. What is the reason? The reason is, in a sentence, the units that can draw the most cognitive attention are meaning groups and the meaning of the clause rather than the morpheme. Consequently, the morpheme's counterpart in the clause is implicit.

On the ground of the above two language materials and three demonstrations, we can, albeit not perfectly, draw the following conclusions: of the morpheme—word—phrase—clause—sentence—discourse levels of language, the part is holographic with the whole; the part embraces the same information as other parts; each holographic node in language system has its counterpart or similar information, respectively, in the whole and other nodes. That is to say, each holographic node of the system becomes, to a different extent, a microcosm of the whole.

The holographic and isomorphic relationship between language system and human body (This is also a content of the law of language holography) has been discussed in Sect. 2, 3, and 4 of Chapter 1: human body has such a dynamically balanced and symmetrically harmonious structure, which creates conditions for and lays the foundation of the states of the inner as well as the outer language holography. Here I will not go into much detail.

4.3 The "non-Holo-Ness in Holography" in the State of the Inner Language Holography

Be that as it may, I also find that in Chinese, the interjection, preposition, conjunction, and modal particle do not have structural counterparts in the clause, or the so-to-speak correspondence is implicit and latent. The same holds to the article, conjunction, and interjection in English. In addition, neither of the morphemes in the two languages has its counterpart in the clause. This situation means that the holographic degree between them is not high, which is also called "non-holo-ness in holography." How to interpret this phenomenon? In my views, there are three points:

In the first place, the function of the holographic node is specialized and is situated in different stages. Since Saussure and beyond, people all acknowledge that language is a system of signs (but they remain to demonstrate this, and Sect. 5 of this chapter will do the work), and that this system is necessarily a functional one. Language is created by human beings, and it is inherently employed to facilitate human beings on thinking about problems, expressing meanings and emotions, and describing the inner and the outer world. This is function. (I would like to mention by passing that it is not occasional that there are fairly many functional linguists in China.) **The functionality of the whole determines that of the holographic nodes in its structural levels. What's more, the function of the holographic node is a specialized one, being situated in different stages of development**. The phone only has the specialized function of itself. The same holds to the phoneme. "The phone is the smallest unit of sound in phonetics, and a sound is a phone. The quality of the phone is determined by its physiological and physical attributes. The phoneme is the smallest unit of sound in the phonemic system of a language, and its fundamental function is to distinguish meanings. The quality of the phoneme is determined by the social attributes of the speech sounds."[20] Both the phone and the phoneme have their respective fundamental functions, to wit., the specialized functions. The syllable's specialized function lies in constituting the word one level higher than it. In this connection, albeit the phoneme and the syllable in a language can form the relationship of mutual embracement, namely the holographic relationship, with the whole system, they are incapable of corresponding to the clause one even two levels higher (there are the levels of the word and the phrase in between) than them. It happens that most interjections and modal particles only have one syllable so, like the syllable, they cannot correspond to or be holographic with the clause at the level of structure, either. Zhang Yingqing who discovered the law of biology holography thus interprets the non-holo-ness of it in his *The Three Laws of the Organism's Structure*: in the sphere of mammal, no holographic node except the embryo can reach the last stage of the development and form a new whole. The holographic nodes all stop at different stages of development due to the fact that the whole of high unity constrains the holographic node's independent and autonomous development. Meanwhile, the regulatory role that the whole plays on the holographic nodes specializes them, for the sake of serving different purposes of usage, to different extents. The specialization as such further obstructs their way to the ultimate stage of development. For the understanding of the phenomenon of non-holo-ness of language, this passage is of great inspirations manifested in two points: first, all the holographic nodes stop at different stages of development; secondly, for the sake of different purposes of usage, the holographic nodes are specialized to different extents. **To language system, specialization is the particularity of the function**.

[20]Zhang. Yanchang, Dai. Shuyan & Li. Bing (1993, p. 50).

In the second place, given that language has different holographic levels, its holography is supposed to be grasped in a holistic fashion. Wang Cunzhen and Yan Chunyou believe, "At the level of cognition, the 'non-holo-ness' is caused by people's confusion of different information levels. They separate the micro, meso and macro levels, putting the concepts suitable for this level to that one. Resultantly, what they see is naturally the 'non-holo-ness'. Since the organism is a whole, it should be grasped holistically rather than being restricted to some aspects or levels."[21] The reason why the article and the conjunction in English cannot find their corresponding points at the level of clause is also supposed to be thus found. In English, the level of clause is indeed what it shows, namely, there are merely five basic forms—SVC, SV, SVO, SVOO, and SVOC. In the clause, there are indeed no explicit positions for the article and the conjunction which can only function in an implicit fashion.

Thirdly, there are implicit and explicit holographic states. When a holographic node fails to find its counterpart at a higher level, it is not absolutely but explicitly "no" and implicitly "yes." "The 'non-holo-ness of holography' is a difference on explicit state. There is the necessity to introduce the concept of "holographic threshold." Holographic threshold is the boundary over which the information needs to rise when it manifests itself or transfers from one level to another. Once it reaches some threshold value, the information will exist in another state, say, the transference from the micro to the meso, from the meso to the macro. The constraint from the holographic threshold gives rise to the difference at the level of quality of the holographic states on both sides of the threshold. Nevertheless, the information of the different holographic states is identical in essence. Within some holographic threshold, compared with the higher level, information exists in an implicit fashion, playing a latent role on the higher level; when the gradual accumulation of the latent information reaches its holographic threshold, whereas, there will emerge a qualitative leap, and the information will leap from the implicit state to the explicit one."[22] That is to say, notwithstanding that the interjection, preposition, conduction, and mood particle in Chinese and the article, conjunction, and interjection in English do not have their respective counterparts in the structure of the clause, the "no" is not absolute in the true sense of the word; rather, it is merely implicit "yes." **When the gradual accumulation of the latent information reaches its holographic threshold, say, the discourse, there will emerge a qualitative leap, and the information will leap from the implicit state to the explicit one.** As a consequence, it will be an easy job to find the corresponding points of the above parts of speech in Chinese and English at the level of discourse.

[21] Wang. Cunzhen & Yan. Chunyou (1995, p. 95).

[22] Wang. Cunzhen & Yan. Chunyou (1995, p. 96).

4.4 *Brief Summary of the State of the Inner Language Holography*

Of the levels of language's substances, namely, morpheme—word—(clause)—sentence—discourse, the part is holographic with the whole; the part embraces the same information as other parts; each holographic node in language system has its counterpart or similar information, respectively, in the whole and other nodes. That is to say, each holographic node of the system becomes, to a different extent, a microcosm of the whole.

Now let us look back at the implications of the poem at the beginning of this chapter: To see a world in a grain of sand, and a heaven in a wild flower, hold infinity in the palm of your hand, and eternity in an hour. It mentions material, biological, spacial, and temporal holographies, in a word, cosmic holography. The most interesting thing is that language (English poem) can be employed to describe the cosmic holography, which is itself a proof that language is isomorphic and similar to and embedded in the cosmos. The poem offers a thorough support for the state of the inner language holography.

5 The argument for the status of the inner language holography in terms of the system theory

Introduction: this section will take another way (namely different from that demonstrating the state of the inner language holography by means of the law of cosmos holography): to argue for the state of the inner language holography by means of the system theory.

If we can succeed in demonstrating that language is a system, that the most prominent prompters of a (any) system emerge one by one in language, we can draw the conclusion that taking the way of the system theory can also reach the theory of language holography. As is indicated in the second one of the ten principles of the theory of cosmos holography: **all the systems are holographic. All the holographic systems are of equivalence** (For details, see Sect. 4 of Chapter 2).

There might be such an opinion: Saussure has early asserted that "Language is a system of signs," why don't you use the ready-made conclusion? What is the need to demonstrate it from the beginning? Is it that Saussure only has assertion but gives no demonstration?

It is Xu Guozhang's contention that "Of the systematicity, discreteness, and learnability of language, systematicity is the most essential."[23] Since it is the most essential, there is all the more the need to ask: Who has ever demonstrated that language is a system?

[23]Xu. Guozhang (1999, p. 21).

It is a fact that Saussure gives this conclusion. It is not problematic to say that language is a "sign" and there is no need to demonstrate this insomuch as language is itself a sort of sign. Who, nevertheless, has ever demonstrated that language is a "system"? The level of sciences in Saussure's age did not permit him to demonstrate his assertion by means of the thought of modern system theory. That is to say, **Saussure remained to demonstrate his assertion by mean of the thought of modern system theory**. As is noted by Li Xiyin, the assertion that "Saussure remained to demonstrate 'Language is a system' by means of the thought of modern system theory" is right. To be sure, structuralism can be said the forerunner of the thought of system theory, and there would be no system without structure; modern system theory however is a new fruit of the development of sciences in the middle and late twentieth century. It is fairly legitimate to demonstrate the predecessors' theories by virtue of the latest theories albeit the later generations are the continuation and development of the predecessors."[24]

To assert that language is a system is the number one problem of language. How can the number one problem be accepted by everyone without demonstration?!

In what follows, I will examine, by means of the thought of modern system theory (For details, see Sect. 5 of Chapter 2), whether or not language structure is a system.

5.1 Language's Wholeness

The most fundamental property of the system is: "The whole is more than the sum of its parts." The quality or property of the system is not the simple sum (algebraic sum) of those of its constituents but embodies the fact that the whole is more than the simple addition of its parts.

5.1.1 Language Structure is of Wholeness

What would be the result if someone pronounces a phone, pauses, and then pronounces one more phone? For instance, if we let out the following phones by means of segregating them: [t]... [æ]... [s]... [i]... [t]..., what would be the result? We certainly cannot hear any meaning. This situation (failing to form a whole) is the sum of the algebraic addition:

$$0 + 0 + 0 + 0 + 0 = 0$$

The algebraic sum is zero. Be that as it may, if these syllables are integrated into a whole flow, and a stress is attached to a syllable therein, say, the two syllables of [tæsit] are integrated which results in a relative whole, "tacit," the sum of their addition is no more zero, namely, they have a meaning: "implied by actions or statements." This is then the case mentioned by J. R. Searle, "Characteristically when one speaks one

[24]Mr. Li Xiyin gave this reply in a letter to me (March 6, 2001).

means something by what one says, and what one says, the string of morphemes that one emits, is characteristically said to have a meaning."[25] Please note the "pronounced bunch of phones," which is a relative whole, a bunch rather than a single one. In this connection, the language flow forming a whole **is no more meaninglessness plus the original meaninglessness…equaling meaninglessness but owns meanings. Here appears a result of the whole being more than the addition of its parts (more than the algebraic sum)**.

In the same way, if someone pronounces some single phones with pauses between them, say, [ʃ]… [i:]… [g]… [i]… [v]… [z]… [t]… [æ]… [s]… [i]… [t]… [k]… [ə]… [n]… [s]… [e]… [n]… [t], the result is naturally that there is no meaning at all. By algebraic addition, the phones segregated and remaining to form a whole result in many meaningless sets as follows:

$0 + 0 + 0 + \ldots + 0 = 0$

The algebraic sum is zero. Nevertheless, when these syllables form the flow of a string of phones with proper stresses and rhythms, namely, when they form a relative whole, they are no longer zero but have meanings: She gives tacit consent. As a result, the language flow forming a whole **is no more meaninglessness plus the original meaninglessness…equaling meaninglessness but owns meanings. Here again appears a result of the whole being more than the addition of its parts (more than the algebraic sum)**.

Needless to say, the case is so in Chinese and any other language. When a Chinese pronounces intermittently the following phones: [ta], [liao], [jie], [liao], [ci], [shi], no one knows what they mean. This is a situation in which a whole remains to be formed. When he integrates these syllables into a whole, matches it with proper tones, gives proper intonation groups, and says "*ta liao jie liao ci shi* 他了结了此事 (He has finished this thing)," the condition that the whole is more than the sum of its parts appears—**meaning is added to the meaningless sound units after they form a whole**.

The transference from meaningless syllables to a meaningful word is the case, that from meaningless syllables to a meaningful phrase is the case, so is that from meaningless syllables to a meaningful sentence or discourse. The originally meaningful parts (syllables) turn into a meaningful whole (word, phrase, sentence, or discourse) after being added. The conclusion is: language as a whole is more than the sum of its parts.

This condition—the originally meaningless syllables (parts) turn into a meaningful word, phrase, sentence, or discourse (They are all relative wholes) after being added—is nothing but "Being comes from Nothing." Here, I think of "Laozi's thought of valuing 'Nothing': Things in the life-world come from Being, and Being comes from Nothing."[26] Laozi has early elucidated "All the beings come from Nothing," so much so that the later generations cannot but marvel at the profoundness and foresightedness of his thought! Language is a case in point of "Being comes from Nothing." The "Being comes from Nothing" as such happens to be identical with

[25] Searle (1965, p. 228).

[26] Hu. Shi (2000, p. 41).

the situation explicated by Stephen William Hawking in his *A Brief History of Time: From the Big Bang to Black Holes*—the cosmos is also a case of "Being comes from Nothing." **The coincidence of the two cases of "Being comes from Nothing" is by no means a generatio aequivoca. This indicates that language structure is holographic with the cosmic one**.

5.1.2 The Whole Meaning of the Idiom is also More Than the Sum of Its Parts

The following situation is also an example of the whole being more than the sum of its parts. Let us have a look at an idiom first: Jones kicked the bucket. The simple addition of parts (added one word by one) results in the meaning of Jones "kicked the bucket." In fact, it is certainly not "kicked the bucket," and anyone with English as his/her mother tongue knows that it means "Jones died." "Jones died" is the extra meaning of the sentence as a whole. In English, there are considerably more such cases (idioms), namely, the meaning of the whole is more than the sum of those of its parts. For instance, the holistic meaning of "cut one's eyeteeth," viz., "to become experienced or sophisticated," has no bearing whatsoever on the respective meanings of the single words, i.e., "cut, one's, eyeteeth," being far more than the sum of the latter. Insofar as the Chinese version of "to become experienced or sophisticated," to wit., *huo de shi shi jingyan* 获得世事经验, is concerned, its holistic meaning—eidetically grasping via practices the experiences and lessons of how to behave oneself—is far richer and more expanded than the sum of the respective meanings of the single characters such as "*huo* (get)," "*de* (obtain)," "*shi* (worldly)," "*shi* (affairs)," and "*jingyan* (experiences)."

5.1.3 The Implication in the Utterance is Another Case of "The Whole Meaning is More Than the Sum of Its Parts"

In addition, whether in Chinese or in English, there are far more conversational implicatures or illocutionary meanings rising over the verbal meanings. In Chinese, for instance, we can say "*zhe ge xiao niu zhang de bi zi shi bi zi, lian shi lian* 这个小妞长得鼻子是鼻子, 脸是脸," or "*nv ren bi jing shi nv ren la* 女人毕竟是女人啦." Neither of their whole meanings is the sum of single characters' meanings but rises over them, being "She is fairly beautiful" and "After all, woman is the weak." According to Searle (1975), "This is not the meaning of the sentence but that of **the utterer**." This notwithstanding, the utterer's meaning is generated on the basis of the verbal meaning. This happens to indicate that in a particular context, the whole meaning of a sentence will rise over the sum of its parts, which is also a case of the whole being more than the sum of its parts.

5.1.4 Davidson the Famous Linguist Answers the Theory of Holism from Another Perspective

Donald Davidson presented the holistic view of meaning. He holds that if sentences depend for their meanings on their structure, and we understand the meaning of each item in the structure only as an abstraction from the totality of sentences in which it features, then we can give the meaning of any sentence (or word) only by giving the meaning of every sentence (and word) in the language. Frege said that only in the context of a sentence does a word have meaning; in the same vein he might have added that only in the context of the language does a sentence (and therefore a word) have meaning.[27]

We still remember that in Sect. 5 of Chapter 2, I mentioned a most typical experiment that Bertalanffy (1733) cited, namely Driesch's famous experiment of the sea urchin. The half gastrula developed into a minor but complete embryo and then a larva at last. Some biologists once interpreted this experiment by means of vitalism or teleology. Insofar as the experiment per se is concerned, it indeed shows the holistic property of the system, namely, it is not the simple sum of its parts. Bertalanffy interprets this phenomenon with "different causes, same result" and equivalence. That which gets me interested is, this experiment is nothing but the manifestation of the law of biology holography. The half gastrula embraces the information of the whole embryo, just like what we discussed afore, namely, the holistic language flow into which meaningless phones are integrated becomes a meaningful word, phrase, sentence, or discourse.

This coincides with the wholeness of the dragon lantern game without precious consultation. On the whole, the ultimate effect of this game is: a dragon is dancing. This effect is more than the mechanic piecing together of the segments of the dragon's body, which is at most equivalent to a dragon-like work of art.

Thus is demonstrated the proposition that language structure is of wholeness.

5.2 *Language's Organic Connection*

The system's wholeness is guaranteed by its organicity. The factors of a system are interconnected and interact with one another. The interconnection between the inner factors of any system with wholeness is organic. The factors are interconnected and interact with one another, constituting the whole of the system. Language's organic connection is manifested in the following three typical phenomena: the first is the endless mutual interpretations between words, the second is the mutually promoting and influencing phonetic changes, and the third is the mutually constraining inflections.

---

[27]Davidson. Donald (1967, 17. p. 308).

5.2.1 The Mutually Interpreting Words

In previous section, I took Chinese and English words as the examples to demonstrate that there is a state of endless mutual interpretations between words, namely the holographic state of you have me and I have you. I will take Russian as an example again to show this: the organic connection between words is exactly manifested via this state. Please note:

The starting word дорога[28]

The first-level interpreting words on which дорога relies:

1. Полоса земли, предназначения для передвижения, путь сообщения;
2. Место, по которому надо пройти или проходить, путь следования;
3. Путешетвие;;
4. Средства достижения какой-н цели, жизненный путь.

The second-level interpreting words on which дорога relies:

The first sense group (interprets every word on the first level):

Полоса: … … …

Земли: … … …

Предназначения: … … …

Для: … … …

Передвижения: … … …

Путь: … … …

Сообщения: … … …

The second sense group (lists every word interpreting it):

Место: … … …

По: … … …

Которому: … … …

Надо: … … …

Пройти: … … …

Или: … … …

Проходить: … … …

Путь: (It appears the second time, which means that circular argument begins.)… … …

Следования: … … …

The third sense group (lists every word interpreting it):

Путешетвие: … … …

The fourth sense group (lists every word interpreting it):

Средства: … … …

Достижения: … … …

Какой-н: … … …

Цели: … … …

Жизненный: … … …

---

[28]The interpretations of дорога are based on *СЛОВАТЬ РУСКОГО ЯЗЫКА.*. Ed. С. И. Ожеков. Государственноеиздательство иностранных и национальных словарей,, М. 1953.

Путь: (It appears the third time, which means circular argument begins again) … … …

The third-level interpreting words on which Дорога relies (interpret all the interpreting words on the second level): … … …

The nth-level interpreting words on which дорога relies: … … …

The interpreting words on which дорога relies can be sought endlessly, albeit the work load is considerably heavy. Be that as it may, this is an era wherein there are computers and lexicons, so it can be accomplished. This indicates: first, one word (partial information) can ultimately embrace the words in the whole language system (whole information). Secondly, all the words in language system rely on and interpret one another. This is the first manifestation of language's organic connection.

5.2.2 The Mutually Promoting and Influencing Phonetic Changes

Phonetic change is also a most typical and representative manifestation of language's organic connection. **That in which I am interested here is not the specific implementation of phonetic change but those factors determining it, namely, the mutual promotions and influences between the parts**. As regards the promoting force of phonetic change, we need only say one word, namely, phonetic change emerges for the sake of convenience and effort-saving. This condition being important notwithstanding, it is not the main goal of our studies here. Nonetheless, **the convenience and effort-saving-ness of pronunciation is exactly determined by the adjacency between phones**.

Take Chinese as an example, the light tone, tonal modification, *r*-suffixation, and the changes of the interjection "*a* 啊" all result from the organically relevant actions of language.

To begin, let us have a look at light tone. Each syllable of Mandarin has a fixed tone, whereas some syllables will lose their original tones in some words or sentences, and will be pronounced with a short and lisped tone. Changes might even occur to initials and finals. This is light reading. It however is not arbitrary but constrained. The constraining law is: it changes along with the previous syllable's tone. For instance, the syllable after the high and level tone is pronounced with a short semi low one, the pitch being 2, e.g., "*zhuō**zi*** 桌子 (table)"; that after the second rising tone is pronounced with a light, short middle one, the pitch being 3, e.g., "*fáng**zi*** 房子 (house)"; the original pitch of the second "*shì*" in "*shì**shi*** 试试 (have a try)" is 51, but it will become 1 when the tone changes into a light, short low one, and the final [i] is virtually inaudible.

Secondly, let us come to "modified tone." In language flow, when syllables are linked, the pitches of some syllables will change under the influences from the adjacent syllables, which is again a manifestation of the mutual reliance between language units. For instance, when two falling-rising tones are linked, the pitch of the former one changes from 214 to 34, approaching that of the second rising tone, e.g., "***kǒu**yǔ* 口语 (spoken language)." When more than three falling-rising tones are linked, the pitches of the former two both change into 34, e.g., "***shǒuxiě**tǐ* 手写体 (handwritten script)." The most interesting is, if all the characters in a sentence have falling-rising tones, then the tone before the pause is pronounced at the original pitch, and that before the original pitch changes into one approaching the second rising tone, e.g., "***qǐng****nǐ* 请你 (Please)/***dǎ****diǎn* 打点 (get some)/ ***jǐng****shuǐ* 井水 (well water), ***wǒ****hǎo* 我好 (so that I can)/ ***xǐ****bǎliǎn* 洗把脸 (wash my face)." If the tones were not changed but were pronounced according to their original pitches (You may have a try), which is a violation of the regularity, you would feel out of breath. What's more, the falling-rising tone will change into a semi one before the non-falling-rising tone, the pitch changing from 214 to 21, e.g., ***shǐ****zhōng* 始终 (all the time)." There are more such cases, say, the change of the falling tone or "*yī*一(one)," *qī* 七 (seven)," *bù* 不 (no)," *bā* 八 (eight)," or the like, as to which I will not go into much detail.

Thirdly, let us come to *r*-suffixation. The pronunciation of the final will change after *r*-suffixation occurs to the latter. The regulation of change is determined by the final's heading and ending. Here I merely give two sorts of conditions as examples for explication: when we pronounce that which has *a, o, e,* or *u* as the kernel vowels and [r] as the ending of final, the [r] indicating the act of retroflection is immediately added to it, e.g., "*shāngēer* 山歌儿 (folk song)" [shan ger]; when we pronounce that which has *i* or *ü* as the kernel vowels, [er] is added to it, e.g., "*xiǎomǐer* 小米儿 (millet)" [xiaomir]; when that which has *in* or *ün* as the kernel final is pronounced, its *n* is omitted and [er] is added to it, e.g., "*jiǎoyìner* 脚印儿 (footprint)" being [jiaoyin-r] originally but changed into [jiaoyier] for convenience. As to this condition, I will give no more examples here.

The change of the modal particle "*a* 啊 (ah)" is also influenced by its previous syllable's last phone, and will be pronounced according to different conditions as "*ya* 呀, *wa* 哇, *na* 哪, *a* 啊," respectively.

In a nutshell, the part to which phonetic changes occur must accept the constraints from the units before and after it. This is exactly the organic connection between the inner factors of the system.

Needless to say, the situations in which the mutual constraints between phones produce phonetic changes are fairly abundant in English, and there are quite a lot of relevant materials at home and abroad, so the readers can find them easily.

The language having more colorful such phonetic changes and inflections is Russian. The voicing of voiceless consonants and the devoicing of voiced consonants in Russian both take the phones before and after them as the objects of reference. The softening of hard consonants is also constrained by the surroundings to a certain extent. In a word, the phonetic changes in Russian embody the regularity of being constrained by adjacent phones.

No phonetic change does not embody the mutual constraints between the inner factors of the system, to wit., the system's organic connection.

5.2.3 The Mutually Constraining Inflections

Inflection is also caused by the mutual constraints between the inner factors of the system. There is no inflection in Chinese, which is a fact. That which can best manifest the mutual connection between parts (namely the inner factors of the system) is the three phenomena of Russian, namely, conjugation of the verb, the declension of the noun, and the division of the adjective into three genders and their plural forms. The conjugation of the verb is dominated by the subject, and я can only be followed by читаю rather than читаешь; the declension of the noun is constrained by the verb, and we can not say книга but can only say книгу (the fourth case, objective case, direct object) after я читаю; the objective (demonstrative pronoun) also must be constrained by the noun it modifies, and must keep coincident with the latter on gender, number, and case. Take та интересная книга as an example, if книга turns into книгу, the та интересная before it must change into ту интересную, say, "Я читаю ту интересную книгу." It is exactly due to this definite constraining relationship that the utterer can change the word order at random without producing confusions of meaning (Of course, it is not suitable to separate the ту интересную книгу which has become a cognitive module except under a few conditions like in poetry). There are more examples like "Читаю я ту интересную книгу," and "Ту интересную книгу читаю я," and so on and so forth, all meaning "I read the interesting book" rather than "The interesting book reads me," even less than the ridiculous "Read the interesting book I." This is the convenience brought by the mutual constraints between the inner factors of language system. It also provides linguists with a beneficial inspiration: there is not the problem of trouble as to the organic connection within language system. So long as you want a system to exist on, in a rather good state, and in convenient and flexible fashion, you cannot but face up to the constraint as such. When you find that a system no longer has this "trouble," that means it no longer exists, being drastically "comfortable."

Albeit the noun in English does not change on gender (Only personal pronouns have the distinction between feminine and masculine, which however differs from Russian. In Russian, the feminine does not necessarily refer to female humans, but also to feminine object nouns, say, она can refer to ручка, and so on), it retains the change of some particular cases (like the noun's possessive case and the objective case of personal pronouns with visible inflections), and that of the number of the verb acting as the predicate (howbeit it is rather simple). In the same way, these changes are all manifested in the mutual constraints between parts, say, the change of the verb is necessarily determined according to the number of the subject, the objective case of the noun is necessarily influenced by the verb or the preposition of the predicate, and so forth. In a word, **none of the infections fails to show the mutual constraints between the inner factors of the system, to wit., the system's organic connection**.

In addition to the above three typical manifestations, language's organic connection is also manifested in those between the inner factors of the system on the one hand and between the outer surroundings and the system on the other. The connection between the system and its outer surroundings means that there are exchanges between it and the outer world at the level of material, energy, and information, corresponding output and input, and the increase and decrease of quantity. As is known, the language of each nation is all the time replenishing new words and eliminating the old ones, which is the exchange of information between language system and human society (crowd, language communities). This quality is very critical for us to understand the gist of language system. Thanks to the information exchange with the outer world, language system will not end up dead.

The organic connection as such is completely identical to the principle of dragon lantern. Each segment of the dragon lantern is interconnected and interacts with the one before or after it. If some segment stops (either due to the player lifting it being exhausted or because of an accident) or its player puts forth his strength reversely (it is not scarcely seen that the player becomes dizzy), it will not merely encumber the segment before it, but also immobilize all those after it and, as a result, the whole dancing dragon is immediately out of shape, and the game no longer exists. The dragon lantern game is an open system the relating mode of which with the outer surroundings is mainly embodied via the players' participation (lifting and waving all the segments of the dragon). That is to say, the subject of this game is the player. Without human participation, the dragon lantern is merely a dead thing. The waving of the players is the material and energetic exchange between them and the dragon lantern system itself.

Thus we say, language is of organic connection.

5.3 Language's Dynamicity

The system's organic connection is not static but dynamic, being related to time. Bertalanffy (1973) holds that the system changes over time. Of the properties of language, changing over time is the most obvious, the earliest felt by the language user, and the first acknowledged and studied by a large number of linguists.

From ancient times till now, as to how many words were added and how many were eliminated in Chinese lexicon, not only linguists can enumerate them, but the native speakers at common cultural level can also list one or two.

The same holds to the fact that word meanings change over time: not only linguists can enumerate them, but the native speakers at common cultural level can also list one or two.

The same also holds to the dynamic change of speech sounds. Compared with the remote ancient time, modern time witnesses the decrease of Chinese pitches into four a proof of which is: in some dialect areas at present, pitches more than the four ones are still reserved.

The dynamic change of sentence structure is also the case, just that this change is not that rapid and obvious as those of lexicon and speech sounds. For example, in the Chinese after the May 4th Movement, Europeanized sentences were added. For another example, there was no "*shi*是(be)" in the ancient judgment sentence and it is in modern Chinese judgment sentence that large quantity of "*shi*" appeared. Some scholar contends that in ancient Chinese literature, the definite usage of "*shi*" in the speech act of judgment first appeared in late Eastern Han Dynasty. The accuracy of this conclusion needs further study in that according to my investigation,[29] even in the judgment sentences in the late Qing Dynasty (with the novels in that period as the materials), "*shi*" appeared not very frequently. Till the period of the Republic of China, in the lecture of Mr's Cai Yuanpei the then president of Peking University, judgment sentences without "*shi*" remained therein—No matter when the changes of the judgment sentence appear, they definitely exist.

In foreign linguistics, there is particularly a historical linguistics, the diachronic study of language, which can prove the dynamic change of the foreign languages. Since Saussure and beyond, there have been so many fruits of the diachronic study of language.

I remain to enumerate specific facts as regards the dynamic changes in the aspects mentioned afore not because I do not have sufficient data but exactly the other way round. It is because any common scholar studying linguistics has such data. The study as such is of a property: it definitely notes that this is language's dynamicity. (Therefore, it will occupy the space of the book to list the data familiar to everyone, which would be unacceptable to readers.)

Language's openness and organic connection stresses the connection and exchange of information between language and the outer world. Dynamicity, whereas, stresses the existing state of the information. What does the existing state of dynamic language as information look like?

In the first place, it is manifested in a relative steady state. Language is relatively steady. Man will never choose an ever changing language as his own, or else how can people maintain daily communications? Say, a thing is called "soap" today, but the "soap" changes into "thin block" tomorrow. When the signified is not fixed, how can the concept is given, and how can the judgment, inference, and conclusion? Won't a language that cannot be used to make a judgment, an inference, or to draw a conclusion bring about social chaos? Change is constant but it stresses continuity namely steadiness.

In the second place, language's steady state is by no means a static one. People must modify the language refusing to change over time. For their convenience (economy principle, least effort principle, etc.), people will continuously modify and change what they are using. Language's steady state is a state of movement embracing the dynamic one. Language's movement refers to the flow of information.

Thirdly, language can evolve. Vemuri (1978) notes that the design of any system whatsoever is supposed to take into consideration the fact that lesions might occur in the future to the system remaining to show any hint. In this connection, the controlling system per se must be capable of evolving so as to effectively deal with the coming

[29]This investigation aimed at demonstrating that the Western ontology cannot be obtained in Chinese even after considerable meditations. The theory of "ou, ont-" in Western philosophy results from the meditations in Western languages. The kernel problem in Western philosophy is to study "ont-" (equaling to being or das Sein). "*Shi*" qua a judgment word appeared late in Chinese, so how can there be "the theory of ont-" in Chinese philosophy? The demonstration is in Sect. 2 (The different language directions of Chinese and Western philosophies) of Chapter 2 (Prospect: inquiries from philosophy to language) of my *Language: the Last Homestead of Human Beings*.

ferment. Language is exactly capable of evolving. The following proofs can be easily found in every nation's language system:

The evolution of speech sounds is directed upon making the movement of human oral cavity and vocal organs become more reasonable, convenient, smooth, and effort-saving.

The changing direction of language structure (sentence and phrase structures) absolutely follows human memory and attention span, being convenient for cognition, conceptualization, and categorization, and hence the changing direction of the structure is necessarily aimed at more convenience and clarity.

I will not use "evolution" to describe lexicon, but merely say the increase and decrease of it, and the parlance more suitable for the system theory is "the old gives place to the new." The lexicon's increase and decrease are most easily predictable since whenever an object (can be an abstract concept or thought) and substance emerges in actual life, a word reflecting it will be added correspondingly, and vice versa, whenever an object and substance in actual life disappears, the corresponding word will follow suit.

This is the situation in which language is evolving. **Moreover, I can predict with complete assurance that the direction of language's evolution is: the evolution of speech sounds and language structure will become more and more reasonable and effort-saving; and the lexicon will become more and more abundant and enormous**.

In the same way, language is coincident with the dragon lantern game on dynamicity. Each segment of the dragon lantern must wave, which is dynamic. Moreover, the process from the starting of the game via the dragon's dancing in full swing to its stop is relevant to time.

On the whole, language is of dynamicity.

5.4 Language's Orderliness

The structure and level manifested by the system's organic connection and the progressive segregation manifested by its dynamicity all characterize the system as orderliness. Bertalanffy (1973) contends that the system's change from disordered to ordered marks the increase of its organizational nature or degree which appertains to both the organic connection between the system's inner factors and its dynamic progression.

5.4.1 Language's Structure and Level Are Distinct

The structure and level manifested by language's organic connection are definite and, due to human's participation, they have progressive directivity. As to language substance, its levels are: morpheme (meaning begins to emerge from this level) →

word → phrase → sentence → discourse.[30] The reverse analysis is also feasible: discourse → sentence → phrase → word → morpheme. This is orderliness. When we make analysis from the discourse downward till the morpheme, we can get a smaller meaningful unit in each substance. Take the phonetic level as another example, from a syllable, we can get, via analysis, meaningless single phones of consonant or vowel, or the like. The structure of the phrase can be analyzed into core and finite elements. In a sentence structure, say, in a Chinese sentence, we can recognize the subject, predicate, and object, or the subject and predicate, or the subject, predicate, and complement; in English, on the other hand, we can have SVO, SVOO, SVOC, SV, and so on. **It indicates that the substances' continuance is ordered when we can get via analysis in them smaller units or elements having independent meanings and being applicable repeatedly and independently**. "Being applicable repeatedly and independently" means that the smaller units or elements with independent meanings analyzed from the bigger substances appear in another space and are combined with other units or elements to form new meaningful structures. Nevertheless, from the occasional human cry, we cannot analyze smaller till the smallest substances with independent meanings, not to mention the re-collocation and repeated application of them. Therefore, such human voices are disordered even if they are reluctantly successive, and hence they are not qualified for entering into language system. The same holds to the noise made by an object dropping to the ground. Such sounds cannot constitute a complex language system as phones do.

5.4.2 Language Structure' Directivity of Progressive Segregation

Language also shows the dynamic directivity of progressive segregation characteristic of the system. This characteristic of human language is as clear. People enable morphemes to constitute a word, many words a phrase, many phrases a sentence, and many sentences a discourse. The situation in which people use sentence structures also shows the directivity in the same way. These cases of directivity are all the best proofs of orderliness. They are the results of human constantly creating and improving language system rather than being inherent in it. It is the language users' purpose that enables language system to have the dynamic directivity of progressive segregation.

5.4.3 Language's Organizational Nature or Degree

Bertalanffy holds that the system's developing from disordered to ordered marks the increase of the system's organizational nature or degree which appertains to both the organic connection between the inner factors of the system and its dynamic process. Language system's organizational nature or degree is manifested in its distinct levels.

---

[30] I originally planned to put clause before sentence in this level but gave up when I considered that cause is after all identical to sentence on pattern.

According to the levels of phonetic substances, the constitutional levels in ascending order are: phone → syllable → phonetic group → language flow; the analyzable levels in descending order are: language flow → phonetic group → syllable → phone. Seen from the levels of language substances, the constitutional levels in ascending order are: morpheme → word → phrase → sentence → discourse; the analyzable levels in descending order are: discourse → sentence → phrase → word → morpheme. To this connection, the organizational nature of language system is quite distinct: on the one hand, these substances are analyzable hence distinct; on the other hand, they can be analyzed in descending order, but they can also be constituted in ascending order. It is my contention that **the analysis in descending order and the constitution in ascending order of language substances are language's organizational nature or degree**.

5.4.4 Language's Direction of Change is Predictable

Then, what kind of inner driving force do language system's orderliness, directivity, and organizational nature have? Zipf's Law tells us: "Any human action will be a manifestation of the Principle of Least Effort in operation. …It is manifested in obtaining the biggest fruit of illocutionary act by means of the least phonetic effort."[31] What is "the lest phonetic effort"? Language is a vocal substance. So to speak, a language system becomes a system as the result of adding meanings to the phonetic system. Therefore, the least "phonetic effort" may as well be equated to the least "linguistic effort." **So long as the awareness of the "least phonetic effort"—i.e., the effortless phonetic activity—is kept, language system will ultimately be optimized by means of least effort principle and economy principle**. What kind of inner driving force is driving language system's orderliness, directivity, and organizational nature? The answer is supposed to be: the phonetic activity with the least effort. How to accomplish the optimization of language system? Language is after all an artificial system, and human beings will adjust very wittingly **its direction of change toward the highly ordered and highly organized state to avoid it being eliminated**.

Why can I predict with complete assurance the direction of language's evolution (the phonetic and linguistic structures will become more and more reasonable and effort-saving, and the lexicon bigger and bigger)? It has itself demonstrated the orderliness of language. If language were of no order, no one could predict something about it. Reversely stated, **any predictable structure is necessarily ordered**.

This highly ordered and organized direction of language is exactly the same as the orderliness of the dragon lantern game. Seen from "The analysis in descending order and the constitution in ascending order of language substances are language's organizational nature or degree," isn't the dragon lantern game the same case? When a beginner plays the game, the immediate expression is that the segments fail to be connected and the direction of the waving fails to be coincident with the strength,

[31]Cf. Zipf (1949).

which is the disordered state of the dragon lantern; when a skilled player does the work, the direction of waving of each segment is coincident with the strength and hence the game is accomplished, which is the orderliness of the dragon lantern system. That is to say, the structures, levels, and dynamicity of this system show the directivity of progressive segregation. The dragon lantern game's change from disordered (the "mess" at the starting stage in the very beginning, or that brought due to the players' exhaustion) to ordered marks the increase of its system's organizational nature or degree, and the organizational nature is embodied by the organization of the players. If the phonetic activity of the least effort ultimately optimizes language system, the waving of the least effort also ultimately optimizes the dragon lantern game (namely, the players make the least effort, and the dragon waves beautifully).

On this ground, language is of orderliness.

5.5 *Language's Purposiveness*

It is Bertalanffy's contention that the orderliness of the system is not that for the sake of orderliness but has a certain direction, nay, this direction is dominated by a certain purposiveness. He notes that the direction of a system is determined by its purposiveness. A system is determined by the actual conditions, but it is also contained by the ultimate state it reaches. Therefore, purposiveness is believed to be determined by the future. That is to say, the direction of a system is determined not only by the actual states (the necessity) but also by the prediction of the future (the occasionality), the unity of both being the purposiveness. Nevertheless, he notes that the finality in the general system theory is purposiveness rather than teleology.

What is the purposiveness of language as a structure? **The direction of a system is determined not only by the actual states (the necessity) but also by the prediction of the future (the occasionality), the unity of both being the purposiveness of language**. It is manifested in two aspects as follows:

First, human's requirement to use language determines its actual state (the necessity);

Secondly, human's further requirement for language, namely, to optimize language system by means of least effort principle and economy principle, determines the prediction of language's future (the occasionality).

One is an actual state, the other is a prediction of the future, and the unity of them is language's purposiveness. Human's requirements for language determine language's status quo and its future direction. This conclusion is of no problem on acceptability. Language system is a completely artificial system. Any artificial system whatsoever is of purposiveness. The direction of an artificial system is determined by the intention of setting it. The purposiveness of language system gradually becomes definite in accordance with human's requirements for language.

Human's requirements for language are: when human needs to think with language, he/she requires that language has **the logic and clarity for thinking**; when human needs to behave with language (performing some speech act), he/she requires that language has **the clarity and abundance of illocutionary act** (Please note: he/she requires not merely simplicity and directness, but also complexity, indirectness, and variation); when human needs to express emotions with language, he/she requires that language has **the exactness and diversity** (including sophistication as an innate nature of human) **for emotion expression**.[32] At the very moment when language first came into being, it took human's requirements as its direction: when human thinks, language needs logic and clarity; when human performs speech acts, language needs clarity and abundance; when human expresses emotions, language needs exactness and diversity, and so on. Language will not develop that which human does not require, and will develop that which human requires. As a consequence, like the development of any other artificial system, that of language system embraces human's purposiveness. Hence: **the choice of language system is that of human, and human's choice is forever of certain motivations**.

The so-called natural language is by no means completely "natural"; the commonly used "natural language" is named for the sake of contrasting with the artificial language (designed by an individual or a group of people according to the law of symbol, say, Esperanto designed by Ludwig Lazarus Zamenhof). De facto, **natural language** (formed gradually by human groups during the long term by means of the process in which accidental variations and choices are combined) is nothing but "human-tural" language. Of course, this human is not an individual (like Zamenhof creating Esperanto), namely, this language is ultimately created via the long-term agreements reached by the groups composed of many people.

The direction of the system is dominated by a certain purposiveness. **The various properties manifesting the direction of language system surely appertain to human's requirements and purposes**. As a matter of fact, we can examine every property of language and will find that human's requirements and purposiveness are surely embraced therein. So far we have found these properties: recursiveness, discreteness, hierarchy, linearity, fuzziness, rhythm, organicity, and arbitrariness (coexisting with motion). As to the properties much discussed (It's fair to say that these properties remain to be all-encompassing, and I believe that more will be found along with the deepening of human recognition. An assertion is, nevertheless, all the properties of language are surely developed in the direction of human's requirements), I will not examine them; rather, I will examine those less mentioned, say, the recursiveness. Form recursiveness, we can see that language's direction is dominated by purposes—specifically speaking, human's purposes. For details about language recursiveness, please see Sect. 2 of Chapter 5 in this book. In brief, language recursiveness refers to **the repetition or mutual embedding of identical structural elements in linguistic structural hierarchy and speech generation**. Why is it so? This is because the recursiveness at holistic level avoids the danger of cumbersome and complex sentence pattern combinations, which makes the sentence pattern limited and simple. The tremendous even whole meaning of language recursiveness

[32] The foregoing requirements refer to the conditions in which language is used as a communicative tool. As to the conditions in which it is not used as a tool, there are detailed discussions in Sect. 1 of Chapter 2 of my *Language: the Last Homestead of Human Beings*.

lies in allowing people to produce limitless sentences by means of a few sentence patterns. Why **can** people **only**, and why **must** they, produce limitless sentences by means of a few sentence patterns (that is to say, why **can** language structure **only**, and why **must** it, be recursive, namely their identical structural elements are repeated and mutually embedded)? The answer is: human's cognitive resources namely memory and attention span are limited. He/She cannot remember so many sentence structures. If a new structure were applied to each sentence in lieu of the present repetitions of several major structures, the sentence pattern combination of a nation's language would become astoundingly cumbersome and inconceivably complex. That de facto proclaims the bankruptcy of that language and the impossibility of its realization. According to the requirements from memory and attention span, the less sentence patterns the better, and the more convenient. Now we are clear: language is of the property of recursiveness due to the fact that human's cognitive capacity and memory are taken into consideration. That is to say, **it is the system's purposiveness that makes language have recursiveness**.

In the same way, **we can retrieve that the other properties of language are also brought by the purposiveness of language system. It is language system's purposiveness that makes language have various properties**.

Reversely, we can say that the various properties of language system embody its purposiveness.

This coincides with the purposiveness of the dragon lantern game. Every player has a definite aim: "I must make the whole dragon dance." For this end, he must immediately follow the previous segment and simultaneously take care of the segment after him. This purposiveness is acknowledged by every player, or else he would not join in and would not be allowed to join in the game. In this connection, the dragon lantern game is ordered along with a certain direction dominated by purposiveness. This is because the ultimate state supposed to reach—dancing—constrains every player.

The five points above indicate that the properties of the system are all manifested in language structure. Now we can say: language is a system.

5.6 *Collateral Evidences*

5.6.1 The Lesions and Disturbances of Language System

As a system, language is supposed to have lesions and disturbances. A language without them is unreliable and authentic instead. In my view, the reason is, **lesions and disturbances are nothing but the signs that the system requires metabolism, the supplement of information and energy, and the external interferences to promote the inner world to make adjustment**. The manifestations of the lesions and disturbances of language are mainly these: (1) modifications without or with bad theoretical motivations are performed on conventional usages, and are spread unchecked. I will merely give several examples here: refusing to rectify the flooding wrong words, to implement orthography, or to carry out received pronunciation, using many wrong words in ads to mislead the schoolchildren, or the authorities let things drift when facing various wrong or nonstandard usages; (2) poor creations (like the implementation of the second edition of simplified Chinese characters); (3) indiscriminate elimination (like attempting to eliminate Chinese characters); (4) refusing and indiscriminately using alien words and sentence patterns; (5) forbidding to use some national language in favor of another one, and so forth.

To be sure, we can reset a new system in lieu of the old one—to replace the old system with a new one. The lesions of language system nevertheless are not supposed to be dealt with in this way. An attemptable alternative method is to perform an "engineering transformation" on language system, namely, to guide it in the "proper" direction such as changing its structure or modifying the input in it or both. To criticize the phenomenon of indiscriminate and unhealthy usages of language, to rectify the tendency of wrong and negative usages of language, to open courses, to intentionally train all the members of language community, to popularize Mandarin, and the like, are all means of rectifying the lesions. Nonetheless, I would like to stress two points: first, it is not very easy to distinguish the lesions from the normal variations in language. Most changes are the results of language's self-organized movement, so it is not supposed to regard any initial self-organized movement in language as a negative lesion. We should be very cautious when defining "lesion." Secondly, **language community is capable of settling lesions and disturbances by itself**. Language community has an innate capacity to gradually resolve its errors and adjust its lesions. The aforementioned means, namely, to criticize and resist the unhealthy usages of language, the wrong and negative tendency, and the phenomenon of indiscriminate usage of language, to open courses, to intentionally train the members of the language community, and the like, are a part of the capacity to settle lesions by itself. This capacity comes from two sorts of wishes: in the first place, language as a life expression of the utterer can obtain the same care of the latter as for life. Refusing to love language is refusing to appreciate oneself or running counter to one's own life consciousness. This is the last choice of anyone. In the second place, the wish to improve the communicative tool (when language acts as this) is not to seek evil. People usually have the wish to improve their tools. This is a giant power resisting lesions and disturbances. The power to resist linguistic lesions and disturbances is as giant as that to resist the social ones. When we see the fact that in the long human history, albeit wars occurred every year, the peaceful ages were always longer than the war years, we will be convinced of language community's capacity to settle its lesions and disturbances by itself.

At the level of fundamental form, the lesions and disturbances in language are the same as those in the dragon lantern game. Be that as it may, to reset a new system in lieu of the old one—to replace the old system with a new one—is easy to the dragon lantern game but impossible to language system.

5.6.2 People Only Situated in One Language System Cannot Perform Genuine Questionings and Value Judgments on It

This situation is not strange to us: scholars of Chinese who only know Chinese but know no foreign language and never take a foreign language for reference, and who study Chinese merely via itself, cannot find great problems as regards Chinese's regularities. Similarly, scholars who only know a foreign language but do not study and never take Chinese for reference, and who study a foreign language merely via itself, also cannot find great problems as regards the foreign language's regularities. Such facts emerge once and again. People entrapped in this situation, whereas, are often so deeply involved that they cannot get away. A positive example is that masters of language such as Zhao Yuanren, Wang Li, Lu Shuxiang, and others, all have particular findings of Chinese, which is absolutely related to the fact that they are situated in more than one language systems.

The structure or configuration of the system cannot perform self-authentication or evaluate itself. "The structure or configuration of the system is rarely self-evident." This is a fairly important property. **On this account, no system can question itself or make value judgment as to itself**.

The collateral evidences can also indicate that language is a system.

5.7 *From the Theory of Language System to the State of the Inner Language Holography*

That which I would like to stress is, to demonstrate that language is a system is not to take the matter on its merits but to carry out the transition to the theory of language holography.

There is no gap whatsoever between language as a system and the state of the inner language holography (or the theory of language holography). The internal relationships of a system are necessarily holographic. The second of the ten principles of the theory of cosmos holography is: all the systems are holographic. This principle indicates that all the martial forms from the lowest to the highest level—the brain and mind—are the microcosms of the cosmos. As a consequence, all the holographic systems are of equivalence (For details, see Sect. 4 of Chapter 2).

The system is necessarily holographic, and holography is necessarily systematic. **The state of language system is that of the inner language holography**. That is to say, on each level of language's morpheme-word-phrase-clause-sentence-discourse, the part is holographic with the whole; one part contains the same information as the others; each holographic node (subsystem) has its counterpart or similar information in the whole and other nodes, respectively, namely, each holographic node in the system becomes, to a different extent, a microcosm of the whole.

References

Davidson. Donald, Truth and Meaning. In *Synthese*. Dordrecht-Holland: D. Reidel Publishing Co., 1967, 17. p. 308.

Hjelmslev, L. *Prolegomena to a Theory of Language*. Madison: University of Wisconsin Press, 1969, p. 3.

Hu. Shi, *The Outline of the History of Chinese Philosophy*. Shanghai: Shanghai Classics Publishing House, 2000, p. 41.

Li. Zhichao, The abstraction of the principle of holography and its philosophical meaning. In the proceedings of The Third National Academic Conference of the Law of Biology Holography. 1985.

Mason. Stephen, *A History of the Sciences*. Shanghai: Shanghai People's Publishing House, 1977, p. 215. Translated from the Chinese version—the translator.

Qian. Guanlian, *Pragmatics in Chinese Culture*. Beijing: Tsing Hua University Press, 1997, pp. 83–89.

Quirk. R., Greenbaum. S., Leech. G., & Svartvik, J., *A comprehensive grammar of the English language*. London: Longman, 1985.

Quirk. R., Greenbaum. S., Leech. G., & Svartvik, J., *A New English Grammar Coursebook*. Ed. Zhang Zhenbang. Shanghai: Shanghai Foreign Language Education Press, 1996.

Searle. J. R., What is a speech act? In *Philosophy in America*. Ed. M. Black. Ithaca: Cornell University Press, 1965, p. 228.

Wang. Cunzhen & Yan. Chunyou, The theory of cosmos holography. In *Natural Information*, 1985, p. 2.

Wang. Cunzhen & Yan. Chunyou, *The Theory of Cosmic Holographic Unity*. Jinan: Shandong People's Publishing House, 1995, pp. 39, 90, 95, 148–150.

Xu. Guozhang, *Xu Guangzhang on Language*. Beijing: Foreign Language Teaching and Research Press, 1999, p. 21.

Yang. Zhenning, Beauty and physics. In *Xinhua Wenzhai*, 1998, 1, p. 212.

Zha. Ruqiang, The assumption of the category system of dialectics of nature. In *Social Sciences in China*, 1985, p. 5.

Zhang. Yingqing, The law of biology holography. In *Potential Science*, 1980, p. 2.

Zhang. Yingqing, The theory of biology holography and holographic biology. In *Potential Science*, 1985, p. 5.

Zhang. Yanchang, Dai. Shuyan & Li. Bing, *Introduction to Phonology*. Changchun: Jilin University Press, 1993, p. 50.

Zhao. Shikai, *The Summary of Foreign Linguistics——Schools and Representatives*. Beijing: Beijing Language Institute Press, 1990, p. 197.

Zipf. G. K., Human Behavior and The Principle of Least Effort, An Introduction to Human Ecology. New York: Hanfner, 1949.

Chapter 4
The Holographic Relations Between Language and Cognition

Abstract The discussions in this chapter are performed for the sake of further demonstrating the state of the inner language holography.

Keywords The hierarchy of cognition · The hierarchy of language · The universality of language · The return of cognition into itself · Part · Whole

Introduction: as regards the seven layers relevant to the cognition of human brain, the language layer (language, sign, technique, and act) is merely one of them. This is a view of the general theory of evolution.[1] According to this view, the layer above language is consciousness (perception, consciousness, emotion, and feeling), that below language is logic (logic, science, religion, and art) belonging to the level of culture, and the language layer is situated between them.[2] Nevertheless, I will not discuss the holographic relation between language and consciousness layers according to this vein insomuch as the language layer is situated in the cognitive activities of the whole human brain, and hence I will focus on the holographic relation between the language layer and the whole cognition. Only when we can demonstrate how language is embedded in the whole cognitive activity, will the holography of language layer itself be sound and reliable. After the demonstrations in this chapter, you will find that language is embedded in and lives in peace with cognition, and that they are merely two Chinese boxes embedded in the biggest one of the cosmos. This Chinese-box relationship enables us to see clearly that the relations between part and other parts, part and the whole, and between part and the bigger whole over the one to which it belongs, are all the overlapping relations of information.

Be that as it may, in the theory of language holography, **the relation between language and cognition is still supposed to belong to the state of the inner language holography. This is because language is a tool to recognize the objective world, but it itself can also act as an object of cognition. Meanwhile, the cognitive process corresponds to and overlaps with language generation, which means that cognition and language must be attached to human body**. Culture (particularly the part of material cultivation) on the other hand can exist independently of

[1]Zhao (1994. pp. 184, 188).

[2]For details, see the figure in Sect. 2 of this chapter.

G. Qian, *The Theory of Language Holography*,
https://doi.org/10.1007/978-981-16-2039-3_4

human body. Therefore, the relation between language and culture is supposed to belong to the state of the outer language holography.

To demonstrate the relationship of being embedded layer upon layer, we must demarcate and innumerate cognitive science, cognitive linguistics, and some surrounding relationships for study, which demands that we should approach, patiently and meticulously, the mutual embedments between language and cognition.

1 Cognitive Linguistics and the Theory of language Holography

1.1 What Is Cognitive Science

Cognitive science, the interdisciplinary study of cognitive phenomena, has its origins in philosophy and can be viewed as the empirical pursuit of age-old questions in the philosophy of mind. Perhaps the word which best captures the field of cognitive science is diversity. Cognitive scientists study a broad range of cognitive phenomena, including attention, perception, memory, language, learning, and reasoning. Moreover, researchers in cognitive science come from a wide set of backgrounds. The field draws from a number of disciplines including philosophy, linguistics, psychology, computer science, anthropology, sociology, and the neurosciences. However, one upshot of the varied nature of the disciplinary backgrounds of cognitive science researchers is the production of a number of complementary research methods.[3]

The disciplinary background develops. Now, these research methods and fruits are employed to demonstrate the holographic relation between cognition and language.

All cognitive scientists are committed to the belief that **the human mind is a complex system involved in the acquisition, storage, transformation, and transmission of information**. Further, most cognitive scientists are committed to the thesis that an explanation of cognitive phenomena involves an account of formal structures and processes, their representational significance, and their physical implementation. The principal characteristics of the field, then, include commitment to some species of mental representation and the tendency to employ formal systems, especially computational models, in their descriptions of cognitive phenomena.[4] These works of cognitive scientists cannot be more closely related to language research. Just imagine, if human's mental process is "a complex system including the picking-up, storage, conversion and transportation of information," isn't language mechanism also nothing but such a system? It can be said that the works of cognitive scientists are exactly the preliminary works that linguists should do. This is the very reason why we say that people could not understand the linguistic process without understanding the cognitive one.

---

[3]Coulson (1995, p. 123).

[4]Coulson (1995).

Seana Coulson notes that **the general objective of cognitive science is to establish a mode connecting the cognitive processes at immensely different levels**. It is never an easy thing to connect the events noted by cognitive neuroscientists with those concerned by cognitive anthropologists. Moreover, between the concept of human brain and that of human mind, there is also a daunting gap of differences on interpretation. Be that as it may, it is of some help to fill the gap via describing cognitive phenomena by means of formal systems. Albeit people are intensifying their efforts to explore which specific formal system is the most effective and whether or not any formal system can function properly, **the inclination to employ formal system is steadfast**. We must be aware that the concepts relevant to the brain are completely different from those to the mind. **Whereas the brain is material, the mind is a nervous activity performed and finished in the brain, and we usually call it cognitive activity**.

1.2 The Theory of Language Holography at the Level of the Influences from Other Disciplines on Cognitive Science

To demonstrate cognitive science's push on the theory of language holography, the first thing we should investigate is how disciplines like linguistics, etc., (philosophy, artificial intelligence, psychology) exerted influences on cognitive science. In effect, it is very necessary to look at the problems reversely. This is because the more inseparable the relations between linguistics, etc., and cognitive science are, the more convenient it is to elucidate the holographic relations between them.

1.2.1 The Contributions from Philosophy to Cognitive Science

Cognitive science involves an empirical approach to questions which have long been considered by philosophers. Perhaps the most notable of these is the mind/body problem concerning the relationship between mental characteristics of mind and physical characteristics of the brain Whereas the philosophical problem involves consideration of whether and why such disparate phenomena might (or might not) be connected, the problem in cognitive science is to characterize the relationship between mind and body for any given phenomenon. Most cognitive scientists have adopted, at least implicitly, one of two positions on the mind/body problem. The first is materialism, and is favored especially by people working in neuroscience. Materialism involves the belief that the only adequate characterization of mental states is in terms of their reduction to physical states of the brain. The second position is functionalism, and is popular among cognitive scientists pursuing questions in psychology and artificial intelligence. Functionalism, although compatible with materialism, differs from the latter in the belief that the essential characteristics of mental states are their informational properties, rather than their physical characteristics.[5] We may as well borrow this train of thought: from "the only adequate characterization of mental states is in terms of their reduction to physical states of the brain," we can deduce that only when the properties of the mental state are sufficiently revealed, can the state of language generation be restored. Even if we cannot completely deduce reversely the generation of language, we can see **the step-by-step corresponding state between cognitive process and language generation. Apparently, this corresponding state can be used to elucidate the holographic relation between them**. Coulson's statement offers a support:

> Other philosophical issues tackled by cognitive scientists include the question of intentionality (how it is that words, actions, and mental representation in general can have content); the issue of whether human knowledge should be characterized as innate or learned; rationalism versus empiricism (the relative importance of the mind as opposed to the external environment in determining our conception of reality); and epistemology (what it is to know something: in cognitive science, this debate has centered on the possibility of building intelligent computers).
>
> As noted above, cognitive science has branched off from its philosophical roots, abandoning the thought experiment for the empirical methods of the natural and social sciences. To some extent, one can conceptualize artificial intelligence (AI) as an extension of philosophy, where the philosophers' logical tools have been automated. **Nonetheless, philosophy continues to have a strong influence on cognitive science in forcing clarity of concepts and the explanatory adequacy of its theories.**[6]

1.2.2 The Push from Artificial Intelligence on Cognitive Science

Perhaps more than anything else, cognitive scientists have been inspired by the invention of the computer and its attendant theoretical constructs, such as information theory and symbol processing. The movement in the 1950s in computer science toward construing computers as symbol processors rather than mere number crunchers led some of AI's founders to a new way of thinking about the mind. The use to which cognitive scientists put the computer is two-fold: first, the computer is employed as an inspiring metaphor for mind. That is to say, cognitive scientists have used the metaphor of mind as a computer to inspire their work. Second, the computer has been used as a tool for building formal models of intelligent behavior.[7] These are not tongue twisters but a quite inspiring assertion. We can thus interpret them: the principle of mental work is like the computer, and the latter is also like a mental generator, i.e., the brain. The brain commands human to utter words, namely, to generate sentences, just like the computer performs arithmetic operations, and that is why the mind is compared to the computer; on the other hand, the formal model of the computer in fact performs intellectual acts, and hence the computer is also a "brain" similar to human's. Tempted by such a consideration, some affirm that the most powerful AI machine could think and speak like human. My assertion in

---

[5]Coulson (1995, p. 124).

[6]Coulson (1995).

[7]Coulson (1995).

Sect. 2, "Robots Can Not Have Human-Like Intelligence and Language" (as one of the two predictions of the theory of language holography), of Chapter 9 of this book, namely, the robot is not at the same level with human in terms of holography, is the answer directed to this temptation.

1.2.3 The Help from Psychology to Cognitive Science

As was stated by Coulson,

> The field of cognitive psychology began mainly as a reaction against the reigning theory of psychology in the 1950s, behaviorism. Profoundly committed to controlled experimentation and the study of observable phenomena, behaviorists considered mental phenomena such as thoughts, images, and ideas to be vague categories whose ontological status was questionable. Because mental phenomena were not directly observable, they were deemed unfit for scientific investigation. However, the development of the computer and concomitant theoretical developments in information theory (Shannon 1949) offered psychologists a new way of discussing mental phenomena. The computer served as an example of a mechanism whose observable, intelligent behavior did not require an appeal to introspective knowledge. Moreover, the behavior of the computer could ultimately be attributed to physical processes. The construal of the human mind as an analogue of the computer thus had a legitimating effect on the status of mental phenomena as potential objects for scientific study. Further, it provided cognitive psychologists with a language for discussing unobservable mental phenoma in a rigorous way. **The human mind is thought of as implementing a formal system**. The cognitive scientist's job, then, is to outline the symbolic representations and transformation of those representations which intervene between environmental input to a given person and his/her behavioral output. **The mind-as-computer analogy has also been used to develop a vocabulary for discussing cognitive mechanisms based on that used to discuss mechanisms in the computer**. For example, programs, compilers, and buffers are often invoked as analogues of human mental processes. Armed with the theoretical machinery of computer science, cognitive scientists have studied human decision making, syllogistic reasoning, reasoning under uncertainty, the organization of memory, problem solving, auditory and visual perception, planning, learning, development, and aging.[8]

Please note: our question is, "Lexicon is an inventory of language materials and vocabularies built by modern people in the computer, so how can it be used to discuss the cognitive mechanisms ('The mind-as-computer analogy has also been used to develop a vocabulary for discussing cognitive mechanisms')? Furthermore, how can cognitive mechanisms be used to discuss the electronic brain, namely, computer ('based on that used to discuss mechanisms in the computer')? This is because the electronic brain can be analogized to human brain, and the second step turns to the discussion of human brain by means of cognitive mechanism. To this connection, by synthesizing these two steps, we can say this: to discuss the cognitive mechanism with language materials (the language materials and vocabularies in the lexicon), and to observe human brain with cognitive mechanism. How, then, is it possible? Doesn't it demonstrate the holographic relation between language and cognition? **If no cognitive information were contained in language, and vice versa, how could you investigate the two opposite movements, respectively? Isn't the mutual**

[8]Coulson (1995, p. 125).

embracement, namely, holographic relation for which we are searching hidden behind the feasibility of the opposing investigation as such?"

Coulson further says,

> Moreover, one of the biggest areas in developmental psychology concerns the question of language acquisition. Though this research has chiefly focussed on the growth of children's syntactic knowledge, the acquisition of pragmatic aspects of language ability has also been addressed. Bates (1976) suggests that children阵 competence with speech acts precedes their acquisition of other aspects of language. Moreover, the child's early communicative knowledge helps pave the way for subsequent language development. Mandler (1991) suggests that, in fact, children 阵 conceptual ability develops quite early, in the form of image-schemas. **Image-schemas are mappings from spatial structure, abstract aspects of trajectories of objects and their interactions in space, onto conceptual structure** (This definition merits heed in that the core concepts of cognitive grammar and cognitive semantics that will appear later exactly appertain to schema). She argues that the perceptual sophistication of very young children is sufficient to support image-schema representation; moreover, she points to the implication of image-schemas in cognitive linguistics and suggests that **the initial stages of language acquisition involve mappings between words and image-schemas.**[9]

It is my contention that this assertion of Mandler is of vital significance for us to understand the holographic relation between cognition and language. The mutual mapping is shown between words and image-schema, then what are words in language? She believes that they are the images, the mapping of schemas which, de facto, means that words are the mapping of the cognitive process. That is to say, the information in the cognitive process embraces words, and that conveyed by the words also embraces images and schemas. The mutual mapping as such is nothing but a holographic relation.

1.2.4 The Push from Linguistics on the Rise of Cognitive Science

I will explicate this problem in "Cognitive Linguistics and the Theory of Language Holography" (the 5th subsection of this section).

1.3 The Relation Between the Theory of Language Holography and Cognitive Science Seen at the Level of the Latter's Development Tendency

It is one of the directions of modern cognitive science that the culture's function in intellectual activities is acknowledged more than before. The solution of many cognitive subjects is due to the aid of instruments or cognitive utensils like book, calculating machine, computer, etc., popularized by virtue of culture. Of course, the most impressive discussions of cognitive activity are usually the results from the cooperation of groups of people on breaking down the technical barriers. Another tendency

[9]Coulson (1995, pp. 125–126).

of cognitive science is the increasing interest in the problem of evolution. The new disciplines like evolutionary biology, physical anthropology, animal psychology, etc., can all provide a clue for people to ascertain the evolution of human cognitive competence by virtue of natural selection. In addition, people have just become interested in the computation mode of the evolution of **their various cognitive competences, notably natural language**. The logic and cultural evolution mechanisms take shape in a new paradigm of artificial life. The emulation similar to life behavior is also a kind of artificial life. It is composed of many systems of semi-autonomous entities of human, and the partial communications between semi-autonomous entities are controlled by a set of simple rules.[10] The main development of this research program indicates that complex and high-level dynamicity and structure are often sudden emerging results from the development of the partial communications.

The most noteworthy parlance herein is "their various cognitive competences, notably natural language." Natural language is considered as the most prominent surface structure of the evolution of cognitive competence. In other words, **cognitive competence can be seen from natural language, and vice versa, natural language can be seen from cognitive competence. The mutual embracement of information as such is by no means accidental. It indicates again that the layer below language, namely, the layer of cognitive competence, is in a holographic relation to language**.

1.4 *Other Aspects in Cognitive Science That Are Concerned with the Theory of Language Holography*

In the first instance, the functionalism in cognitive science can clearly explain the intimacy between language and cognitive competence. Seana Coulson notes,

> The functionalist, then, is concerned with **what sorts of representations are involved in the phenomena and which processes operate on them**. A functionalist might develop theories by building computational models of psychological processes, and later testing those theories by conducting experiments. A functionalist might also be inclined to employ the methods of linguistics, developing theories to account for linguistic facts and testing them via linguistic intuitions. Because the functionalist is less interested in the physical instantiation of cognitive phenomena, s/he will not concern him/herself with questions about the neurophysiological details surrounding that phenomenon.[11]

Here, that which draws my attention is, as a school of cognitive linguistics, functionalism merely looks backward at the cognitive law from the functions revealed by language, namely, how language representations are embraced in cognitive phenomena ("what sorts of representations are involved in the phenomena").

---

[10]Langton (1988).

[11]Coulson (1995, p. 132).

So to speak, each process of language is usually handled together with cognitive phenomena. What does this intimate relation indicate? Why do the functionalists in cognitive linguistics examine their theories by means of language intuition? Why are they inclined to employ linguistic methods when improving and examining the theories interpreting language facts? This shows nothing but the fact that **language activities are in a state of completely mutual corroboration with cognitive phenomena and they both look backward at themselves from the signs in the other party, namely, they are in a holographic state**.

In the second instance, it is about cognitive modularity. As was says by Coulson,

> One issue which polarized cognitive scientists in the 1980s and continues to figure prominently in psycholinguistics concerns Fodor's (1983) characterization of cognition as **modular**. Fodor's proposal is that cognition is **the interaction of a large number of autonomous, highly specialized input modules with a general purpose central processor**. Input modules can be conceptualized as an array of autonomous black boxes, each of which transforms a particular sort of inputs from the world into representations which can be handled by the central processor. Input systems are referred to as black boxes because they are informationally encapsulated with respect to the central processor as well as with respect to each other. Moreover, the central processor has access only to the outputs of the input modules and not to the intervening representations in the modules themselves.
>
> **A modular approach to language processing** involves the assignment of low-level aspects of processing (such as parsing and word recognition) to informationally encapsulated input modules while leaving the higher-level aspects such as semantics and pragmatics to the central processor. The difference between a modular account of language processing and a non-modular account chiefly concerns the time-course of processing. In the modular account, lower levels of processing occur autonomously and are integrated only later by the central processor. However, on a non-modular account, the lower levels of processing are not independent of higher levels but interact continuously with them in the processing of a sentence. Thus all parties agree that **the various levels of linguistic analysis interact**, while making different predictions about when the results of higher-level analyses become available. The controversy concerns whether or not higher-level contextual factors can influence processing at lower levels.[12]

As to this, I believe that the theory of language holography can accept it. In Sect. 4 ("The Argument for the State of the Inner Language Holography in Terms of the Law of Cosmos Holography") of Chapter 3 ("The Inner Language Holography") in this book, I have particularly demonstrated how the levels of language interact with one another from which we can conclude that the contextual factors of the high levels can influence the processing at the low ones.

1.5 Cognitive Linguistics and the Theory of Language Holography

To properly demonstrate that cognitive phenomena support the theory of language holography, we must have profound knowledge about cognitive linguistics. Now

[12]Coulson (1995, p. 133).

I will briefly introduce cognitive linguistics on the basis of Dirk Geeraerts' (1995, p. 111) account before gradually transferring to how it supports the theory of language holography.

1.5.1 Introduction

Cognitive linguistics is **an approach to the analysis of natural language that focuses on language as an instrument for organizing, processing, and conveying information. Methodologically speaking, the analysis of the conceptual and experiential basis of linguistic categories is of primary importance within cognitive linguistics**: it primarily considers language as a system of categories. The formal structures of language are studied not as if they were autonomous, but as reflections of general conceptual organization, categorization principles, processing mechanisms, and experiential and environmental influences. Because cognitive linguistics **sees language as embedded in the overall cognitive capacities of man**, topics of special interest for cognitive linguistics include:

The structural characteristics of natural language categorization:

prototypicality,
systematic polysemy,
cognitive models,
mental imagery and metaphor;

The functional principles of linguistic organization:

markedness,
iconicity and naturalness;

The conceptual interface between syntax and semantics:

Langacker's cognitive grammar,
Fillmore's frame semantics,
construction grammar;

The experiential and pragmatic background of language-in-use; the relationship between language and thought:

relativism,
conceptual universals.

Of them, the several subjects like syntax metaphor, conceptual structure, categorized prototype theory, image-schema, syntax iconicity, and the like, are the foci of studies in recent years.[13]

Here, I would like to insert an important comment: t**he view that "cognitive linguistics sees language as embedded in the overall cognitive capacities of man"**

[13]Geeraerts (1995, pp. 111–112).

is of critical importance for us to recognize the theory of language holography. My previous four passages of similar discussions can explicate one another:

First: "Only when the properties of the mental state are sufficiently revealed, can the physical state of the brain be restored. Even if we cannot completely deduce reversely the generation of language, we can see the step-by-step corresponding state between cognitive process and language generation. Apparently, this corresponding state can be used to elucidate the holographic relation between them."

Second: by synthesizing the two steps, we can naturally say this: to discuss cognitive mechanism by means of language materials (language materials and vocabularies in the lexicon), and to observe human brain by means of cognitive mechanism. If language did not embrace cognitive information, and cognition did not embrace linguistic information, we could not investigate the two opposite movements, respectively.

Third: here the most noteworthy parlance is: "the evolution of various cognitive competences, particularly of natural language." Natural language is considered as a most prominent surface structure of the evolution of cognitive competence. In other words, cognitive competence can be seen from natural language, and vice versa, natural language can be seen from cognitive competence. The mutual embracement of information as such is by no means accidental. It indicates again that the layer below language, namely, the layer of cognitive competence, is in a holographic relation to language.

Fourth: so to speak, each process of language is usually handled together with cognitive phenomena. What does this intimate relation indicate? Why do the functionalists in cognitive linguistics examine their theories by means of language intuition? Why are they inclined to employ linguistic methods when improving and examining the theories interpreting language facts? This shows nothing but the fact that language activities are in a state of completely mutual corroboration with cognitive phenomena and they both look backward at themselves from the signs in the other party, namely, they are in a holographic state.

I must stress that cognitive linguistics is not a sub-discipline but a school of linguistics. It studies language on the ground of some sort of experience and cognitive method and strategy. The experience refers to ours of the world, and the method and strategy to that by means of which we perceive and conceptualize this world.[14]

Cognitive linguistics came into being in the 1970s and early 1980s, and the driving force of its development came from two different sources. On the one hand, it keeps the interest in the phenomenon of meaning (it belongs to the typical generative semantics within generative linguistics). Nevertheless, compared with generative semantics, cognitive linguistics is completely outside the tradition of generative linguistics. On the other hand, cognitive linguistics gets inspirations and enlightenment from psychological linguistics based on the prototype of categorized form. The leading people of cognitive linguistics are George Lakoff, Ronald W. Langacker, and Leonard Talmy.

---

[14]Cf. Zhang (1998, p. 3).

Let me take two examples, i.e., categorization and metaphor mentioned afore, to indicate cognitive linguistics' support for the theory of language holography. The preposition is a part of speech of the most distinct characteristics and the most complicated meanings in any nation's language. Traditional grammar merely concentrated on the central usage of a preposition, often regarding its other usages as the phenomena of unison containing no inner connections whatsoever. Whereas, the insight of cognitive linguistics into the principle of categorization enables it to see the highly structured essence through the external messy conditions. Seen from the view of categorization, the most frequently used terms of meaning are nothing but those situated at the center of the category, being the prototypes most characterized by prototypical structure, whereas those so-called irrelevant unisons are on the periphery of the category. The center and the periphery being different on meeting the necessary and sufficient conditions of the definition notwithstanding, they are interlinked with one another on information. The situation of linkage on information does not merely exist in the category of preposition, but it also exists in different parts of speech. For instance, "overall" emerges in the dictionary (e.g., *Oxford Advanced Learner's English-Chinese Dictionary*) as two different parts of speech: one is adjective, being interpreted into "including everything; total," and its Chinese paraphrase is "*baokuo yiqiede* 包括一切的, *quanbude* 全部的"; the other is noun, being interpreted into "a loose-fitting coat worn over other clothing to protect it from dirt, etc.," and its Chinese paraphrase is "*changzhaoyi* 长罩衣." Seen at the level of metaphor, isn't the second term of meaning, viz., "*changzhaoyi*," the metaphorical extension of "including everything; total"? The interlinkage of information is situated in nothing else than the extension of metaphor.

From the above we can see that **the information landscape revealed by the cognitive view of metaphor is**: metaphor is universal,[15] which makes possible the universal connection of information; its systematicness enables information to communicate with one another and to form a system; it is characterized by being conceptual—more than a linguistic topic, metaphor is all the more a thinking mode. That is to say, the thinking process is itself metaphoric, and the conceptual system on which we rely to think and act are mostly constructed and delimited in a metaphorical fashion for the sake of agglomerating the communicative information into a conceptual block.

1.5.2 Cognitive Linguistics and Cognitive Science

Cognitive linguistics differs from the method (a broader sphere) processing natural language as a mental phenomenon. In a more rigorous sense, cognitive linguistics is merely a method of cognitive science on processing language, needing distinguishing from many research modes of language in the spheres of generative grammar and artificial intelligence. What, then, ultimately determines the particularity of cognitive linguistics in cognitive science? To answer this question, two more specific questions

[15] Lakoff and Johnson (1980).

need discussing: what is the concise meaning of "cognitive" in cognitive linguistics? How does this meaning differ from the constructing mode of other forms of linguistics (also as cognitive disciplines)?

The answer to the second question is supposed to be specifically connected with generative grammar. Admittedly, another key factor of the rise of cognitive linguistics is the development of Chomsky's generative grammar. When it comes to cognitive science using the concepts of computer science's automatic control theory, and to treating natural language as a string of signs describable as a formal system, Chomsky's views of language can be said a case. Albeit early Chomskian mode (in this mode, the syntax of natural language was processed as a pure form) played a critical role in the early development of cognitive science, the later development focused more on the connection between form and meaning. 25 years of development in the sphere of cognitive semantics amounted to a research procedure the results of which were directly applied to cognitive science. Under such a conception, the function of language is to establish the sentence's syntax construals, coordinate with each sphere, and to construct a mental space of the accessing, spreading, and viewpoint of information. When language is understood in this way, natural language provides us with such a means to trigger the complex structure crossing the discourse. The results obtained in accordance with this train of thought include the studies showing the important roles played by the metaphoric mapping in lexical semantics. The obtainment of the abstract schema in semantic structure is also proved very useful to analyze similar thoughts.

Now let us get back to the point.

In which sense do we say that cognitive linguistics belongs in cognitive science?

In the background of the fundamental qualities of cognitive paradigms in cognitive psychology, philosophy of science, and relevant disciplines, some viewpoints adopted by cognitive linguistics can be delimited more definitely. **Cognitive linguistics is the study of language in its cognitive function**.[16] Here, cognition refers to the critical function of the intermediary information structure when we meet the world. Cognitive linguistics is identical to cognitive psychology on the mode of cognition: their hypothesis is, the interactions between us and the world are realized via the intermediary function of the information structure in our thinking. Nevertheless, when particularly observing natural language qua the means of organizing, processing, and conveying information, cognitive linguistics is more concrete than cognitive psychology. In this way, language can be considered as a storeroom of the worldly knowledge and an aggregate of meaningful categories. The storeroom and aggregate can help us deal with new experiences and maintain the information of the old ones.

How do we recognize all things in the world? The conventional answer was: we observe with the five sense organs, infer with the brain, and hence we recognize the world in an intuitive or abstract way (the abstract way is more profound hence more meaningful). Cognitive linguistics however tells us that when recognizing the

[16]Geeraerts (1995, p. 112).

world, we are not directly faced with it or think bare-handedly but make use of the medium of natural language ("Their hypothesis is, the interactions between us and the world are realized via the intermediary function of the information structure in our thinking"). Natural language becomes the intermediary information structure for human to recognize the world. The function of the intermediary informant structure is critical. What kind of means does natural language have on accomplishing the task of such a recognition (of the world)? It can organize, process, and convey information. Therefore, when recognizing the world, we put the results (the worldly knowledge) into a storeroom or an aggregate helping us deal with new experiences and maintain the information of the old ones. The storeroom or aggregate as such is natural language. The function of a storeroom is understandable, but what is "an aggregate of meaningful categories"? When recognizing the world, a thing we must constantly do is: to perform classification, to categorize the things in the world, namely, to perform meaningful classification—it is not that the world reveals the grids it has early classified, but that human's thinking distinguishes and responds to the universal essences of the objective things. For instance, the recognition of the matter's movement is classified as "physics," the research of the inner changes (the synthesis and the decomposition) of the matter as "chemistry." Some regularities in economic life are generalized as "market economy." The cat and the tiger are classified as "felidae family." Nevertheless, no one will bracket the computer and the biscuit since it is a meaningless categorization. In this way, for the sake of helping us to recognize the objective objects, the world is classified by us into hundreds and thousands of indistinguishable meaningful classes and categories (say, some "system," "-ization/-ification," "-ology," "theory," "level," ad infinitum) like phyla, classes, orders, genus, species, and so on. We thus gradually agglomerate the views of the world and form our knowledge. When reviewing language in this way, we find that we study language in its cognitive function (not the communicative one). Cognitive linguistics is the study of language is this way (What are the structural traits of the categorization of natural language? What are the functional principles of language organization? What are the conceptual interfaces between syntax and semantics? What are the experiential and pragmatic backgrounds of language in use? What, moreover, is the relationship between language and thinking?...).

From the overview above, we can get three fundamental properties of cognitive linguistics: the primacy of semantics in language analysis, and the encyclopedic and the subjective perspectival natures of language meaning. The first one merely states that the fundamental functions of language includes meaning; the other two reify the properties of the semantic phenomena; the priority of semantics in language analysis is immediately obtained from the cognitive perspective; if the primal function of language is the categorization (of the world), meaning is necessarily the primal language phenomenon. The encyclopedic nature of language meaning is derived from the categorizing function of language: if language is a system categorizing the world, there is not the necessity to presume a level of the system or structure of language meaning (this level again differs from those connected with worldly knowledge and language form). The subjective perspectival nature of language meaning means that this world is by no means objectively mapped in language: **when performing the**

function of categorizing the world, language foists a structure on it rather than merely mapping the objective realties. Specifically, language is a mode weaving knowledge, reflecting the needs, interests, individual experiences, and cultures of human world.

As regards the thought that language meaning has subjective perspectival function, cognitive linguists making theoretical elucidations of it from philosophical and epistemological stances include Lakoff, Johnson, and Geeraerts. Such stances are explicated by virtue of two traits: negatively, it is refusing the objectivism of epistemology; positively, it is empiricism (the viewpoint of which is: human's inference is determined by the work of our own organs and by the individual or collective experiences).

1.5.3 The Main Research Areas of Cognitive Linguistics

As has been noted afore, cognitive linguistics is by no means an independent and single linguistic theory but an aggregate of many relevant research methods. The following investigation might not exhaust the various methods, it however can roughly depict the research train of thought within the framework of cognitive linguistics.

The overall research strategies of cognitive linguistics are manifested in the two properties as follows:

To begin, the research of the lexicon's categorizing process (the process of its classification) is generally regarded as the starting point of the methodology employed to research the categorizing process of grammar. If the categorization of language is a main focus of cognitive linguistics, researching lexicon first is a feasible procedure: the categorizing function of lexicon is attached more importance by linguistic tradition than that of grammatical structure. The intention to study the grammar of some language along the same route as lexicon apparently leads to a particular grammatical theory **which holds that grammar, like lexicon, is constructed by an inventory of symbolic elements, viz., meaningful units**. This idea is expressed in the clearest and most detailed fashion in Langacker's cognitive grammar and Fillmore's construction grammar. The symbolic and construction-based perspective recognized by these modes also indicates how the aspects remaining to pay sufficient attention to the procedures and algorithm of grammar, namely, the units paying little attention to the inventory of symbolic elements, are merged into a bigger structure—such as the phrase or the sentence.

In the second place, people systematically research the categorizing function of language units from three different perspectives: (1) the inner structure of the separately processed category; (2) the bigger conceptual structure merging many individual categories into a coherent mental mode; (3) the relationship between form and meaning. The research of the category's inner structure is primarily performed in the prototype theory. As to the relevant works, see Lakoff, Taylor, Tsohatzidis, Geeraerts, Grondelaers and Bakema. The researches of the bigger conceptual structures merging many specific categories are all the time performed from different perspectives. The common research areas include metaphor research (more specifically, that in the theoretical mode of common metaphor), and frame semantics. When these bigger conceptual structures are put in the situation relevant to cultural surroundings, the research is expanded into the cultural mode. The mental mode merging single categories is not necessarily of permanent nature as the research methods mentioned so far. The mental space theory accomplished by Fillmore describes how the mental mode is constructed in the discourse as a tentative structure. At last, the relationship between the form and the meaning of language is researched under the general topic of motivation—more specifically, it is in the mode of iconicity.[17]

In a word, the core problems of cognitive linguistics are: categorization theory, metaphor system, image-schema, and syntactic iconicity. These problems are supposed to be considered as the quintessence of cognitive linguistics.

1.5.4 The Communications Between the Main Principles and Ideas of Cognitive Linguistics and the Theory of Language Holography

According to Haiman (1985a) and Geeraerts (1990)'s theories, cognitive linguistics agglomerates some fundamental views of language, epistemologies, and methodologies with respect to cognition. They are:

First, natural language is both a production and a tool of human's cognitive activities. Its structure and function are supposed to be regarded as the result and response of human's general cognitive activities. Human's linguistic competence should not be considered as a completely self-contained and self-sufficient gifted part independent of other cognitive competences and knowledge in human brain but as closely related to general cognitive competence. Language mechanism is supposed to be a part of the universal cognitive one, and they are supposed to be combined for research. **It is this point that supports the theory of language holography. Inside language system, in each link of language, the part and other parts, the part and the whole (the part is a microcosm of the whole), and this holographic node and that one are communicative with one another. Not only that, outside language system, linguistic competence is also relevant to other cognitive ones**. Secondly, syntax is not concerned with any transformed part. The surface syntactic structure is a fundamental unit of syntactic description, and it directly corresponds to semantic structure. Thirdly, language meaning is not based on the objective truth condition, nor can semantic structure be simply transformed into an arrangement of the truth condition in that it does not correspond to the objective outer world but to the non-objective projected one, and is directly related to the conventionalized conceptual structure. Fourthly, semantics and pragmatics constitute a continuum and both act upon language meaning. Fifthly, since language's fundamental function is to convey meanings, the distinctions on form are advisable only when they reflect the differences at the semantic, pragmatic, or discourse level. Sixthly, language universals and

[17]Cf. Haiman (1985a, b).

the general laws of language are usually manifested in some tendency rather than absolute rules. Seventhly, neither the formalization of language laws nor the interpretation of language universals in the mode of structure formalization is interpretation in the authentic sense; rather, they are merely descriptions or modelings. The more meaningful interpretations of language universals can only be found outside the form, say, in language meaning, expressive and communicative function, cognitive competence, strategy, or the like. Eighthly, the categorization in language is not completely determined by sufficient and necessary conditions. A category often includes the central and the extended peripheral parts. Therefore, some principles of categorization are based on schema, others on prototype. Ninthly, like the lexical item, grammar format is also the pairing of form and meaning.

2 The Hierarchy of Cognition and That of Language

2.1 The Hierarchy of Human Brain's Cognitive and Thinking Process

Now we can present a proof to demonstrate that language mechanism is situated in human brain. This parlance might provoke a burst of ridicule: isn't this asking for trouble? Does it need demonstration that language mechanism is situated in human brain? Can it be situated at the tongue?

There are too many such things taken for granted in the world. For instance, according to the fact that the sun rises in the east in the past hundreds and thousands of years, people affirm that tomorrow it will still rise in the east. In the eyes of natural scientists, nevertheless, it remains to be demonstrated as to whether or not the sun will rise in the east tomorrow. Leave it alone.

If we can prove that cognition and language closely fit one another at the level of hierarchy, we can prove that language mechanism is indeed situated in human brain (rather than at the tongue). Of course, this is a secondary task of this section. The most important task is to demonstrate the holographic relation between the hierarchy of cognition and that of language.

Zhao Nanyuan thus starts his demonstration of the hierarchy of cognition: it is not very helpful to understand human brain via regarding it as a system constituted by ten (one hundred?) billion neurons, and to regard human as a composition of cells or to directly analyze the society into individuals will bring about confusing relationships, which will do harm to the understanding and grasping of the system. In this connection, to the considerably complicated system, it is easier to realize the evidence of analysis to divide it into a few subsystems before further dividing the latter into sub-subsystems, ad infinitum. This "seniority" relationship in the process of analysis constitutes the system's hierarchy which, with the help of exponential explosion,[18] enables us to grasp the considerably complicated big system with a few common principles and mechanisms. This is the necessity of the hierarchy analysis when we analyze the complicated big system, which can be called layered reductionism. For instance, we can divide human body into the subsystems of alimentary system, circulatory system, nervous system, respiratory system, reproductive system, among others, which can be further divided into organs, tissues, and cells layer by layer. In this way, human body can be divided into the four layers of system, organ, tissue, and cell, which is easier to understand than is done directly from the cell (We will see in what follows that the layered recognition as such will offer fairly clear inspirations to the hierarchy of language—the author). Each layer has its own principles and mechanisms, and the principles of the upper layer can be interpreted by those of the lower one, say, the functions of the subsystems therein, the relations between them, and the like. **As regards the adjacent layers, the lower one has strong interpretative power of the upper one**; as regards the non-adjacent layers, whereas, it is usually very hard to interpret the upper layer by means of the lower one's principles, or else the layers in between would become unnecessary.

The concepts with regard to cognition can be divided into seven layers.

Zhao Nanyuan notes that as to the complex functions in the considerably complicated system like human brain's cognitive and thinking process, layered interpretations are necessary for overall elucidations, and insufficient layering might bring about theoretical difficulties. He divides the concepts with regard to cognition into seven layers which can be further grouped into four levels.

culture:	logic, science, religion, art
	language, symbol, technique, behavior
psychology:	perception, consciousness, emotion, feeling
	nerves, classification, prediction
physiology:	neural network, mode, association
	neuron, excitation, depression, sensation
physics:	biophysics, biochemistry

Illustration: of the layers above, the layer of "language, symbol, technique, behavior" crosses the cultural and psychological levels, that of "nerves, classification, prediction" the psychological and physiological levels, and that of "neuron, excitation, depression, sensation" the physiological and physical levels. Zhao Nanyuan thus explicates the hierarchy of cognition: **the fundamental principle of the layering is that the concepts in the upper layer can be interpreted by those at its adjacent lower layer**. Due to the fact that the concepts are concerned with more than one layer, and the layers also interact with and influence one another, it is not supposed

[18]Zhao (1994). In ancient China, the thought about exponential explosion could be seen in the story of "A lamb goes astray on a forked road": someone lost his lamb, so he asked the villagers to help him look for it. He soon came back depressed. Someone else asked him, "It is just a lamb, so why are you so depressed?" He said, "It is not the problem of the lamb. What is in my mind is, there is a forked road, and more ahead of it, so no matter how many people I ask, it is not enough." Of course, it is possible to find the lamb in real life. This is merely a thought experiment showing the difficulty of exponential explosion.

to consider this layering as absolute. It merely offers relative positions in general to illustrate the upper-lower relationships between these concepts.

From the bottom up, the first layer is of biophysics and biochemistry, which belongs to the physical level. It corresponds to semiconductor physics explaining the working principles of the transistor in terms of computer and television.

The second layer is concerned about the physiological and physical levels. In the case of computer and television, this layer is equivalent to the working principles of single transistor.

The third layer is of the neural network, etc., belonging to the physiological level. It can correspond to the layer of fundamental circuit in computer or television. The learning and memory at this level are mainly manifested in some fundamental functions of the neural network, say, the functions of self-organization, mapping and function approximation, associative memory, to name a few.

The fourth layer is of nerves, etc. It is equivalent to the functional parts like memory, arithmetic unit, control unit, interface, etc., of the computer, or to those such as high and media frequency lines, video amplification, audio amplification, color decoding, line scanning, kinescope, etc., of the television. The relevant learning and memory are manifested in the generating process of these functions.

The fifth layer can be called the layer of consciousness. This layer is situated at the core of the psychological level, so its themes are essentially coincident with those of psychology. It corresponds to the whole structure of the computer or television. The layer of consciousness determines the overall structure of the intelligent system. The learning and memory in this layer are manifested in consciousness' role of evading from the exponential explosion in the learning process.

The sixth layer is that of language. This layer is concerned with the psychological and cultural levels, being relevant to the hardware structure of the cognitive system (referring to the nerves one layer below and the neural network one more layer below and the neuron still one more layer below) but being less influential than the consciousness layer (which is situated in between: "as regards the non-adjacent layers, whereas, it is usually very hard to interpret the upper layer by means of the lower one's principles, or else the layers in between would become unnecessary"). The language layer corresponds to the operating system of the computer or the system of the television. The main research objects of this layer are language, symbolic expression, the advancement of the technique, and the like. Symbolic expression is the popularization of linguistic concepts, including such means as gesture, figure, countenance, etc., and the comprehension of them. Language is merely a special case of symbolic expression. Technique refers to the skilled behavior produced by the actions organized in a complex fashion. The capacity of symbolic expression or the usage of language is also a technique. The capacity to grasp language appertains to the hardware, relying on the speech center of the cerebral cortex and its motor center operating the vocal organ, but the choice of language is determined by the cultural surroundings. On this account, linguistic competence is biologically genetic whereas specific language structure comes from the culture's evolution. The same holds to other techniques including symbolic expression, namely, they rely on the hardware of the cognitive system or the brain on the one hand, and are determined by the cultural surroundings on the other. Like the operating system is the interface between the computer's hardwares and softwares, **the layer of language is the interface between the psychological and cultural levels**. The learning and memory at the language layer are manifested in some specific applications and complex combinations at the psychological level, and in things relevant to learning at the cultural and psychological levels.

The seventh layer can be called the logic layer, and it belongs to the cultural level in toto. This layer is equivalent to the application softwares in the computer or the telecasts in the television. The learning and memory in this layer are manifested in culture's evolution process, or the like. That I call this layer the logic layer is of particular intention: it stresses that **logic is the product of cultural evolution, being the superstructure rather than the foundation of cognition**. The name of the language layer is of the similar meaning, namely, **cognition is the foundation of language and symbol**. The understanding of the psychological level of cognition helps to explicate language, symbol, and logic ("As regards the adjacent layers, the lower one has strong interpretative power of the upper one"—the author); contrariwise, it is extremely hard to explain the cognitive and thinking process by means of language, symbol, and logical reasoning ("as regards the non-adjacent layers, whereas, it is usually very hard to interpret the upper layer by means of the lower one's principles"—the author).

Where is the position of the language layer?

It is of vital significance to find the position of the language layer in the seven ones of cognition. Achieving this, we will be aware of these: the interrelations between the language layer (the sixth layer) and other cognitive ones; what problems in the lower layers (the bottom level is the psychological one, namely, the layer of consciousness: perception, consciousness, emotion, feeling, and the lower level is…) must be settled before the necessary preparatory knowledge is obtained; the studies at the layer of language are the preparatory conditions of the other tasks at the higher layer (the top layer is the cultural level, namely, the logic layer: logic, science, religion, art, and there is no higher one); and what research directions and conclusions are important and to what.

In addition, only when we understand the position of the disciplinary studies at the language layer in cognitive science, can we decide effective research guidelines pertinent to the disciplines at this layer. In virtue of the respective positioning of the whole cognitive hierarchy and the language layer, we will have a clear idea as regards the position and importance of each research area relevant to cognition in the overall theory, their interrelations, and the order of relevant researches.

The following discussions (the holographic relation between the hierarchy of cognition and that of language) are orderly exactly because they take the sixth layer (the position of the language layer) as the point of departure.

2.2 *The Holographic Relation Between the Hierarchy of Cognition and That of Language*

The following is my discussions with respect to the hierarchy of cognition. I focus on three aspects: (1) the relations between the sixth layer, namely, the language layer and other ones are exactly holographic; (2) those between the four factors (language, symbol, technique, behavior) at the sixth layer are holographic; (3) those between the hierarchy of cognition and that of language are holographic.

(1) The relations between the sixth layer, namely, the language layer and other ones are exactly holographic. Where is the position of language in cognitive process? Now I will present a part of the previous figure again:

logic, science, religion, art
culture
language, symbol, technique, behavior
psychology perception, consciousness, emotion, feeling
……………………………………………………………………

The lower neighbor of the language layer (the sixth layer) is the layer of consciousness (perception, consciousness, emotion, feeling belonging to the level of psychology), and the upper neighbor of it is the layer of logic (logic, science, religion, art belonging to the level of culture).

Now we can see why we must study psychology when studying language, and why there are psycholinguistics, experimental psycholinguistics, and applied psycholinguistics. This is because the lower neighbor of the language layer is the level of psychology. To interpret the language layer by means of the consciousness layer is the most intimate and supportive relationship. That is to say, human's language is holographic with his/her mind. Seen from the status quo of cognitive science, Zhao Nanyuan contends, the most important cognitive level is that of psychology. "This is because the levels of physiology and physics below the psychological level have established advanced research areas with comparatively complete research methods and many fruits",[19] and hence we can make use of them. Albeit "the level of psychology remains essentially in a situation of "the blind man feeling an elephant"—to take a part for the whole, offering merely some scattered conjectures and remaining to become systematic, which, as a result, makes the researches at the layers above it relatively hard for lacking necessary foundation",[20] namely, albeit there are many difficulties, we must make clear the problems at the level of psychology before claiming that we understand language well. As has been said by me previously, "To interpret the language layer by means of the consciousness layer is the most intimate and supportive relationship," and that is why psychological terms permeate linguistics. Thus we can say that to fully understand psychological linguistics qua the guideline of linguistic studies is a correct decision.

---

[19]Zhao (1994).

[20]Zhao (1994).

Now we can see, again, why we must study culture (logic, science, religion, art) when studying language, why language is the carrier of culture, why studies as regards the relations between culture and language have reached their height, and for what reason anthropological linguistics, ethnolinguistics (a branch of anthropological linguistics, and linguistic anthropology came into being. **This is because the upper neighbor of the language layer is the cultural level. To interpret the cultural level by means of the language layer is the most intimate and supportive relationship**. That is to say, human language is holographic with his/her culture. Hence, to fully understand the relations between psychological linguistics qua the guideline of linguistic studies and culture is a correct decision.

To this connection, **the language layer is the interface or bridge between the levels of psychology and culture**.

It is easy to see clearly the holographic relation between the language layer and the cognitive ones (the cultural level above it and the consciousness layer below it) closely adjacent to it, it however is not that easy to see clearly the relationship between it and other levels (the physiological and physical levels) albeit it is also holographic. This is because they are not that closely adjacent to one another.

The sixth layer lives in all the seven ones, namely, **the language layer lives in the whole cognitive hierarchic system**. Now we can see why we must study the cognitive laws when studying language, and for what reason cognitive linguistics and cognitive pragmatics came into being. This is because **cognition is the foundation of language and symbol**, and there are the levels of psychology, physiology, and physics below the language layer—they build the foundation of cognition layer by layer. The understanding of the psychological level of cognition helps to explicate language, symbol, and logic. This is to say that **cognition is holographic with language**. In the same way, to settle linguistic problems from the relations between cognition qua the guideline of language research and language is a correct decision. Moreover, we can say that it is never excessive to stress the importance of the relations between cognition and language. Cognitive linguistics is the most fundamental discipline of linguistics, and the reason is: the language layer lives in the whole cognitive hierarchic system.

We can also say that **psychological linguistics and all the language researches pertinent to psychology, and cultural linguistics and all the language researches pertinent to culture are all the constituents of cognitive linguistics**. The reason is: the levels of psychology and culture are also included in the seven layers of cognition.

Starting from the position of the language layer in the whole cognitive hierarchy, we can affirm that the three areas, namely, **the disciplines at the top layer with regard to the relations between culture and language, those at the bottom layer with regard to the relations between psychology and language**, and **cognitive linguistics**, are **the three major fundamental disciplines of language**.

(2) What are the relations between the four factors (language, symbol, technique, behavior) of the sixth layer itself? We merely need to see that starting from language, linguistics is included in semiotics (thus are settled the relations between language and symbol), language is also a technique (thus are settled the relations between

language and technique), and that people must study human behaviors so as to study language, anthropologists consider studying language as their duty, linguistic scholars should study human behaviors (e.g., the speech acts studied by pragmatists), and so forth (thus are settled the relations between language and behavior). The horizontal relations between them can occur due to the fact that **the four embrace one another**. **This relation of embracement indicates that the relations within the sixth layer are also holographic**.

(3) The holographic relation between the hierarchy of cognition and that of language

We have given detailed analyses with respect to the hierarchy of cognition afore, so next, let us have a look at that of language.

As has been demonstrated previously, the word is equivalent to the cell, the phrase to the tissue, the sentence pattern to the organ, and the whole language substance to the system. This hierarchic relation, viz., cell → tissue → organ → system, strongly resembles that between the earth and its environment (for details, see Sect. 5 of Chapter 5, "Language Hierarchy"). On this account, we can say that language hierarchy comes from the cosmic one.

Now let us concentrate our sight on human brain. It is never a coincidence that both cognition and language structure show the property of hierarchy; rather, it is a fact that the hierarchy of language is embedded in that of cognition, they two being in a Chinese-embedded-box relation hence being holographic with each other. The similarity in their hierarchies is nothing but the representation of their holographic relations. They lay foundations for and interpret each other. Furthermore, their hierarchies exactly conform to that of the cosmos outside human brain.

2.3 Again on Language's Position in Cognition and the Holographic Relation Between Them

As was stressed afore, language's position in cognition is of vital importance. The importance is manifested in these: only when we know the position of language in cognition, can we know what research directions and conclusions are important and to what, and can we formulate effective research guidelines relevant to language-oriented disciplines. It is starting from the position of the language layer in the whole cognitive hierarchy that we believe, "The disciplines at the top layer with regard to the relations between culture and language, those at the bottom layer with regard to the relations between psychology and language, and cognitive linguistics, are the three major fundamental disciplines of language."

That which can offer a rationale to the conclusions above is the positions of language in the 12 subjects of Norman's (1981) cognitive science. Let us have a look at them first:

Belief systems
Consciousness

Development
Emotion
Interaction
Language
Learning
Memory
Perception
Performance
Skill
Thought

As to the two subjects of language and perception, he thus comments: the importance of them has been attached enough even, so to speak, too much importance. Therefore, there sometimes appear some tendencies in cognitive science, holding that the latter is the research about these two subjects. De facto, the case is certainly not so. I think it is a tragic thing that this incorrect idea prevails. Language and perception are themselves quite complicated topics in which many different aspects of cognition are mixed together. Any subject in cognitive science is in the case, and these aspects support one another, the research activities of one of them being enriched by the knowledge and properties of the other areas. Hence I believe, before substantial progress is obtained in the other ten subjects of cognitive science, the attempt to interpret language and perception cannot succeed.[21]

There are two noteworthy points in the previous comments. The first is, the relationship between language and other subjects is "these aspects support one another." Seen in the view of the theory of language holography, this is exactly the manifestation that the information of language and the other eleven subjects is mutually embraced ("The research activities of one cognitive area are enriched by the knowledge and properties of other ones), namely, they are holographic. The most powerful proof is, the theoretical linguistics at present all connect, hundreds and thousands of times, language with belief systems, consciousness, emotion, interaction, learning, memory, perception, performance, skill, and thought for study, and none of them remains to use these terms hundreds and thousands of times (so frequently that they have thought that these terms originally belong to linguistics)! What does this reflect? These subjects embrace one another. May I ask: which one of them can do without another one? For instance, we take language as the point of departure: language expresses belief systems; that which is prior to language is consciousness; emotion is inferior to language and language also expresses it; language is accomplished via interactions; it is acquired and consolidated through learning; learning a language needs memory (including the short-term and long-term ones) and there would not be language without memory; we must come through the stage of perception before acquiring or learning a language; speech or speech act is performance; language is manifested in skill, and only when a language becomes a skill can it be effectively used; language is all the more closely related to thought, namely, either language

[21] cf. Norman (1981).

expresses and converts into thought, or thought formulates or constrains language. These interrelations embrace one another, you being in me and I in you.

3 Cognition and the Universality of Language

The problem that all languages share something in common, namely, they have universality, universal, universal grammar, and universal tendencies, is one of the most lively argued topics in the twentieth century. People generally acknowledge that this topic appertains to the transformational generative grammar presented by Chomsky.

There are not a few sceptics and supporters. Of the supporters, there is Gennaro Chierchia, the writer of the total entries of *The MIT Encyclopedia of the Cognitive Sciences*. His words are not supposed to be underestimated albeit they remain to carry sufficient weight. He says: the various common points between languages indicate that people's speech acts show clear-cut and complex laws. The same holds to all languages in the world. As a matter of fact, such a tendency seeking common ground shown by language typology is of profound significance.The common points on language structure that he lists are manifested in the following several aspects:

The mode of word order is quite limited. The most commonplace fundamental orders of the main sentence components are "subject-verb-object" (usu. SVO) and "subject-object-verb" (usu. SOV). It is rarely seen that the object is located prior to the subject.

Another common language phenomenon is that all languages have the method of modifying the noun by means of the clause. Needless to say, English and Chinese are also the case.

Such structural properties are common to all the existent speakable languages, but the same also holds to sign languages, e.g., visual-gestural languages.

Chierchia continues with a fairly interesting word:

"It seems plausible to maintain that **<u>universal tendencies in language are grounded in the way we are</u>** (The bold and underline formats are made by me); this must be so for speaking is a cognitive capacity, that capacity in virtue of which we say that we 'know' our native language. We exercise such capacity in using language",[22] and he further says that a term often used in this connection is "linguistic competence." The way we put such competence to use in interacting with our environment and with each other is called "performance."[23]

There are two levels of logic reasoning in the above paragraph:

First, the universal tendencies in language are grounded in the way human beings are;

[22]Chierchia (1999, p. xcii).

[23]Chierchia (1999).

Secondly, this is because speaking is a cognitive capacity; in virtue of that capacity, we say that we "know" our native language. Reversely, we exercise such capacity in using language.

The conclusion we draw according to the first reasoning is: language embraces the way human beings are and vice versa. **In language, there is the information with respect to the way human beings are; in the way human beings are, there is also the information with respect to language**. They are in a relation of you in me and I in you. **The present condition of language structure**—the mode of word order is quite limited. The most commonplace fundamental orders of the main sentence components are "subject-verb-object" (such structural properties can also be found in sign languages)—**has early been deposited in the information of the way human beings are. That is to say, human language is holographic with the way they are**.

For instance, there is SVO structure in Chinese, English, Russian, and so on. We regard Chinese, English, Russian … as individual holographic nodes and the whole human language as a big system. The individual holographic nodes horizontally corresponds to and embraces one another, and each node is of course holographic with the whole language system a level higher.

According to the second reasoning, we can also draw the conclusion that language is holographic with cognition. Speaking is a cognitive capacity in virtue of which we know our native language. Reversely, we exercise such capacity in using language. Seen in this line, **language is a product of cognition, but it is also a tool to reform, deepen, and sublimate cognition**.

In human's cognitive hierarchy, language is the closest to cognition. As to the holographic relations between them, detailed discussions have been given in last subsection, to wit., "The hierarchy of cognition and that of language," so I will not repeat them here.

4 The Return of Cognition into Itself

There are at least two paths to study the connections between cognition and language.

In the first instance, it is to cognize the objective and possible world by means of language, namely, to cognize the world with language as a tool. Thus appears the signifier—signified (concept)—signified (material object) relation. Nevertheless, there is no immediate connection between the signified and the referent, namely, the head is not linked up to the tail, so the three are not in a triangle relation, as shown in Fig. 1.

Li Xiyin thus explicates this:

The signified (concept) is an abstract product which reflects (or names) the class of the material object. In everyday discourse, nevertheless, the name of the class can definitely and accurately signify something in concrete surroundings. This is why the word is entangled with the object and why some people misunderstand that word meaning is directly related to the objective thing (e.g., considering that

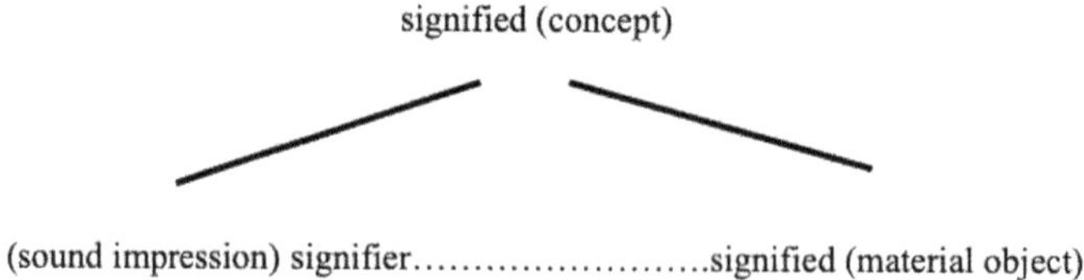

Fig. 1 The signifier—signified (concept)—signified (material object) nontriangle relation

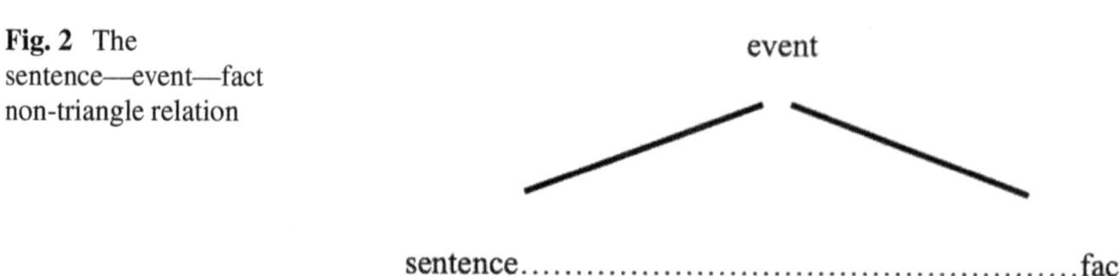

Fig. 2 The sentence—event—fact non-triangle relation

"radio" is directly related to radio). Or there might appear the sentence—event—fact relation. This is because there is no immediate connection between sentence and fact, namely, the head is not linked up to the tail, so the three are of course not in a triangle relation, either. This is the same as the non-triangle relation in Fig. 1, only differently elucidated, as shown in Fig. 2.

As is explicated by Li Xiyin again, the sentence is a language unit higher than the lexicon, and they express the actual fact in concrete communicative activities. People however cannot express the fact until they cognize it. In other words, expression must rely on the medium of "cognition." For the moment, **we call the fact in cognitive state an "event"** (The bold and underline formats are made by me). The event is the referent of the sentence, and its relation to the fact is exactly the same as that between concept and material object (see Fig. 1): **the event is the abstraction of the fact at the level of cognition** (The bold and underline formats are made by me), or, differently put, the former is the class or set of the latter.

That which I would like to stress is, cognition occurs at the link of "signified" (see Fig. 1) or "event" (see Fig. 2). The expression (of sentence) must rely on the medium of "cognition." Cognition is inserted between the expression (of sentence) and the objective world (fact). More often than not, nevertheless, people directly connect the semantic true/false of the sentence (or proposition) with the state of the objective world. That is to say, the intermediary link (people's cognitive state) goes ignored.

The point is, this intermediary link by no means aims to produce isolation or hindrance between the expression and the objective world. This requires that the signifier and the signified or the sentence and the event are considered as being equally situated at the level of symbol.

Li Xiyin thinks so, too.[24] In the two figures above, both the signifier and the signified are at the level of symbol, and the same holds to the sentence and the event.

[24]See the letters between us in October, 1998.

In this connection, cognitive theory is interlinked with semiotic theory. It is thus clear: the ordinary parlance of "There is no organic connection between symbol and material object" is supposed to mean "There is no organic connection between the signifier of symbol and material object, and they must rely on the medium of the signified." The sentence can also be considered as a symbol, and so can the discourse. Friedrich Frege says, the signified of the sentence (or proposition) is its truth-value. The sentence's truth-value is de facto the corresponding fact. Take "It rains" for an example, its truth-value is true, if it rains in fact; its truth-value is false, if it remains to rain in fact. This indicates that the symbol is connected with the objective world via the event (concept), or that **the signified (event) of the linguistic symbol is the result of the cognition of the material object**. Only in this way can it be possible to take natural language as a tool to cognize the objective world. Were there not necessary connections between the linguistic symbol and the material object, namely, were they irrelevant to each other like an apple and an oyster, how could we study the material object by means of the linguistic symbol? Mr. Li's statements above hit the point, or else wouldn't the interconnections between cognition and language be nonsense?

By citing Li's statements here, I aim to note that it is at the level of event that cognitive linguistics can get involved. A conclusion relevant to this section can thus be derived: to a certain extent, to confirm that language is a tool to cognize the objective or possible world is a fact. The fact is, one of the paths to connect cognition and language is to cognize the objective or possible world by means of language, namely, to cognize the world with language as a tool.

As is stated afore, "**to a certain extent**, to confirm that language is a tool to cognize the objective or possible world is a fact." This is a qualified parlance insomuch as language is indeed vulnerable to a certain extent when it is taken as a tool to cognize the world. Starting from this point, we can criticize somewhat the view of language as a tool in terms of its definition. To be sure, language is of the function of communication, to define language according to its function (say, "Language is …a communicative tool") however is faced with the challenges from the Western linguistic philosophers. I will not go further into how to criticize and reflect on the view as such, but will discuss it in detail in the subsection of "Criticisms of the view of language as a tool in terms of its definition" of Chapter 2, i.e., "Prospect: inquiries from philosophy to language," of my *Language: The Last Homestead of Human Beings*.

In the second place, it is to consider language as an object of cognition, namely, to cognize language itself. This results in linguistic relevances: the first level includes grammar, syntax, lexicology, semantics, and phonetics the common points of which are static structures and definite laws; the second level includes the disciplines resulting from the overlapping of language on the one hand and sociology, psychology, mathematics, anthropology, etc., on the other, respectively, and the common points of them encompass language itself and other perspectives; the third level includes the comprehensive disciplines of language functions like pragmatics, etc., It is characterized by taking human factors into consideration, and hence it is dynamic. All these three levels are the results of the consideration of language as a cognitive object.

An increasingly frequent parlance with respect to cognition is, "Cognition can be an object in linguistic research." Jan Nuyts[25] a researcher of the Center for the International Pragmatics Association thus thinks. The first subhead of Sect. 1 of Chapter 1 in his *Aspects of a Cognitive-Pragmatic Theory of Language* is "**Cognition as an object in language research**."

Now, let us have a look at how Jan Nuyts explicates this in detail. He starts from Toulmin's words. Toulmin notes that the clarity and coincidence of goals are the most fundamental prerequisites for the development of a full-scale science. Nevertheless, it seems that language research is lack of this. If we are here merely restricted to theoretical studies, most scholars would agree to this parlance, namely, in any science, the goal is to describe and explain the objects (of the research). Nevertheless, the crux exactly lies in the fact that the things (language researches) concerned are lack of coincidence. This is because the studies of the various sub-disciplines of language remain to have a conglomerate…Language research is basically cognitive research. Jan Nuyts says that he cannot agree more to this view. It can thus be seen that "cognitive science" can be called an appropriate umbrella of the different sub-disciplines albeit the concept of it might be very different from the actual conditions at present. This idea per se becomes reasonable on the basis of the following simple observation: language is a pattern of human's systematic behavior. Chomsky's criticisms on behaviorism indicates that the complexity of linguistic behavior forces you to accept this fact: there is some (confusing) infrastructure (inner or latent structure). The infrastructure makes possible linguistic behavior. It is the "linguistic cognition." Furthermore, the interpretative descriptions of natural language are supposed to reproduce that with which linguistic cognition is concerned, and how linguistic cognition provokes the systematicity in linguistic behavior. This is "a cognitivist view of language" in his terminology.

His meanings can be summarized into the several points as follows:

1. Linguistic research is fundamentally cognitive;
2. "Cognitive science" can be called an umbrella of the different sub-disciplines;
3. There is some infrastructure called "linguistic cognition";
4. "a cognitivist view of language."

Apparently, his core view is "Cognition can be an object in linguistic research" which further means "Linguistic research is fundamentally cognitive." If this core view, notably "Linguistic research is fundamentally cognitive," is true, a very interesting phenomenon would appear: when people take language itself as a cognitive object (please imagine the production of grammar, or the like) (rather than cognizing the objective world with language as a tool), cognition becomes an object of linguistic research. That is:

[25] Nuyts (1992).

man (subject)→cognition→language (object)

During the course in which **one returns from the cognitive state of language to cognition itself**, language merely acts as a springboard on which one does nothing but changes the supporting foot. **This course can be called "the phenomenon of the return of cognition to itself in linguistic research" ("cognitive self-return" for short)**.

At present, the significance of cognitive self-return to linguistic research remains to be estimated properly. Roughly, it might be thus:

1. Linguistic research is fundamentally the research of cognitive laws;
2. To research cognitive laws is to research human him/herself;
3. Hence: to research language is to research human him/herself.

How to understand human via understanding language? The answers from Western philosophers usually include the following four points: first, to understand language is to understand human's feelings and presentation of his/her existence; secondly, to understand the sequence of language is to understand human's logic and mind and his/her cognitive mode of the world; thirdly, to understand language is to understand human's behaviors; finally, to understand the language of a nation is to understand its culture (and to understand a person's choice of words is to understand his/her cultural conditions). The two aspects mentioned by me are: to know about a person's linguistic conditions is to know about his/her life conditions; the cosmos' structure is supposed to be understood via language's since the former is holographic with the latter. The four aspects mentioned afore all remain to be unfolded and developed as the difficulty lies in the fact that it is indeed a big unsettled problem as to whether or not human can cognize him/herself.

Can human cognize him/herself? According to Ouyang Kang, when human cognizes him/herself, he/she will be faced with three strange cognitive circles. The first one is, cognitive subject and object in social cognitive structure are self-related; the second one is, social cognitive activities are intertwined with the social historical ones; the third one is, cultural intermediary and the two corresponding poles in social cognitive structure are self-twined. Of these strange circles, the kernel is **the self-relation of cognitive subject and object**. Han Minqing contends that human's cognition of him/herself cannot be completely outside the object (i.e., him/herself) in that cognition is confused with comment, object with subject, and history with reality, which makes it hard to perform the cognition in the normal fashion. There is one more difficulty allowing no ignorance in human's cognition of him/herself, that is, the tendency of diversification of cognition. Ernst Cassirer calls this tendency "the crisis in human's knowledge of him/herself." He thinks that the cognition of human him/herself opens a new road, that is, a road of symbolic philosophy. He employs symbolic philosophy to study human, and presents his particular anthropological philosophy of culture, viz., anthropological philosophy of symbol.[26]

Human at last opened a new road to cognize him/herself via symbols. Why can he/she achieve this? We can catch a glimpse of this answer from the semiotics of art and literature founded by Cassirer and others (like Susanne K. Langer). When summarizing the properties of Western semiotics of art and literature, Dong Xuewen and Wang Kui mention that the theory of semiotics regards art and literature as symbolic modes expressing human's emotions. The literary and artistic works are a sort of artistic symbol, a symbolic system. **It is in symbols that the subject (human) and the object (works of art created by human) achieve perfect unification**. The importance attached to artistic symbol by semiotics of art and literature promotes the progress of noetic science, linguistic science, and brain science. It **directly** combines the discussions of the essence of art with **those of human nature**. Human is an animal symbolicum. The various forms of human culture—myth, religion, history, language, science, art, industrial product, to name a few, are all human "products" via his/her own symbolized activities. **Human nature is manifested in the fact that he/she can create culture by means of symbols. On this ground, all the cultural forms are both the realization of symbolic activities and the objectification of human's natural power**. Cassirer contends that human relies on symbolic activities to create culture. Human is an animal symbolicum. "The symbolic thought and symbolic behavior are among the most characteristic features of human life."[27] He thinks that human lives in a complex symbolic world rather than a simple physical one. **Language, religion, myth, etc., are each a part of the symbolic world, a net interwoven by human experiences.** Symbolic behavior is one of the marks distinguishing human from animals, and is a necessary medium connecting human and culture. He contends, "Art can be defined as a symbolic language," and "Beauty is necessarily and essentially a symbol."[28] From Cassirer's expounding, we can get these inspirations: (1) since human can reach the perfect unification with his/her creations in symbols, he/she can also cognize him/herself therein; (2) to probe into the essence of artistic symbol is to probe into human's nature; (3) human's symbolic behavior externalizes human nature; (4) that which can represent human's characteristics is the symbolized thought and behavior—human's thought is understandable insomuch as it does not appear in bare form (of thought) but in the form of symbol. On the other hand, human differs from animals on behavior in that the former's behavior is of the property of symbol whereas the latter's is not; (5) as one of the most important parts of symbol, language is a net interwoven by human experiences and, reversely, we can also review human experiences in linguistic net. All these inspirations help to recognize the proposition of "To research language is to research human him/herself."

As a consequence, such a conclusion can be drawn: human communicates with others via language, human presents "existence" with language, and, in language,

[26]Han (1998).

[27]Cassirer (1944. p. 45).

[28]Qtd. from Zhu (1984).

human also has an insight into and illuminates him/herself. When researching language, human finds that he/she is researching him/herself, just like the monkey de facto sees itself when it sees "another monkey" in the mirror. **Such multiple relations between language and human go beyond the interpretative reach of "the view of language as a tool."** Human virtually takes language as his/her homestead. Only in this way can we have the insight into the relations between human and language. The phenomenon of cognitive self-return we are discussing here and now is also a powerful support for the proposition of "Language is the last homestead of human beings."

References

Cassirer. Ernst, *An essay on man: An introduction to a philosophy of human culture.* New Haven: Yale University Press, 1944.

Chierchia. Gennaro, Linguistics and language. In *The MIT encyclopedia of the cognitive sciences.* Cambridge, MA: The MIT Press, 1999.

Coulson. Seana, Cognitive science. In Jef Verschueren, Jan-Ola Ostman, Jan Blommaert (eds), *Handbook of pragmatics.* Amsterdam and Philadelphia: John Benjamins Publishing Company, 1995.

Geeraerts, D., *Editorial statement, cognitive linguistics,* Vol.1, 1990.

Geeraerts. Dirk, Cognitive Linguistics. In Jef Verschueren, Jan-Ola Ostman, Jan Blommaert (eds), *Handbook of pragmatics.* Amsterdam and Philadelphia: John Benjamins Publishing Company, 1995

Haiman, J., *Iconicity in syntax.* Amsterdam: John Benjamins. 1985a.

Haiman, J., *Natural syntax.* Cambridge: Cambridge University Press. 1985b.

Han. Minqing, *Modern philosophical anthropology.* Nanjing: Guangxi People's Publishing House, 1998.

Lakoff, G. & Johnson, M., *Metaphors we live by.* Chicago: Chicago University Press. 1980.

Langton, C. G., Artificial life. In C. G. Langton (ed.), *Artificial life.* 1988.

Norman, D. A., *Perspectives on cognitive science.* Ablex Publishing Company, 1981.

Nuyts. Jan, *Aspects of a cognitive-pragmatic theory of language.* Amsterdam and Philadelphia: John Benjamins Publishing Company, 1992.

Zhang. Min, *Cognitive linguistics and chinese nominal phrase.* Beijing: China Social Science Publishing House, 1998.

Zhao. Nanyuan, *Cognitive science and the general theory of evolution.* Beijing: Tsing Hua University Press, 1994.

Zhu. Di, *Modern western aesthetics.* Beijing: People's Publishing House, 1984.

Part III
The Outer Language Holography

Chapter 5
The Outer Rootstock of the Different Properties of Language

Abstract The outer language holography is discussed from Chapter 5 to 8. Inside China, discussions are mainly directed upon language's properties of linearity, fuzziness, and arbitrariness. Here the readers are supposed to pay particular attention to language's holographibility, recursiveness, discreteness, hierarchy, and organicity. This is because they have never been mentioned inside China or, if any, have never been demonstrated in a rigorous fashion. Not only that. For what I can tell, linguists outside China have also never treated holographibility, recursiveness, and discreteness as the essential properties of language. I ask for your, the readers', attention, hoping that it can provoke your interest in giving criticisms. In addition, that which merits heed is, by discussing these properties, I primarily aim to seek outward (i.e., outward the system, and toward the cosmic structure) for their holographic background.

Keywords Language holographability · Language recursiveness · Language discreteness · Language hierarchy · Language linearity · Language fuzziness · Language rhythmicity · Language organicity · language arbitrariness

The outer language holography is discussed from Chapters 5 to 8. **Outer language holography refers to the holographic state between language system and the world (cosmic structure) outside it: language structure is isomorphic and similar to and embedded in the cosmic one.**

Language repeats the evolution of the cosmos, to wit., the holographic law of it. In this connection, many properties of language can find their origins in the law at issue. Language is a system, and hence it is of the properties of a system. When expounding the six key points of his "theory of linguistic prototype-model," Zhang Jin who presented the "Hypothesis of Thought Module" says, "All things display once and again their respective 'prototype' according to the norms of module before producing their own qualities, properties, figures, and appearances."[1] The "prototype" in his terminology refers to the objective physical as well as mental worlds, the "module" to language and parole. That is to say, he believes that the present appearance of language (quality, property, figure, and appearance) is the result of the repeated

[1]Zhang (1998).

G. Qian, *The Theory of Language Holography*,
https://doi.org/10.1007/978-981-16-2039-3_5

displaying of the worlds as such according to the norms of module. "Language repeats the evolution of the cosmos" can be produced from within this proposition, which hence upholds our idea that "Language repeats the law of cosmos holography."

1 Language Holographibility

Language holographibility refers to the property displayed by the states of the inner as well as the outer language holography. It merely stresses the facet of language property. As was stated afore, in essence, the theory of language holography is identical to **the law of language holography or holographibility**, all referring to the states of the inner as well as the outer language holography.

As to the inner language holography, please see Sect. 4 of Chapter 3, namely, "The demonstration by means of the law of cosmos holography," and Sect. 5, namely, "Re-demonstration by means of the system theory." No more repetition will be given hereafter.

As to the outer language holography, please see Chapters 5, 6, 7, and 8.

2 Language Recursiveness

I will treat in a definite fashion recursiveness as one of the essential properties of language, just like language arbitrariness and linearity, before putting more stress on the explications of the fact that linguistic recursiveness originates from the holographic relationship between language structure and the cosmic one.

2.1 Theoretical Introduction

In Western literatures, when the phenomenon of recursiveness in the application of language is mentioned, it is merely considered as a grammatical attribute of transformational generative grammar. This attribute introduces the primal sign S as a selective element into the rule of expansion, which, as a method, makes possible the generation of innumerable sentences, and hence amounts to innumerable times of employment of the previous rules. This indicates that Western linguists remain to definitely treat recursiveness as an essential property of language.

In more than one place, Chomsky points out "recursive devices," "recursive processes," "recursive aspect," and "recursive tense system," generally regarding recursiveness as a grammatical attribute of his transformational generative grammar. He thus says, "A grammar without the recursive devices (a closed circle...) would become inconceivably complex. On the other hand, if it indeed has some recursive device, it would generate infinite sentences." Here he already connects the capacity to generate infinite sentences, the simplicity of grammar, and recursive devices which, undoubtedly, is of profound significance. He says, "The presumption that language is infinite can simplify the description as such (i.e., it is conceivable that grammar has recursive devices so as to generate infinite sentences)," "Therefore, generative grammar cannot but be a system of rules capable of generating innumerable structures." In another place, he further points out, "Seen in this connection, a set of grammars project the acts of the utterer who can generate and understand infinite new sentences. Furthermore, when a sort of knowledge has a language, it necessarily contains this capacity." It is believed that this concept hits upon the fact that all languages are creative, "These languages provide such methods, namely, being capable of expressing infinite thoughts, and of always giving proper corresponding methods in infinite changing situations." This all-important passage has, so to speak, shown in itself that recursiveness is an essential property of language; nevertheless, Chomsky remains to note that there is a direct relationship between this essential property and recursive devices, which puzzles me a lot. In addition, he notes, "The technical devices for expressing a system of recursive processes, as developed in mathematics, not only account for sequences longer than any ever before produced, but offer an explicit formulation of creative processes."[2] On the whole, that which Chomsky intends to express via these thoughts is: Why humankind is capable of speaking infinite sentences with finite means? The reason lies in the fact that language has a certain recursive device. As to what recursive devices are, and what language recursiveness is, I will explicate them in what follows.

Chomsky substitutes language competence for Saussure's language, language performance for Saussure's parole. Language competence is the bottom system of rules grasped by the utterer, and language performance is the specific application of such rules. Chomsky thus criticizes Saussure, "He regards language as a sign storehouse characterized by grammar, namely, in this storehouse there are reserved elements similar to vocabularies, fixed word-combinations, or presumably things similar to phrases. In this vein, he has no idea settling the recursive process of sentence formation. It seems that he regards forming sentences as parole rather than language, as a free and arbitrary creation rather than a systematic rule. In Saussure's system, he is lack of a concept, namely, creativeness restricted to rules. Individual creation is still permitted in the system of rules. Several finite rules can be set to generate infinite sentences. It is not that hard to accomplish this. **So long as several recursive rules are applied repeatedly, various sentences in which relation clauses modify the noun can be obtained**. The last point remaining to be the generalization of recursiveness notwithstanding, it can offer many tips to us. For instance, what kind of rule is recursive? Why can this rule be applied repeatedly? In the fourth part of this section, namely, "The demonstration of linguistic recursiveness," the formation of a long sentence is the result of the inspirations from Chomsky.

---

[2]Chomsky (1965a, p. 8; 1965b, p. 17).

Jef Verschueren once noticed the phenomenon of linguistic recursiveness. When discussing implied meanings, he points out that background information in a certain extent must be presumed as co-owned by the utterer and the interpreter. Such a presumption is concerned with some sentence types of recursive and mutual embedding. His example is: I know that you know that I know, etc. It is widely acknowledged that the sentence type as such is one of the typical recursive types, but it is also a typical structure of "Chinese embedded box" (see below), to wit., the repetition of identical structures (e.g., Somebody knows that). In another place where he discusses the various expressions of the utterer, he points out another situation, namely, in writing utterances, the complex pattern of the utterances is embedded in the main one. He notes that in this book of his, the simple definition of an "utterance" is: an utterance expansion generated by the same person(s) and with relatively clear beginning and ending. To this connection, an utterance might be a speech turn in the conversation, or a trilogy of 1000 pages. Trilogy includes innumerable embedded utterances provided by innumerable main utterers (i.e., the authors of the trilogies). Needless to say, such an utterer of the embedded utterance can also speak in various expressive ways. Verschueren notes that such a situation expresses the possible recursiveness of the entire structure. As to these statements, my understanding is: a discourse is first and foremost the author's utterances; secondly, a great many people's utterances are embedded in the work, which is the "embedded utterances" in Verschueren's terminology. These embedded utterances are identical on structure, which hence constitutes the recursiveness of the entire structure. In a word, the main utterer cites other utterers ("embedded utterers"), and utterances are embedded in utterances ("embedded utterances"). Be that as it may, I would like to stress that the crux lies not in utterances being embedded in utterances, but in the fact that the embedded utterances employ in a repeated fashion identical structures, and repeat the structures embedded layer upon layer (If the structures are not identical, how can they be embedded layer upon layer?).

When discussing the complexity of scale-category, Western systemic functional grammarians introduced recursiveness. It is their contention that the complexity of structure can be manifested in repeated appearances of the structural elements, and this phenomenon is called recursion. Recursion is classified into sequence parallel recursion and sequence subordinate recursion, and the former can be further classified into order parallel and apposition parallel recursions.

2.2 Some Typical Forms of Recursive Structure

The domain in which the aforementioned recursive phenomena appear is by no means available everywhere. In some discourses, the repeated appearance of structural elements cannot be guaranteed. According to me, "This is a dog. Beware of it!" or its Chinese version "这是一条狗, 小心!" is not supposed to be a recursive structure. Albeit they are complete discourses, there is not the repetition of structural elements. Nonetheless, recursive structure can be found in virtually all the bigger discourses. This judgment is generally identical with the recognition as to the typical sentence type of recursiveness discussed in transformational generative grammar. The typical sentence type is: NP + VP ∈ N'P' + V'P' + N"P" + V"P". Its simple transformational process is thus:

1. S → NP + VP
2. VP → V + NP
3. NP → Det + Nom + (S)

Since S can be embedded into NP, the following sentence is thus generated: The man (who kicked the ball) scored the goal (that won the game). In this sentence, "The man scored the goal" is an NP + VP, "who kicked the ball" is another N'P' + V'P', and "that won the game" is still another N"P" + V"P". Therefore, the whole sentence becomes a bigger NP + VP in which two smaller ones are embedded. The whole situation can be expressed by: NP + VP ∈ N'P' + V'P' + N"P" + V"P". This is a typical recursive sentence type in which identical structures are embedded layer upon layer.

Another typical sentence type showing recursiveness is: I know that you know that I know, etc.

Still another typical type is "recursive field": This is a book on AIDS (A). I hate it (B). That is a CD disk (C). I like it (D). In this discourse, (C) repeats (A), (D) repeats (B), but (A) is not recursive to (B), neither is (C) to (D). The intermingled recursions and non-recursions constitute a recursive field. "Recursive field" refers to a discourse in which recursions and non-recursions are intermingled. A language is so to speak a biggest recursive field embracing innumerable smaller ones. Recursive field exists in a large quantity and in a universal fashion.

I will not cite other typical sentence types one by one.

2.3 *The Definition of Linguistic Recursiveness*

It can be seen from previous discussions that language recursiveness is supposed to be thus defined: the repetition or mutual embedding of identical structural elements in linguistic structural hierarchy and speech generation.

This definition is coincident with Zhou Haizhong's expounding.[3] He notes that recursion is a nomenclature of recursive theory (also known as "recursive function theory" or "effectiveness theory") which, nevertheless, is a branch of mathematical logic, focusing on the study of computability theory. It studies whether or not there are algorithm solutions to problems; if not, what is the extent of non-solvability. Its main method is to reveal in depth, by virtue of studies of number theory, the essence of the solvable process so as to forcefully settle many important mathematical problems. Its calculation of function value is as a rule obtained via recurring to the known value, and hence people call this theory "recursive theory." Recursive theory is mainly

[3] As to Zhou Haizhong's statements of recursion, see his letter to me on May 23, 2000.

applied in computer science to computational complexity theory. The mathematical concept of "recursion" was introduced into linguistic studies via generative grammar. It refers to a grammatical means generating infinite phrases or sentences by virtue of recursively employing identical rules.

2.4 *The Demonstration of Linguistic Recursiveness*

2.4.1 Holistic Recursiveness

In this vein, many seemingly complex problems become simple and clear. This is why no matter how many sentences there are in English discourses, they are all the time sorted into the five basic sentence types, namely, SVC, SV, SVO, SVOO, and SVOC. This is also why no matter how many sentences there are in Chinese discourses, they are all the time sorted into thematic sentences and agentive sentences (more specifically analyzed, there are merely about a dozen of types, respectively, belonging to subject-predicate sentences and the non-subject-predicate ones). That is to say, hundreds of thousands of English sentences mainly rely on the recursive mutual embeddings of the five types with identical structures, and hundreds of thousands of Chinese sentences mainly rely on nothing other than the several sentence structures. This is the "Chinese embedded box" structure, constantly copying the same information and duplicating the same pattern, recurring to itself and being embedded into itself. In a word, the recursive structure of language is the repetition of that of the cosmos.

To a person having the experiences of listening, speaking, reading, and writing Chinese or English, this fact (the repetition of identical structural elements) is not supposed to be strange. For instance, in "We saw him come," "we saw" and "him come" can be regarded as the duplications of two "S + V" structures. In Chinese, the sentences constructed by the duplication of two such "SV" structures (provoked by telescopic forms) are everywhere, say, "我请你来 (I invite you to come)," "上头命令他办 (The head ordered him to handle this thing)," and the like.

To Chinese literati accustomed to reading, this fact is already quite familiar. For instance, in the first section of *The Analects*, there are "…isn't it pleasant…isn't it delightful…isn't it superior-man-like." Aren't these triple sentences the recurrences of the identical structural elements? In the last section, Confucius says, "He who knows little about fate is not qualified for a superior man. He who knows little about rituals is not qualified for a mature man. He who knows little about the verbal skills is not qualified for understanding others." In this part, "…knows little about…is not qualified for…" recurs trice. Isn't this a recursive structure? I would like to note in passing that the triple sentences at issue are everywhere in *The Analects*. Such recursive sentence types are where generations after generations of Chinese literati get immersed.

Anyone capable of reading and writing in English can piece together the following infinite long sentence (which is de facto a word game, one capable of revealing the recursive phenomenon):

This is a ***cat***[4] that can be defined as a small, domestic, fur-covered animal often kept as a pet, to catch ***mice*** which are sorts of small ***rodent*** (house one, field one, harvest one) e.g., a rat, rabbit, squirrel, or beaver, which gnaws things with its strong teeth specially adapted for this ***purpose*** which is thing that one intends to do, get, be, etc.; ***intention*** which can be explained as intending; thing intended; ***aim*** which can be paraphrased as purpose; ***object*** which can be defined as ***person or thing*** to which something is done or some feeling or thought is directed; thing aimed at; ***end***…

So long as he who plays this game has the time and interest, he can continue from "end" the description, constraint, fulfillment, and supplement, and can develop it by means of for example adding when-clauses, various other clauses, and participle, adjective, noun, etc., independent sentences, and so on and so forth, until exponential explosion is caused by the ramification and extension as such.[5] This passage can be extended in an infinite fashion without the worry that it might reach the end of the player's wit. (Incidentally, in this infinite recursion, a word can exhaust all the dictionaries for interpretation. This is the situation discussed in Chapter 3, "The Inner language holography," namely, the part embraces the whole, the part embraces the parts, and the part is the microcosm of the whole.) Moreover, the identical structure of "which/that can be defined as something" is constantly embedded layers upon layers. Of course, I never mean that only this structure is recursive. De facto, any bigger discourse has repeatedly appearing identical structures. For another example, we gather materials on the spot by employing a passage I wrote afore. When we examine it and number the sentences therein, we will see the obvious recursive phenomena between sentences:

> "(1) In this vein, many seemingly complex problems become simple and clear. (2) This is why no matter how many sentences there are in English discourses, they are all the time sorted into the five basic sentence types, namely, SVC, SV, SVO, SVOO, and SVOC. (3) This is also why no matter how many sentences there are in Chinese discourses, they are all the time sorted into thematic sentences and agentive sentences (more specifically analyzed, they are merely about a dozen of types respectively belonging to subject-predicate sentences and the non-subject-predicate ones). [That is to say], (4) hundreds of thousands of English sentences mainly rely on the recursive mutual embeddings of the five types with identical structures, (5) and hundreds of thousands of Chinese sentences mainly rely on nothing other than the several sentence structures. (6) This is the "Chinese embedded box" structure, (6a) constantly copying the same information and (6b) duplicating the same pattern, (6c) recurring to itself and (6d) being embedded into itself. [In a word], (7) the recursive structure of language is the repetition of that of the cosmos."

Intuiting the above sentence types, we can see that (3) repeats (2), (5) (4), (6b) (6a), and (6d) (6c). This is a sort of recursion.

---

[4]The interpretations as regards cat, mice, rodent, purpose, intention, aim, object, person or thing are all adopted from *Oxford Advanced Learner's English-Chinese Dictionary*, Fourth Edition, The Commercial Press and Oxford University Press.

[5]Cf. Zhao (1994).

This apart, there is another sort: (1), (2), (3), (4), (5), (6), (7) are all subject-predicate sentences, namely, the same type is repeated seven times.

In addition, seen from the property of the predicate, sentences from (2) to (7) are all nominal predicate sentences (be + noun), namely, this type is repeated six times. This is the third sort of recursion.

The fourth sort: (6a), (6b), (6c), and (6d) are appositives, and predicative parts as well. Nevertheless, (6b) repeats (6a), (6d) (6c).

Isn't this embedding layer upon layer? Isn't this a "Chinese embedded box" structure?

2.4.2 Partial Non-recursions

That which merits heed is, albeit the respective recursiveness of the cosmos and language on the one hand and the holographibility of their recursiveness on the other are factually indisputable and are everywhere, the two systems of the cosmos and language are extremely complicated (the latter being contained in the former), and hence the structural recursion is varied rather than being one and the same. Consequently, at the interface of two different recursive modes are located partial non-recursions. It is impossible that people only say "This is a…," "That is a…," "They are…," or "I do….," "She does…," "They do…," or the like. This is because if the recursiveness remains this way, how can we speak of the complexity of the cosmos or language? The world was not the case from the very beginning; it is a multiple unity. It is impossible that any two sentence types with coherent meanings are repeated. Take for example the two coherent sentence types, "这是一本讲艾滋病的书。我不喜欢 / This is a book on AIDS. I hate it." The two coherent types remain to overlap, neither in English nor in Chinese which, in this connection, belongs in partial (a small "field" consisting of two sentences) non-recursion. This notwithstanding, if we say "这是一张CD盘。我喜欢 / This is a CD disk. I like it" after the aforementioned two sentences, the four constitute a recursive field. The case holds true in both English and Chinese.

2.4.3 Why Recursiveness Is One of the Essential Properties of Language

We now proceed to how Chomsky's assertion, namely, "That which the child learns from finite utterances is a set of complete grammatical knowledge, and it expresses infinite thoughts with finite means," becomes possible and how it must be so. Why infinite thoughts can be expressed with finite means? This is because identical structural elements can be repeated in an infinite fashion.

Why language must be recursive?

When discussing the dynamic property of language, Gennaro Chierchia thus says, "Another important aspect of linguistic dynamism is that the utterer can speak and understand infinite sentences whereas he merely occupies finite cognitive resources, namely, memory, attention span, and the like." He continues, how can this be possible? We must presume that such a thing occurs, as is inferred, in such a way: We can add two numbers never added together before. We can accomplish this insomuch as we have grasped a set of composition mechanisms, viz., algorithm. Be that as it may, it is through trainings under clear-cut rules and regulations that we learn algorithm whereas the composition mechanism of utterance is automatically generated in one's childhood. Such a set of algorithm is capable of creating and generating our linguistic competence.

We notice in the previous statement these words, "finite cognitive resources, namely memory, attention span, and the like." It is exactly because human's cognitive resources and attention span are finite that he/she cannot remember so many sentence structures. Be it English, Chinese, or any other language, if each utterance in it employs a new sentence structure rather than being in the previously mentioned situation, namely, several main sentence structures appear repeatedly, a nation's linguistic agglomeration of sentence types would become incredibly colossal and unbelievably complex. De facto, that proclaims the bankruptcy and unattainability of that language. According to the requests of memory and attention span, the lesser sentence types are remembered, the better and the more convenient. Language must take this way: to create infinite sentences with finite linguistic means. As a matter of fact, a person is absolutely incapable of changing a new sentence type each time he/she utters a new sentence in a discourse and doing so constantly; but rather, he/she can only repeat identical sentence types in quantities. On this account, recursiveness is one of the essential properties of language. This is due to language's principle of economy, which reflects human's nature of seeking simplicity. With respect to the topic that infinite sentences merely need finite means, Chomsky thus holds, so does Humboldt who says, "It is due to the fact that language is a capacity of the brain that the utterer can create infinite linguistic acts with finite linguistic means."[6]

Fortunately, language is the very case in effect. Differently put, the existence of language is supposed to be owed to its recursiveness. We may even say that language is what it is—infinite language is expressed with finite means—due to the fact that there is structural recursiveness. The holistic recursiveness of language averts the danger from colossal agglomeration and complexity of sentence types, and hence makes sentence types finite and simple; the partial linguistic non-recursion enriches language within finite means. This is exactly where the necessity of language recursiveness is located.

2.5 The Source of Linguistic Recursiveness: Language Structure is Holographic with the Cosmic One

It is my contention that linguistic recursive structure can be introduced in a direct fashion from the cosmic one in that the two structures are supposed to be coincident.

[6]Cf. Robins (1982, pp.74–78).

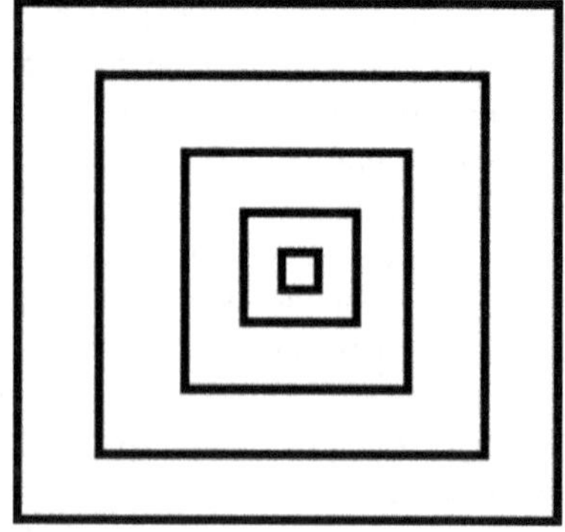

Fig. 1 Chinese embedded box

The most general rationale is: a subsystem (holographic node) is the rapid and simple repetition of the parent system, the two being holographic with one another.

What is the cosmic recursive structure?

> "The macro cosmos embraces innumerable micro ones, macro system innumerable micro ones, and the topmost level innumerable lower ones. Each microcosmos, micro system, or low level is the microcosm of the larger one. We call this 'Chinese embedded box' structure holographic recursive structure."[7]

What kind of a structure is "Chinese embedded box" structure? Such a structure must be: (1) identical or similar at the level of construction (composition, frame, model, and mode); (2) embedded layer upon layer. It is my contention that to compare "'Chinese embedded box' structure" to recursion can be said mutually enlightening, which makes them both more understandable. The structure of "Chinese embedded box" is supposed to be shown by the Fig. 1.

"If the cosmos is infinite, the information is located in each holographic node or locus by way of the holographic recursive structure of infinite layers; …The holographic cosmos shows a rather complicated structure which, nevertheless, is constructed in accordance with the simplest law, namely the constant duplication of the same information, following the principle of extreme economy."[8] What is the "simplest law"? It is the "the constant duplication of the same information." Isn't this the repetition of identical structures? Isn't this the embedding layer upon layer? "The holographic repetition law of the cosmos means that the progression of subsystems is a microcosm of the system's developing history, even of the cosmic evolution history, the rapid and simple repetition of the latter. Moreover, the constituting mode of subsystems is the duplication of that of the system.…We can also say that the cosmos is a recursive structure of holographic repetition.…The cosmos is always recurring in itself. Such a self-twining 'Chinese embedded box' structure is a sort of mysterious 'strange circle'".[9] The duplication of mode and the recurring in itself are

[7]Wang and Yan (1995, p. 54).

[8]Wang and Yan (1995, p. 61).

[9]Wang and Yan (1995, p. 198).

equivalent to being of the same structure and being embedded layer upon layer. "In its eternal cycling movement, the cosmos is always repeating itself in a holographic fashion, being engaged in eternally cycling and infinite self-recurring movement."[10] Recursion is being embedded in the self. "...the infinite holographic recursive structure...Any physical system whatsoever embraces infinite layers of information each of which is again the microcosm of all the other layers of information, namely, each layer of information embraces infinite ones, and the former is also infinitely embraced by the latter. In this connection, the layers infinitely reflect one another and recur ad infinitum."[11]

The repeated descriptions can be concluded thus: being identical on structure, and being embedded layer upon layer. Since the cosmic structure is manifested in embedded layers upon layers, so is language structure. That is to say, language recursiveness originates from the holography between language structure and the cosmic one.

Conclusion:

Facts tell us that the whole language structure and speech generation are located in the repetition and layers of embedment of identical structures. Language recursiveness originates from the cosmic recursive structure, viz., the law of cosmos holography. **Cosmic information and structure are condensed into language structure**.

The great even the whole significance of language recursiveness rests in it permitting people to generate infinite utterances with only a few sentence patterns, which hence frees their communications of constraints.

3 Language Discreteness

Language discreteness is a new topic. We need to start from discrete mathematics and combinations.

Prof. Zhou Haizhong who presented the conjecture of "the distribution of Mersenne Primes" notes that discrete mathematics is an important branch of modern mathematics. It is gradually established along with the progression of computer science, and is an emerging instrumental discipline. It riches in content and covers a wide range. So to speak, any mathematics with the discrete magnitude as its object belongs in discrete mathematics. Human, book, integer, course, computer, sesame, and the like, are all discrete magnitudes. That which runs counter to discrete magnitude is continuous quantity, say, real number, body temperature, sesame jam, among others. The fundamental content of this mathematics includes set theory, number theory, graph theory, mathematical logic, algebraic structure,

[10]Wang and Yan (1995, p. 215).

[11]Wang and Yan (1995, p. 309).

formal language, automata theory, and so on. Zhou believes that discrete mathematics already offers a scientific and effective method to formal grammar, transformational generative grammar, text generative grammar, Montague grammar, dependency structure grammar, precedence grammar, to name a few. Set is the primal object of set theory. A set treats distinctive things in a certain range as a whole, and the things are called the elements of this set. Discreteness and set are the fundamental existing forms of objective things, being a unity of contradictions. Whereas discreteness is absolute, set is relative.[12]

The elements (i.e., individuals) in each set are discrete to each other. The case is so among positive integers (1, 2, 3…) in that numbers with decimal points between 1 and 2 are omitted. All the scores in the school reports of students are discrete, say, one course is marked 85, another 76 between which there is no continuity at all. Every Chinese is discrete from any other one, and so is the case of all the concepts in each book. For another example, the connections between the Stone Age, Bronze Age, and Iron Age in China are discontinuous, which can also be called "discrete." This is because the spatio-temporal connection between process A (e.g., the Stone Age) and process B (e.g., the Bronze Age) does not mean that A will necessarily lead to B, but that B will necessarily replace A,[13] and so on and so forth.

That which runs counter to discrete magnitude is continuous quantity. Distinguishing them is of critical importance for us to recognize language discreteness. A person's body temperature is continuous, increasing or decreasing little by little but being incapable of bypassing any numerical phase. It is the continuous quantity that records, by means of numbers, the changes of a person's body temperature: continuous increment or decrement. The incremental quantity of the population however is not continuous, say, Chinese population can only increase or decrease according to the order of positive integers, increasing from 1.2 billion to 1.2 billion plus 1 during the course of which a fairly tremendous order with decimal points (Here I merely cite several numbers amidst them: 0.0001 person, 0.01 person, or 0.5 person, or the like) is bypassed. In this vein, the relationship between 1.2 billion (people) and 1.2 billion plus 1 (people) is discontinuous, i.e., discrete.

Apparently, the words uttered by people are discrete, to wit., discontinuous, to one another.

Someone says, "语法枯燥 (Grammar is boring)."

Another one says, "This, my Lord, is a perilous and tremendous moment."[14]

Still another one says, "Эта точка зрения очень высока, но полна, не самая высокая…".[15]

In this connection, we can see that a bunch of utterances of an individual, i.e., a short discourse, can be, respectively, regarded as some tiny sets, namely, subsets. In the subset as such, there is not any relationship whatsoever of continuous incremental or decremental quantity between the two successive (or up-down, left–right)

[12]These statements come from the letter to me from Prof. Zhou.

[13]Cf. Ye (1998).

[14]William Pitt (1989, p. 82).

[15]В. И. Ленин, *Философские мемрабц*, 1947, стр. 143.

language units (e.g., "This" and "my," or "my" and "Lord"), which can be seen as a manifestation of language discreteness.

When there is not the relationship of continuous incremental or decremental quantity between any two linguistic units, we call this property of language "language discreteness."

Language discreteness is first and foremost manifested in the level of utterances generated instantly by the individual.

To interpret the passage above, we can also follow this thought-train: the semantic connection between any two uttered units does not own previous prescriptiveness, namely, the semantic connection between the former and the latter language units is instantly selected according to the subjective will of the utterer. For instance, in "语法枯燥," 法 (rules) does not necessarily emerge after 语 (linguistic/ language/ verbal/ -)[16] (and it is the utterer's instant will to give 语法, and there is not necessity), many characters can be uttered after it, say, [语] 流 (flow), 言 (speech), 病 (error), 词 (word), 调 (tune), 音 (sound), 感 (sense), 汇 (vocabulary), 句 (sentence), 库 (repertoire), 料 (material), 录 (record), 气 (mood), 塞 (loss), 素 (morpheme), 文 (Chinese), 系 (family), 序 (order), 义 (meaning), 意 (sense), 源 (source), 种 (type), and so on. No matter which language unit it is, it is temporarily released by the utterer out of his subjective need. It can be seen that the relationship between 语 and 言 or between 语 and 录 is discontinuous.

In the same vein, "am" does not necessarily emerge after "I," and it might be replaced by "was," "were," or "be," even by "is" (e.g., "I" is a word). "Do" might also emerge after "I," or the like.

Again in the same vein, there is not any continuous quantity whatsoever between Я and слушаю, and цитал or some other verb or hundreds and thousands of other words might also emerge after Я.

The discreteness as such is manifested in the most clear-cut fashion in the relationships between all the words in a dictionary where there is no process of continuous quantity at all.

Language discreteness is also manifested in language's structural levels.

In all the phoneme sets of a language, there is not incremental or decremental continuous quantity between any two phonemes whatsoever. The distinguishability and analyzability of speech sounds can also be regarded as a discrete state.

Between two successive language units, there is a proper phonetic blank or pause, which is a discrete state as well.

As a circumstantial evidence, the discreteness in the sign system underpins that in natural language.

We can give one more support, with the discreteness of a sign (data signs or operational language, mathematical or chemical symbols, inter alia) associated with natural language, for the discreteness of language equally belonging to sign system.

---

[16]In Chinese, 语 is ambiguous, having many meanings, particularly when it is matched with the following characters in the present context. Therefore, I present four main meanings of it, of which the "-" means "void" since sometimes the English counterpart of Chinese characters are not identical with the latter on number—the translator.

All the previously given signs can be seen belonging to one formal system where they all have clear notions, constituting a process of derivation. These derivations have their own rules, and after many times of them and a series of operations having recursiveness and theoretical predictability, a self-sufficient sign system is formed. There is also no incremental or decremental continuous quantity between any two signs within this system, which stands in contrast to the derivation of a theory by means of natural language itself. That is to say, the discreteness in sign system underpins that in natural language.

Where did language discreteness originate?

To begin, we need to find the causes inside the cosmic construction. All the natural languages are the calling for and expressions of the concrete things and abstract concepts within the cosmos. The cosmos is a giant set. Inside it, all the elements in each set of visible things are definite individuals different from one another and showing the state of discreteness. Language, whereas, is a subset of this giant one, and hence becomes a holographic node. A holographic corresponding relationship is formed between this holographic node and other ones in the cosmic system. To this connection, words within language system are also discrete. This means that language structure must correspond to the discrete structures of the things (individuals) in each subset of the cosmos.

Is it, then, that the elements in each set of visible things within the cosmos are some definite things (individuals) different from one another? This seems to be a sheer fact. The case is so among a flock of sheep or among the people of a country, and the same also holds to stars and sands, respectively. So long as they are in a set, the elements are discrete from each other. Of course, there are also continuous quantities in the cosmos, say, positive number, body temperature (the measurement of temperature must employ positive numbers), and the like, which are not discrete. Positive number however is not physical, nor is it visible; but rather, it is a concept designed by human brain.

The discreteness between things in the cosmos is of its origin. Take the organisms as an example, "Albeit biological systems differ from each other, they share inside the cells the copy of information inherited from their common ancestors, and the difference is merely on the extent and direction of its manifestation. This macro evolution of organisms is the discretization among individuals, and the realization of the broad group. During the individual discretization as such, the independence among individual organisms is strengthened, and their mutual reliance is weakened."[17] This is to say that the difference between organisms on the extent and direction of manifestation provokes the discretization between individuals, namely, it produces "definite things different from each other."

In addition, "Holographic order stipulates the length of the information wave expressed by each holographic grid, namely, the threshold of holographic grid's manifestation. Once the information action of some holographic grid reaches the stipulated threshold, it will manifest itself upward or potentialize itself downward,

[17] Wang and Yan (1995, p. 97).

and, as a result, things show another state."[18] That is to say, the threshold of the manifestation of the holographic grid produces a thing in another state, namely, another thing discretes with it.

These two reasons are the origin of the production of "definite things different from each other" in the cosmos. Since language is holographic with the cosmos, it is supposed to be, and it is de facto so, discrete.

In the second place, we need to find the causes inside language structure. That which is situated between linguistic syllables must be "definite things different from each other," or **the borderlines between the syllables would not be clear-cut, which would not embody the distinctive function of phonemes**. Where would language be located when there were no distinctive function between phonemes? "Animals' calls or features are an inseparable continuum. Scientists have tried every method but failed to find how the animals manage to make any separable unit in this continuum into a new combination. To the contrary, even when faced with a strange language in toto, linguists are capable of singling out its phonemes and words according to certain procedures, and generalize their rules of combination."[19] This notwithstanding, that there are clear-cut borderlines between language structures results exactly from the promotion by the fact that language is holographic with the cosmos, being identical to the latter on property as well as structure. In the final analysis, therefore, the origin of language discreteness is located in the law of cosmos holography.

The cosmos is discrete as well as collective. Language is also of collectivity, or there would not be utterances or discourses; language is of discreteness as well, or the linguistic units would not be dissembled or assembled without obstacles.

Thirdly, what is interesting is, this correspondence of language to the cosmos at the level of the discreteness between things (individuals) in the sets is also a protective reaction. This is because if natural language is not the case, language would lose the raison d'être to exist. Both the creation and the application of language as a tool are directed upon the convenience of self-control and information communications (which is the so-called sociality). Whether the other (asking to communicate information) or the utterer himself (asking others to answer) has the say, the topics—for instance, discussing about the stars in the sky, speaking of the insects on the earth, expressing one's own feelings, or asking about others' ideas—always correspond to the discrete and manifold (but ordered) states of the objective world. When language takes the form of continuous quantity, it will run counter to the discrete state of things. If so, how can a thing of continuous quantity correspond to the discrete universe? In this vein, it is impossible for language to appear.

---

[18] Wang and Yan (1995, p. 57).

[19] Xu (1999, p. 2).

4 Language Hierarchy

The holographibility between linguistic layers is called "the inner language holography." It is nothing else than the repetition of cosmic holography. As regards the demonstrative process of the holographibility between linguistic layers, please return to Chapter 3, the core of this book, and I will not go further here. Originally, Chapter 3 was supposed to be put here, but due to its vital importance and extraordinary kernel location, I made the independent expounding of its content in advance. That which is mentioned here again is merely the content of the property. That is to say, the inner language holography includes the following contents: of the layers of language, to wit., morpheme—word—phrase—(clause)—sentence—discourse, the parts are holographic with the whole; the parts share the same information with one another; each holographic node (subsystem) in language system has its counterpart or similar information, respectively, in the whole and other nodes. That is to say, each holographic node of the system becomes, to different extents, a microcosm of the whole. To put it in another way, language's layers repeat the holographibility of the cosmos'.

This conclusion makes a great step forward compared with Roland Barthes' which merely goes, "Language is similar to any form of social behavior whatsoever at the level of structure and organization."[20] At present, whereas, albeit lack of complete certainty, we can say so in a confident fashion: more than being similar to any form of social behavior whatsoever at the level of structure and organization, language is isomorphic and similar to and embedded in the cosmos.

The holographibility between language's layers indicates that language is hierarchic.

As regards the forming process of linguistic hierarchy, we can make the descriptions as follows:

Yuan Yulin once made a rough comparison between linguistic and signal hierarchic system on the one hand and the biological one on the other.[21] He holds that in a non-strict sense, word is analogous to cell, **parts of speech** to tissues, expression or phrase to organ, and sentence type or pattern to the system. This analogy is of its rationale, namely, language system is in the same cosmos with the biological one, being holographic with the latter. Nevertheless, there is a difficulty remaining to be settled in his comparison as such: "Whereas tissues are the constituents of the organism, parts of speech are not those of language. ..."[22] Rather than an entity, a part of speech (a verb, noun, or adjective, etc.) merely exists in a human's (i.e., the linguist's) consciousness (say, the demarcation of the parts of speech), and hence remains to match up with a biological entity. Presumably, Yuan does not think that there is a counterpart in language to biological organism, namely, the "word" in the upper level corresponds to cell, "phrase" in the lower level to organ, but there is nothing (voidness) that can correspond to organism. In other words, voidness corresponds to the organism of the biological individual, so "parts of speech" is employed

[20] Barthes (1987, p. 3).

[21] Yuan (1998).

[22] Zhao. Zhongde, Hierarchic system and the theory of intermediate perspective of language.

to correspond to organism so as to fulfill this voidness (This train of thought is correct in that just like there is no vacancy in the periodical law of elements, there must be some new materials remaining to be discovered). It is my contention that the settlement can thus go: word is equivalent to cell, expression or phrase to organism, sentence type or pattern to organ, and the whole linguistic entity to the system—the oft-recounted "language system" is nothing else than the whole linguistic entities. In this vein, the problem of voidness is settled.

Apparently, the thought of language's hierarchic system can find its origin in the comparison between language system and the individual life's hierarchic system. Yuan stratifies the latter into cell → organism → organ → system. Insofar as the fairly complicated system is concerned, to disintegrate it into several subsystems and then sub-sub-systems even sub-sub-sub-systems will make it easier to sense the clarity of the individual life structure. For instance, human body can be classified into alimentary system, circulatory system, nervous system, respiratory system, reproductive system, and the like, which can be further classified into organs, organisms, and cells in successive fashion. In this way, human body can be stratified into system → organ → organism → cell. Plainly, such a hierarchy is not unique to organisms since, say, the hierarchy of matter is molecule—atom—nucleus—particle....

Zhou Shuoyu gave another type of description of hierarchy[23] in re. The hierarchy of the planet and its surroundings is: the Galactic System—the Solar System—the ionosphere—the stratosphere—the troposphere—the earth's crust—the earth's mantle—the earth's core; that of organisms' genetic relationship is: phylum—class—order—family—species; that of ecological environment is: biosphere—ecosystem—coenosis—population—the individual; and, socio-economic systems are also universally of hierarchic structures. For instance, a large factory may have the hierarchy of head factory—branch factory—department—workshop—team, and so on and so forth.

It goes without saying that language's hierarchy is in close relation to the hierarchies listed above. The relevance between them, viz., the strong resemblance on hierarchy, exactly illustrates the holographibility between language and the whole cosmos.

On this account, the thought of language's hierarchic system apparently comes from the comparison between language system on the one hand and individual lives and the hierarchic systems of many other matters in nature. The comparison results in the fact that we discovered the linguistic hierarchy. **Language hierarchy refers to the relationship of embedding layer upon layer in language's structure.**

Just like the physical forms in nature are always located in certain systematic hierarchies, language hierarchy exactly corresponds to the micro, intermediate, and macro levels in physical phenomena. **The whole cosmos is a tremendous embedded box, and the embedded box relationship tells essentially the origin of language hierarchy**. No non-embedded box structure is permitted in the layers of embedded box. Differently put, a non-embedded-box structure cannot be inserted in

[23]Zhou (1998).

an embedded-box one. Such incompatibility does not result from the lack of room, but from the contradiction between the two structures.

5 Language Linearity

The objective world visible to human is three-dimensional. According to the law of cosmos holography, "The cosmos is an n-dimensional holographic body," namely, the objective world is stereoscopic even supra-stereoscopic. The cluster of verbal signs, on the other hand, is one-dimensional and linear (In Chinese linguistic sphere, people are not much accustomed to "linearity.").

There are two key points of language linearity: one is that the form of its speech sounds determines its auditory receptivity; the other is that it develops in temporal dimension.

We come to speech sounds first. Given that it is sound, it is sensed via ears, and hence it is necessarily linear. Music takes the form of sound, and is auditory-oriented, so it is linear. Some might base their rationale on the fact that more than three notes can be heard in a split second in for example a symphony, and thus argue that music can be three-dimensional. My answer is: the fact that more than three notes can be sensed within a split second rests in the symphonic state of affairs, namely, many instruments or many human sounds occur simultaneously. To the extent that an individual person or instrument produces sounds, the sounds are still linear. When more than two persons say the same in toto at the same time, e.g., they recite the same sector of a poem with the draft in hand, the recital also owns the properties of a symphony (Note: many people can only produce one syllable in a split second). At the level of auditory sense, any sort of sound in nature, say, the rolls of thunder, the crashing and hitting noises of two things, the tolls of a bell, or the like, is linear.

A matter sensed via eyes (it will necessarily occupy some space) can be linear, planar, or three-dimensional. For example, a laser beam is generally seen as a line. For another example, a lightening is sometimes seen as a line but sometimes a flat. For still another example, a concert hall is flat when some merely see one facet of it; seen from another perspective, whereas, it might show three facets, namely, it might be sensed in a three-dimensional fashion.

Essentially speaking, language is sensed via ears, and hence is linear. Be that as it may, when such sound signs are recorded and then converted into written signs (they become the signs of the sound signs), they are sensed via eyes hence can be observed at planar level. At this time, one can read ten lines at one glance, and one can also skip through the writings. Under such circumstances, linguistic signs become planar. Therefore, when written words are considered as signs of signs, language qua the secondary product (the readable one) is of planarity. Readers' particular heed to this is required.

In the second place, spoken language is a sign unfolded in the milieu of time. That which can merely be unfolded in time but not simultaneously in space can only be linear. Human can, and can only, pronounce one syllable but never two or more within a split second (or an instant), and, as a result, the successive adjacency at temporal level is produced, which is called language linearity. Saussure who discovered language linearity notes that in parole, the signifier is a sound that can only appear one by one chronologically and no two elements can appear simultaneously. In this connection, it is a time span, a line, or a linkage (i.e., linear nature). Different from visual signs, auditory signs can only proceed in time, and hence they are one-dimensional. Saussure makes use of this property to distinguish two relations between linguistic signs: one is syntagmatic relation, the other being associative relation. When the utterer speaks, one sign appears at one time, and the signs appear successively before forming a sequence. Each sign opposes to the signs before and after it as a result of which it obtains its value. The relation as such is called syntagmatic relation.

Things unfolded in space might be linear or, more possibly, planar or three-dimensional. Language is not unfolded in space, so it cannot be planar or three-dimensional.

Language is sensed via ears, and is unfolded in time, so it is only of linearity. It shares this point with all other things sensed via ears and unfolded in time in the physical universe. The pronunciations given chronologically are never unprovoked. The process as such is exactly where the cosmic holographic order works. "Since each locus or each thing in the cosmos is a holographic set, why can people only sense finite information? This is due to the fact that information is hierarchic. Information's holographic expression is ordered, and the mechanism controlling it is holographic order. Each information layer is called a holographic grid. Explicit things are all located in time and space. Any time and space whatsoever is finite....Such finiteness is nothing but the demand from the orderly expression of holographic order. ...To be ordered, information can only be displayed layer upon layer. In this connection, under the control of holographic order, the holographic grids can only show themselves sequentially and express partial information within finite time and space, which is just like we can only recall limited things within limited time and space."[24] Such parlances, namely, "Information is hierarchic," "Holographic expression is ordered," "the orderly expression of holographic order," "the control of holographic order," or the like, are of the same meaning: **within finite time and space, only finite information can emerge**. To be sure, explicit things are all located in finite time and space, but is speech explicit? Of course yes. All explicit things are sensible. Speech is invisible, so it is visually implicit; it however can be heard, and the explicitness at auditory level is also sensible. Speech is also a sort of explicitness, a finite one expressed within finite time—but not in finite space.

In addition, it is my contention that the control of holographic order is nothing else than a self-protective response of the cosmic information. Human can only recall limited things within an instant, which is also a response of maintaining the order, a self-protection of his/hers. The loss of control of information would bring about information jam, frenzy, and chaos, which de facto means non-information, zero-information, and invalid information. Of course, the cosmos is what it is exactly

[24] Wang and Yan (1995, p. 57).

because it is the result of the control of holographic order. In the same vein, if human could recall or utter unlimited things or perform unlimited speech acts in a split second, these would only result in the frenzy or chaos of his/her thinking and speaking, or the disappearance or jam of them, or even the explosion of his brain but nothing else. Of course, human is who he/she is exactly because he/she is also the result of the control of holographic order. On this account, that human can only produce one syllable in a split second is also a protective response. **If one abruptly produced many syllables, or if many people produced different syllables, in an instant, no syllable (It would be a "voice" in that no syllable would be distinguished) would exist**, which is of course unconceivable. Choral speaking is appreciated exactly because many people can only produce one identical syllable in a split second. In a word, an orderly syllable cluster will naturally become a linear sequence of speeches.

The above is the rationale of the discussions with regard to the origin of language linearity.

For more holographic analyses of the syntagmatic relation of language linearity, please cf. my holographic observations of Saussure's theory of language in Sect. 2 of Chapter 6.

6 Language Fuzziness

As regards language fuzziness, Wu Tieping has performed investigations in considerably great depth. In terms of the fact per se (There are many linguistic materials), no one will question it. What is more, the forms of language fuzziness, e.g., some, most, all; adolescent, youth, the middle-aged, the old, or the like, are not the ultimate objects of the holographic theory of language, either. To this connection, I cannot enter into more details now with respect to language's form but merely concentrate on the holographic explications of the origin of its fuzziness.

Systemic linguists like M. A. K. Halliday employs the concept of "cline" to interpret the fuzziness in linguistic facts. He believes that the descriptive categories created by linguists are usually not that definite (not because they do not but because they cannot attain that), and the concept of cline can interpret these ambiguous phenomena. A cline is a scale on which all the things **gradually** develop into other ones. The two poles of a scale are fairly different from one another, but it is hard to tell where their boundary is. By means of "cline," Halliday intends to explicate that some linguistic units belong in category A, some in category B whereas some others are located between A and B. The principle of "All the things on the scale gradually develop into other ones" reveals in toto the holographic relationship between linguistic units on the same scale. I would like to ask, why will it gradually develop into some other thing? When a linguistic unit does not contain the information of both poles of the scale—both A and B, what is the internal rationale for it to gradually develop into another thing? Why is a linguistic unit ambiguous? **If it merely contained the information of one pole without being concerned with that of the**

other pole, it would have a definite categoric end, and there would not be fuzziness. The indefiniteness of the category and the boundaries between the linguistic units on one scale is exactly due to the fact that **the category contains the information of both poles**. In my view, this is the holographic phenomenon between linguistic units: the part embraces the whole and, a fortiori, the whole embraces the parts.

With respect to fuzziness, Li Xiaoming contends that it runs counter to accuracy, indicating "the indefiniteness of the object's boundary distinction in people's cognition, namely, the object's definitions in terms of classification and behavior, etc., are inaccurate and unclear." "Fuzziness refers to the indefiniteness in people's cognition at the level of the object's boundary classification and behavior." As to the objective origin of fuzziness, he thus says, "In the purely objective world, there are neither the so-called definiteness and indefiniteness nor accuracy and fuzziness. The opposition between them is at the premise that cognitive relations occur between things and human beings, namely, it is meaningful merely in epistemological scope."[25]

According to Li Xiaoming, there is not the difference between definiteness and indefiniteness or between accuracy and fuzziness in the objective world, and it is human who is trapped into fuzziness when he/she cognizes the objects. He thus holds that fuzziness is "the indefiniteness of people's cognition at the level of the object's boundary classification and behavior." In this connection, language fuzziness can be described as follows:

Language fuzziness refers to the description of the indefiniteness of people's cognition at the level of the object's boundary classification and behavior by means of a series of words with different values.

The description as such suspends the question as to whether or not the object's boundary classification and behavior are indefinite, and hence avoids the disputes with respect to the origin of the fuzziness, which can be said an effective method. The question is, is it a fact that "There is not the difference between definiteness and indefiniteness or between accuracy and fuzziness in the objective world"? According to Li Xiaoming's introduction, the prevailing view abroad on this question is that fuzziness is a sort of subjective indefiniteness, whereas the domestic view holds that it is first and foremost the inner attribute of the objective thing itself.

"Seen from the perspective of the theory of cosmic holography, there is no independent or fixed substance whatsoever in the cosmos. No system is of an absolute boundary in that the substance is merely a sort of agglomerating and scattering relationship. Things are nothing but the aggregation or a network of such relationships. Once the relationships are cut off, this particular system would disintegrate. This is the nonlocality or universality of the holographic node. Holographibility is exactly the origin of the fuzziness of things. This is because holographibility shows that things are in the state of 'one in two, two in one', or 'you in me, I in you' and, this apart, things are merely an agglomeration of relationships which nevertheless are forever various and indefinite. Indefiniteness is one of the properties of fuzziness."[26] To this connection, by virtue of the law of cosmos holography, it is not that

[25] Li (1987, pp. 9–13).

[26] Wang and Yan (1995, p. 54).

hard to decide whether fuzziness is the indefiniteness of subjective cognition or the inner attribute of the objective thing. The holographic node of the cosmos is of the property of nonlocality or universality, and holographibility is exactly the origin of fuzziness. Fuzziness originates from the cosmos itself. The cosmos is holographic with language. On this account, language fuzziness corresponds to the cosmic one.

We are thus inclined to this description: **language fuzziness refers to describing the indefiniteness of the object's boundary classification and behavior by means of a series of words with different values**.

Another rationale of language fuzziness rests in human's cognitive style (which is also holographic with the cosmos), to wit., fuzzy inference. Strange to say, it is some scientists who went to extremes, arbitrarily denying the scientific nature of fuzzy inference, denying that the latter is also an inferring mode of cognition. In the eyes of some scientists, with the approach of the digital revolution in the twenty-first century, it seems that people in modern society can only check in at the window of 0 and 1. On many an occasion, some people claim that a science without mathematics is not a science in the true sense of the word. At the frontage of the Social Science Research Building at the University of Chicago, a word is thus inscribed: "When you cannot measure, your knowledge is meagre and unsatisfactory." It is particularly surprising that such a word appears at the frontage of the Social Science Research Building. Its premise asserts precision and mathematization's monopolization of sciences and cognition. It denies the diversity of cognitive styles, the multiplicity of the world, and the large quantities of undetermined but scientific synthetic grasping and judgments of people in the sphere of social sciences. Notwithstanding that, human's imprecise synthetic judgments are not merely scientific but also fairly necessary.

It is my contention that of human's cognitive approaches, there is an "unnecessary measuring approach." It can cognize the object in a more rapid and correct fashion than the common measuring approaches. It is only that the mechanism of such an "unnecessary measuring approach" remains to be clear. Apparently, the baby does not completely rely on the measurement to distinguish its mother. Not merely the baby, even an adult need, and only so, rely on "the unnecessary measuring approach" to identify his/her mother. If we cannot but rely on measurement to identify our own mother, we must follow such an index so tremendous hence beyond our capability: the shapes of her eyes, mouth, nose, ears, face, and wrinkles; other properties of the face; the various indices of her voice, breath, figure, speeches, behaviors (at least footsteps), way of suckling, the properties of her relations to her husband (i.e., the baby's father), among others. If a baby performed the measurement according to the indices above, we can affirm that it could never identify its mother. Under normal circumstances, a baby or anyone can immediately identify his/her mother at the first sight or hearing, which shows the magical power and greatness of the "unnecessary measuring approach." **It is not uncertain** (please associate Heisenberg's uncertainty principle) **but unnecessary to measure**! Anyone can cite a great many such facts of "unnecessary measuring approach." Behind this approach lies unnecessary precision. In the section of "The troubles of pragmatic inferential model" in *Pragmatics in Chinese Culture*, I explain that a wanted circular will never give precise numbers (e.g., the height of 1.753) of a criminal's characteristics since the precise numbers will only hinder the identification. I then note that **the fuzzy inference of the brain is incompatible with meticulosity**. Fuzzy inference is itself scientific. It is a pity that I was incapable of noting this inferential mechanism when writing that book. Now I can say that **the fuzzy inference of the brain is incompatible with measurement**. It is said that in Suzhou embroidery, a cat's whiskers are embroidered on the frame by means of a silk of 14 split from a single thread. To be sure, notwithstanding that the whiskers are precise in the true sense of the word, Qi Baishi's Chinese painting of shrimps also gives one the same feeling of vividness albeit it seems to be merely manifested in several brush drawings with fuzzy and rough lines. De facto, cognitive approaches are not supposed to be restricted to a common paradigm. The world is complex and plural to which cognition is supposed to correspond. Therefore, cognitive styles should also be plural.

Since human has the "unnecessary measuring approach" of cognition, the fuzzy remarks and words in language certainly have their legitimacy. As has been discussed afore, the legitimacy already found its rationale in the cosmos' structure.

7 Language Rhythmicity

Language's rhythm refers to the regular phenomenon that strong and weak syllables, or long and short vowels, emerge alternatively. Every nation's language can be compiled into songs, which exactly does justice to the harmony between linguistic and musical rhythms, or to the holographic relationship between them. Music consists of melodies and rhythms. An utterance (only) has rhythms but no melody insomuch as once the melody partakes in the rhythmic utterance, the latter becomes a song. As regards linguistic rhythm, I thus note in my *Aesthetic Linguistics* when discussing the beauty of rhythm of utterances: when speaking, people usually make prominent the beauty of rhythm via the following three modes: first, they give proper numbers of syllables; secondly, they make the sentence type ordered and symmetric; thirdly, they arrange the order of the wording. The three conditions amount to a language quite pleasant to ear hence striking, and English, notably Chinese, are cases in point.[27]

Where does language rhythmicity come from?

Large quantities of scientific experiments prove that molecules, atoms, elementary particles, even all the wave fields jitter in their respective frequencies, and in a rhythmic fashion, which is called by scientists "pulsation." The micro world is generally the case, and the same holds to the macro one. The expansion and contraction of the big celestial bodies are also rhythmic. The sun's "heart" beats once per two hours and forty minutes, so does its surface. Man's heart and pulse beat rhythmically, and the idealist pulsation is 74 times per minute and, simultaneously, the heart is holographic with the pulse.

"The sum of the pulses of any thing is a microcosm of that of the cosmos. As a consequence, the whole cosmos is equivalent to an immense holographically pulsing

[27]Qian (1993, pp. 310–315, 201–202).

network on which any pulse at a lower level becomes a dynamic knot."[28] Linguistic rhythm is nothing but a microcosm of the sum of the cosmic pulses, a dynamic knot on the holographic pulsing network. Language is a layer embraced in the whole network of the cosmos' pulsation, existing in a rhythmic state and wandering amidst rhythms. Its rhythm is coincident with the cosmic and the human ones. The "cosmic rhythm" with which it is coincident refers to the pulses of the big celestial bodies and the sun; by saying that it is "coincident with the human rhythm," I intend to note that human is him/herself regularly pulsing, so his/her language cannot have disordered rhythms, and man's regular pulsation also "orders" his/her language to be rhythmic to a certain extent. Human is always trying every means to "set the voiced linguistic sequence to music" or, even if he/she fails to attain this, he/she will try to make the voices pleasant to the ear and the rhythms harmonious as much as possible. I have stressed once and again this point in *Aesthetic Linguistics*, say, "One will feel pleased on hearing symmetric and balanced melodies and rhythms, and will feel disturbed on hearing the uncoordinated (dissonant), unharmonious, and unbalanced ones."[29] Seen in the view of the law of cosmos holography, doesn't the former (symmetric and balanced melodies and rhythms) exactly result from the coincidence with, and the latter (the three "un-s" of melodies and rhythms) from the violation of, human rhythms? Human is further coincident with the cosmic laws (being holographic with the cosmos) and, as a result, the time when human "feels pleased on hearing the symmetric and balanced melodies and rhythms" is exactly that when he/she is coincident with the law of cosmos holography, and the time when human "feels disturbed on hearing the uncoordinated (dissonant), unharmonious, and unbalanced melodies and rhythms" is exactly that when he/she violates the holographibility between language and the cosmos. This reversely proves that language's rhythms originate from the law of cosmos holography.

In addition, relevant to this, we find that the periodic law (displacement and rhythm) of the cosmos is also repeated by language.

The rising period of big rivers is 1 year, the activity period of sunspots is 11 years, global natural disasters are periodic, human body has the so-called mood, intelligence and physical periods, and so forth, which all indicate the periodicity of the movement of things. "In the cosmos, every system, even the whole cosmos, is a complex of various periods. Additionally, the sum of periods of each system is relevant to and integral with the sum of the whole cosmos' periods, the former being the microcosm of the latter, the latter the expansion of the former. This law is called the periodic law of the cosmos."[30] **Language rhythmicity, i.e., the regular phenomenon that strong and weak syllables, or long and short vowels, appear alternatively in language, exactly corresponds to the periodicity of the cosmos' pulsation**. It is the periodic transience that is manifested in the application of stress in pronunciation, the arrangement of stressed (strong) and unstressed (weak) syllables, the adjustment of long and short vowels, and the like. Nonetheless, the alternative appearances of

[28] Wang and Yan (1995, p. 238).

[29] Qian (1993, p. 49).

[30] Wang and Yan (1995, p. 431).

strong and weak syllables or long and short vowels are performed intentionally by human, belonging to human's intentional acts. Human is a minor cosmos in the true sense of the word, and owns all the information of the various periodic movements of the whole cosmos. On this account, the transient periods of the rhythm of language application ultimately partake in the complex of the various periods of the whole cosmos, but they are also integral with the sum of the latter periods.

8 Language Organicity

As for "language's organic relevance," I note in Sect. 5 of Chapter 3 that it is manifested in the following three typical phenomena:

First, it is the endless mutual interpretations between words.
Secondly, it is the mutually promoting and influencing sound changes.
Thirdly, it is the mutually constraining morphological changes.

The "language organicity" discussed here is a category resulting from the comparison with natural organisms. This notwithstanding, language's organism is supposed to be coincident, at least on a par, with the organic relevance of language system. Man is a natural organism as to which Kant[31] pointed out in 1790 that in an organism, each part acts as a means of and generates another one, and vice versa. The case is not so to machines. In a machine, a part is an effective cause of the movement of another one, but it is by no means the generator of the latter. A machine has its organization and systematic construction but has no **self-organizing** capacity; an organism has its organization, but it is also capable of adjusting the organization and compensating the defects of organs and functions by itself. Whereas the motive power of a machine is given from outside, that of an organism is inherent. Differently put, a machine exists due to the other-cause whereas any organism whatsoever is for itself and is of purposes. On the whole, the following two points also manifest language organicity:

Fourthly, the various traits of language at the levels of sound, tone, and breath are also a sort of language organicity, please cf. Sects. 2 and 3 of Chapter 1 of *Aesthetic Linguistics* in which I employ the term of "the life-consciousness of speech." When analyzing the manifestation of the life-consciousness at issue, I focus on the various traits of language's sound, tone, and breath, so I will not repeat the procedures here.

Fifthly, another manifestation of language organicity is its **self-organizing** capacity. What is self-organizing capacity? Apart from the aforementioned Kant's remarks, namely, "A machine has its organization and systematic construction but has no self-organizing capacity; an organism has its organization, but it is also capable of adjusting the organization and compensating the defects of organs and functions by itself," we can also cf. Xu Shenghuan's essay of "Language deviation and language system" in which he elucidates and predicts language deviation by virtue of Hermann

[31] Cf. Kant (1991). Also cf. Yao (1998). All the citations from German scholars in this section come from this essay and I will not repeat this later.

Haken's synergetics and Ilya Prigogine's theory of dissipative structure. Xu thus says, "The (language) deviation is of its direction and purposes but is not completely random and arbitrary or determined by external factors. When we observe language's deviations in the framework of this theory, we will find that deviation is performed on the basis of the original structural pattern of language system. The deviation is aimed at the legitimate reorganization of the structure, and it is supposed to be based on the original one."[32] Given that I have also discussed "the dynamic balance of language structure at the level of the self-organizing process of language system" in *Aesthetic Linguistics*, I will also not enter into more detail here.

Language structure fairly resembles natural organisms. We may as well call this phenomenon "language organicity."

F. Von Schlegel says in *On the Language and Wisdom of India* that the structure of Sanskrit "was formed organically," which means that language expresses various grammatical relationships by virtue of the internal changes of reflection, to wit., language root. That which runs counter to this is the "mechanical" mode, namely, that the language root does not change in itself but expresses the grammatical meanings by dint of the added affixes or particles (Partikeln).[33] He holds that the organicity of language is manifested in the following three points: (1) The root of a word is like the bud of a life. "In Sanskrit or Greek, just like what the word 'root' means, each root is a living bud in the true sense of the word." (2) The fundamental property of "bud," "seed," or language root is being reproductive. Reflection is produced inside language root, being an organic constituent of the latter, like a branch produced from a tree; affixes and particles on the other hand are like a pile of scattered "atoms," being mechanically attached to the word and removable at any time. (3) The animal has developmental stages, so does language. In the light of animals' stepped arrangement from low to high, Schlegel demarcates language at the level of grade and type. The isolating language is at the bottom stage (like Chinese), in the mediate stage is the agglutinating language, and the inflecting language (like Greek) is at the top stage. His theory of language stages was coincident with the popular cognition of the then biology as regards the origin of species.

Humboldt thus considers the organicity of language:

Different from Schlegel who merely found "the organic structure" in inflectional languages, Humboldt contends that languages "are all organisms." "Language is the immediate manifestation of the organism [of man] in perceptual and spiritual activities, so it is naturally of the nature of all the organic lives."[34] Here I would like to note two points: first, these discussions de facto already suggest that human body is holographic with language. Secondly, these assertions are in essence identical with those produced as regards the beauty of language and speeches in *Aesthetic Linguistics*: "Given that human is in this case (i.e., a dynamic balanced system), he/she owns the internal prescription of aesthetics; given that language is in this case

[32]Xu (1991, p. 2).

[33]Cf. Schlegel. Karl Wilhelm Friedrich, *Über die Sprache und Weisheit der Indier*, pp. 41–42.

[34]Cf. A. Flitner and K. Giel (Eds.), *Wilhelm von Humboldt. Werke in fünf Bänden* (1960–1981, Band IV, S. 218). Stuttgart (Annual Report to the King. Works In five Volumes), Vol. 3, pp. 2–3.

(i.e., a dynamic balanced system), it owns the internal prescription of beauty. The two internal prescriptions of the same structure correspond to, tally with, hence provoke one another, and the beauty of language and speech is thus produced, respectively. In the final analysis, the effects of the beauty of speech and the structure of the beauty of language are supposed to be a part of the harmonious state of human life." I further note, "The effect of the beauty of language is supposed to be a part of effect of the harmony of human life in that the aesthetic choices at each level of language, respectively, reflect the harmonious state of life."[35] That is to say, as a matter of fact, my discussions here already reveal the holographic relationship between human body and language.

In the end of the eighteenth century, some scholars like August Schleicher the German linguist, William Dwight Whitney and Philipp Wegener the American linguists, and Georg von der Gabelentz the German sinologist, and others, thus recognized language "organism":

On the whole, they believe: (1) The generation and development of language are of certain purposes. All the languages regard as their goal clearly and definitely expressing thoughts, but each language has its own way toward this goal, and hence the effects of the expressions are different. (2) Language has many types ranking in a step-like fashion from low to high. (3) Language is "lived," functioning and developing in accordance with its inherent laws. (4) Language is all the time an "organic" whole all the constituents of which rely on each other and cannot be separated.

Let us proceed to Schleicher's ideas on language organicity: after the publication of Darwin's *The Origin of Species* (1859), Schleicher published his *Die Darwinsche Theorie und die Sprachwissenschaf* (*Darwin's Theory and Linguistics*) in 1863, intending to interpret, by means of Darwin's theories, the generation, development, and changes of language. Schleicher contends that Darwin's theories are generally applicable to "language organism." He says, "Language is an organism the production of which does not rely on human will. Language progresses in accordance with definite laws, continuously developing, gradually aging, and ultimately coming to an end. The series of phenomena usually called "life" can also be seen in language."[36] The similarities between a "language organism" and a natural one are as follows: (1) They both gradually change and continuously evolve according to certain laws, and the existent languages and species are all the results of the long-term evolution; (2) Just like all the natural organisms originate from single cells, all the "language organisms" originate from simple roots equivalent to "language's cells" (Sprachzellen); (3) In some phase of the planet's life history, the single-cell organisms once developed in large quantities. Similarly, in the history of language, there was also a phase whence large quantities of simple ideographic roots were produced. Afterwards, natural organisms developed in different directions and ways and, similarly, the ideographic roots also expanded in a diverse fashion; (4) Category descriptions can be made on language as on the organisms. The series of concepts in biology, say,

[35]Qian (1993, pp. 50–74).

[36]See Schleicher (1873, S. f7).

genus, species, subspecies, etc., all have their parallel expressions in linguistics: genus (Gattung) = language family (Sprachstamm), species (Arten) = languages (of the same family), subspecies (Unterarten) = dialects or colloquial expressions, varieties (Varietaten), heterogeneity (Spielarten) = minor local dialects, and individuals (Individuen) = individual speeches; (5) According to Darwin's theory, a **species** is produced gradually and changes slowly, and when it changes, many a new form will be produced from the original one. In the same vein, a basic language (e.g., the primary Indo-European mother tongue) will also vary, which results in the emergence of many sublanguages; (6) The forms differentiated from one species are similar as well as different, and there is no definite boundary between **species** and sub**species**, or between subspecies and varieties. In the same vein, the boundaries between language, dialect, subdialect, local dialect, or the like, are also indefinite insomuch as the developing phases of language expressed by them penetrate each other; (7) Just like the generation and variation of species are determined to a certain extent by the surrounding factors, language also changes due to the differences amidst the surrounding conditions; (8) During the struggles for survival in biological sphere, many organic forms were eliminated and only small quantities of superior species managed to survive and proliferate. In the same vein, during the lengthy pre-historic period (about tens of thousands of years) of human world, there must have been many languages eventually vanishing, whereas some other languages with strong vitality succeeded in being disseminated. Due to the fact that **"language organism" resembles so much the natural one**, Schleicher firmly believes that there should not be difference on methods between linguistics and natural sciences, and that the former should be added into the list of the latter.

The ideas of Whitney, Wegener, and Gabelentz on language organicity are thus: after Schleicher, "organism," "organic organization," "organic," etc., became important concepts indispensable to linguistic theorists, and the "life" and "growth" of language were prior issues of many works of linguistic theory. For instance, Whitney the American who accepted linguistic trainings in Germany published *The life and Growth of Language*,[37] and Wegener *Investigations Regarding the Fundamental Questions of the Life of Language.* When it comes to "language organism" and the "life" of language, most scholars make investigations out of the interest in language history, some other scholars on the other hand stress that "language organism" should first and foremost be understood as a state or a system. For instance, in *Die Sprachwissenschaft: Ihre Aufgaben, Methoden Und Bisherigen Ergebnisse*, Gabelentz notes that like the natural organisms, language "is a (relatively) complete system in each phase of its life, relying on itself in toto; all its constituents interact with each other and all its life-expressions (Lebensausserungen) originate from the interaction as such."[38] He further points out that language is not a thing of independent life; but

[37] *The life and Growth of Language* was published in London in 1875, and the German version translated by the renowned German linguist A. Leskien emerged in the following year.

[38] See Gabelentz (1891, S. f9).

rather, it is "human spirit—the capacity and function embraced in the organism's nature."[39]

Seen at surface level, linguistic system has no relevance whatsoever to (natural) organisms; in the view of the law of cosmos holography, whereas, so long as things are located in one and the same cosmos, these two things are holographic and closely related to each other even if they are on different levels or in different systems. As is introduced in Sect. 4 of Chapter 2, "One of the fundamental theories: the law of cosmos holography," in this book:

> "The law of cosmos holography includes the following fundamental contents: all the things are four-dimensionally holographic; **mutual holographic relationships exist** everywhere, between the parts and the whole of the same individual, things at the same level, **things at different levels and in different systems**, the beginning and ending of a matter, the macro and micro progressions of a thing, and between time and space, and the like; each part embraces, and is simultaneously embraced by, other parts…"
>
> "The law of cosmos holography means that the cosmos is an n-dimensional holographic unity. **Any constituent of it is a condensed information cosmos**. The cosmos is the complex of innumerable information cosmoses. In brief, **any system whatsoever embraces all the information of the cosmos as a whole**."

Your particular heed is required to be paid to the previous statements in bold: "mutual holographic relationships exist…, things at the same level, things at different levels and in different systems"; "any system whatsoever embraces all the information of the cosmos as a whole." Language system and natural organisms exactly coexist "at different levels and in different systems," namely, between an apple and an oyster, of the cosmos. The theory of cosmic holographic unity however holds that they "are mutually holographic." On the other hand, be it language system or natural organisms, it is a "condensed information cosmos," and it "embraces all the information of the cosmos as a whole." With the view of the theory of cosmic holographic unity, it is not that hard to understand why there are so many miraculous similarities between language and natural organisms.

Why, then, don't we call it language's organism-ness? This is because language system is not a proteosome, nor is it a natural organism. Just as is noted by Gabelentz, language is not a thing of independent life; but rather, it is "human spirit—the capacity and function embraced in the organism's nature."

9 Language Arbitrariness

According to Saussure, language arbitrariness means that "the relationship between the signifier and the signified is arbitrary." My understanding of it is: there is not a necessary connection between some phonetic shell (the signifier) and some signified object. For instance, the English speaker will associate [buk] with "book"; in Chinese, "书" is associated with the pronunciation of [shu]; a Russian speaker

---

[39]Gabelentz (1891, S. f17).

whereas has "книга" corresponding to it. What is the cause to this phenomenon? Xu Guozhang once asked, "Since language is a rational act, why does it embrace arbitrary elements?" I think this is a profound question.

Ludwig von Bertalanffy holds that the developing direction of a system is determined at once by the factual states (necessity) and the predictions for the future (contingency) the unity of which is purposefulness. Bertalanffy also says that the world of the organisms appeared a product of chance, accumulated by the senseless play of random mutations and selection; the mental world as a curious and fairly inconsequential epiphenomenon of material events. ...Nevertheless, these aspects exist, and you cannot conceive of a living organism, not to speak of behavior and human society, without taking into account what variously and quite loosely is called adaptiveness, purposiveness, goal-seeking, and the like. ...What should be stressed, however, is the fact that teleological behavior directed toward a characteristic final state or goal is not something off limits for natural science.[40]

A conclusion can be drawn from the above discussions: the formation of any system whatsoever in the world of organisms is accumulated by the senseless play of random mutations and selections.

Is this conclusion suitable for the mental world and the artificial system? Is any system whatsoever in the mental world also "accumulated by the senseless play of random mutations and selections"? Bertalanffy's answer is "mental world as a curious and fairly inconsequential epiphenomenon of material events." That is to say, there are also random elements in the formation of the systems in the mental world.

If so, does the artificial system also have random elements? As is known, the artificial system necessarily accompanies, in fact stretches cross, mental phenomena (human's thinking and idea activities) and the physical world, so they must have random elements during the process of formation.

Needless to say, language theories belong to the system of concept, i.e., a system of the mental world. Nonetheless, language per se is an entity having audible sounds, the performance of it is an illocutionary act or behavior rather than a conceptual deduction, and the formation of language configuration is not a product of logical deduction, either. The formation of language performance and configuration is established by the people through long social practices, the performance of recognized customs and rules. There are of course mental elements in language phenomena. It is a mental phenomenon the performance of which however is not based on logical inferences; but rather, it merely follows the agreed rules by people (There are large quantities of activities violating or ignoring logic).

Language is based on human's mental and psychological acts, and sets rules by means of the sounds produced by physical, namely, vocal organs, which is established by people through long social practices. At the beginning of language's formation, randomness is exactly manifested. The randomness as such all the time accompanies human selections. Take people of Chinese nationality as an example. Initially, there might be a lot many names, callings, or nomenclatures, etc., of rice (*dami* 大米)

[40]von Bertalanffy (1968. pp. 45–46).

as the food served on the table to keep body and soul together; later on, people made their choices, including the aesthetic one, according to their various feelings; and, at last, the candidate items were reduced to several kinds according to most people's selections, say, rice (*dami)*, the meal of rice (*damifan* 大米饭 / *mifan* 米饭), meal (*fan* 饭), or something. Indeed, this is a process "accumulated by the senseless play of random mutations and selection" and accompanied by "a curious and fairly inconsequential epiphenomenon."

This is to say that language system is also accumulated by the senseless play of random mutations and selection. Be that as it may, language arbitrariness is merely manifested in a relationship between pronunciation and the signified rather than in the internal running of the system. Once a language system accomplishes being selected, its internal running becomes necessary. As expected, people have discovered some linguistic similarities in recent years, namely, the legitimacy of and necessary connections between pronunciation and the signified (thing). Language arbitrariness and legitimacy necessarily coexist.

The formation of any system whatsoever (natural system including that of the organisms and the artificial system) is accumulated by the senseless play of random mutations and selection. Language system is no exception. In terms of the formation of language system, randomness is already an attribute of it ab initio. Randomness is an attribute of the system, and it is necessarily that of language system. Given that all the parts inside a system are necessarily holographic with one another, randomness becomes one of the attributes of the holographic language system. **Language arbitrariness originates from the accumulation of the senseless play of random mutations and selection**.

10 Other Properties of Language

The phenomenon of "one word, two poles" is one of the other properties of langue as it differs from those universal and regular ones.

We already find the following phenomenon at once in Chinese, English, and Russian, etc.: one word form has two opposite semantic items. It is suggested that the word as such be called "two-pole word." The phenomenon at stake can be called that of "one word, two poles." One of the rationales of this suggestion is, some people interpret such words into "the polarization of word meaning" (полярзация).[41] The experts of exegetics in China call this phenomenon "*fanfupangtong* 反复旁通" (same word, opposite meanings) or "*xiangfanweixun* 相反为训" (mutual interpretation of two opposite meanings in one word) called "*fanxun* 反训" (enantiosemy) for short.[42]

That which needs explanations is, the phenomenon of "one word, two poles" is not necessarily recorded in dictionaries given that many such words are discovered

[41]See Д. З. Розенталъ и М. А. Телекова. *Словаръ-справочник лингвистических терминнов.*

[42]Qian (1994, pp. 1–3).

in practices. There are not a few of them, say, Xu Shirong has collected 500 Chinese enantiosemy characters.[43]

As regards the two-pole word, Qian Zhongshu gave the following interpretations and examples (the underlines in bold form are made by me):

As is known, one character can have many meanings all of which can be used simultaneously, which is called "many facets are combined" into "one character." Hegel despised our Chinese language, believing that it was unsuitable for speculations; he also bragged that German embraced rules and could express delicate meanings. He gave as an example "Aufheben," contending that the one and the same word contained two opposite meanings (ein und dasselbe Wort fur zwei entgegengesetzte Bestimmungen), and that even Latin remained to have so profound connotations. Since he knew no Chinese language, we do not blame him; as to the common attitude of some experts or giants of thought, namely, being arrogant and indulged in verbiage because of ignorance, it also does not deserve blames; nonetheless, provided that a scholar considers the similar ideas between the East and the West as the differences between the South and the North like those between an apple and an oyster, we cannot but feel pity for him.

A Chinese character usually has more than one meaning. There are roughly two relevant phenomena: one is parallel polysemy. For instance, in *The Analects* · *Zihan* 《论语・子罕》, there is an expression "*kongkongruye* 空空如也" (empty as such) in which the "*kong* 空" means "empty," but it also means "honesty," the two meanings being different and sharing nothing in common. **The other is contrary or bifurcated polysemy**, say, "*luan* 乱" (messy) simultaneously means "ordered," and "*fei* 废" (abolish) simultaneously means "set up," and *Mozi* · *Jing* 《墨子・经》 has early given an example: "*yi* 已: accomplish, fail"; **the "*fanxun*" in ancient people's terminology means that two meanings complement as well as oppose each other**. Here I am specially interpreting this style. When it comes to practical use, only one meaning is adopted at one time and hence it cannot be said containing many meanings in a false fashion. The mental and physical ideas overlap, some are like the ice being incompatible with the fire or the glue being inseparable from the lacquer, some others are like the pearl adding reliance to the jade or the pipe being harmonious with the bell, still others are like chicken dwelling in the same cage with rabbit, or cattle living in the same stable with horse, and so on and so forth. On the whole, many meanings are combined into one character, and the parallel and bifurcated polysemy are interpreted on the same level, which results in the fact that different meanings become harmonious, and contrary meanings become coincident with one another….In the case of "Aufheben," Hegel notes that it has the two meanings of "put an end to" (ein Ende machen) and "sustain" (erhalten); in philosophical works, whereas, we find that one meaning is adopted at one time.

As to how Qian Zhongshu criticizes Hegel for his nonsenses (say, he recklessly says that in Chinese there is no character "containing two opposite meanings in itself") in the above quotation, we suspend it. That which draws my attention is his examples, definitions, and interpretations as regards the two-pole characters (e.g.,

[43] Xu (1980).

"*luan*," "*fei*," "*yi*," etc., mentioned afore). With respect to definition, he cites examples and says, "The '*fanxun*' in ancient people's terminology means that two meanings complement as well as opposite each other." The two meanings of a two-pole word must be complementary as well as opposite to one another as to which he makes the aforementioned interpretations at mental and rational levels.

In his *Fuzzy Linguistics*, Wu Tieping defines the two-pole word as "a word having two opposite meanings in itself." He makes large quantities of demonstrations and cites some two-pole words in various languages. Below is a small part of the Chinese examples:

tao 陶: "happiness" and "sorrowful";
she 舍: "stop" and "release";
guai 乖: "violating the reason" and "being obedient";
chou 仇: "an unhappy couple" and "a happy couple"…

Now we proceed to more examples:

"*pi* 披": it has two opposite semantic items of "cover" and "open" (clear away). The expressions belonging to the former include these: "披(上)雨衣 covering oneself with a raincoat," "披(上)斗篷 covering oneself with a cape," "披星戴月 being covered by stars and the moon," "披挂 (整齐、上阵) covering oneself with a suit of armor (in order or for the battle), "披红戴绿 covering oneself with red and green clothes," "披麻戴孝 covering oneself with mourning apparels," "披甲 covering oneself with the military attire," "披坚执锐 covering oneself with a suit of armor and arming oneself with weapons," "披肩 covering oneself with a cape on shoulder," and the like. On the other hand, the expressions belonging to the latter include these: "披卷 (先打开书籍再阅读) opening the reading materials" (opening the book before reading it), "披览 opening and scanning," "批阅 opening and giving remarks," "披露 opening and revealing," "披肝沥胆 opening one's heart," "披怀 (敞开胸怀) opening one's breath of mind" (being broken open), "披荆斩棘 clearing away brambles and cutting thistles," "披沙淘金 clearing away sands for golds," and such like.

"*jiu* 救": it has two opposite semantic items of "saving the object" and "avoiding, putting out, or eliminating the object." As to the former meaning, we have "救民 saving the people," "救生 (圈) lifesaving (ring)," "救命 saving the life," "救国 saving the nation," "救世 saving the world," among others, where the people, life, nation, world, etc., as the objects need saving and aiding; as to the latter meaning, we have 救死扶伤 "avoiding death and saving the wounded," "救火 putting out the fire," "救荒 eliminating the famine," "救苦救难 eliminating the sufferings and the miseries," "救灾 eliminating the disaster," or the like, where the death, the wounded, the fire, the famine, the sufferings, the miseries, the disaster, etc., as the objects need not saving but avoiding, putting out, or eliminating. In *Modern Chinese Dictionary* compiled by the Linguistics Institute of Chinese Academy of Social Sciences, "*jiu*" has two interpretations: "first, save so as to bring… out of disasters or dangers; second, help people and things to avoid (disasters or dangers)." Such a distinction remains to be sharp. The crux lies in the fact that the results are not considered from the perspective of the object. Contrariwise, the parlance of "it has two opposite semantic items of 'saving the object' and 'avoiding, putting out, or eliminating the object'" can enable the learner to instantly grasp the essence of the opposition at stake so as to rapidly distinguish the items.

"*bai* 败": it has the two opposite semantics items of one's own failure on the one hand and one's defeating the rivals (which, to him, is not failure but victory) on the other. The former means "one's own failure in the battle or competition," which is so popular that there is no need to give examples; the latter means "defeating the enemies or the rivals." Defeating the rivals means winning the battle with them, say, "utterly defeating the aggressors" is equal to "utterly wining the battle with the aggressors." For another example, the meaning of "败火 defeating the fire" is never situated at literal level but means defeating the inflammation in the body and reaching the effects of eliminating the internal heat, cooling the blood,[44] and detoxifying the body.

"*chule* 除了": its including and excluding modes oppose each other. As to the former, we have for example "Tom also attended class besides (*chule*) Dick," which does not mean "excluding Dick" at literal level but rather includes him. As to the latter, we have "Every one has come except (*chule*) Tom." Why don't the Chinese think it equivocal when understanding it? It is because the anaphors after "*chule*" help. In the case of the former meaning of *chule*, the anaphor is expressed by "also…besides" in which "also" is added as a hint. The premise at which "also" here appears is to suggest that the previous object is a thing or a person surely included. In the case of the latter meaning of *chule*, "every one has…except" is an anaphor containing two opposite meanings in which the object of "*chule*" is opposite to "everyone has" and, by virtue of intellectual interference, the hearer will infer that the object at stake is excluded. The case is not so to English "except" which only means "exclude(ing)."[45]

There are also two-pole words in English.

ambition (n.): (a) strong desire to achieve sth., e.g., filled with ambition to become famous, rich, powerful, etc.; (b) particular desire of this kind, e.g., **have great ambitions**. In the view of a native English speaker, to make himself famous, rich, and powerful is a manifestation of a normal person's individual values, namely, the formal development of individualism. This meaning is supposed to belong in the semantic item of (a), being equivalent to "*xiongxin* 雄心, *baofu* 抱负" in the cultural circles of Chinese language, and hence it is approving. Contrariwise, if someone wants to invade and occupy another country, or to proclaim himself king by means of subverting the legitimate government, it is "a particular desire of this kind," so the meaning of "ambition" belongs in the semantic item of (b). It is equivalent to "*yexin* 野心" in Chinese language, and hence it is derogative. When a word simultaneously contains the approving meaning (to become famous, rich, powerful, etc.) of "*xiongxin*" and the derogative one (invading the country or proclaiming oneself king by means of subverting the legitimate government) of "*yexin*" for a human being, it is supposed to be a two-pole word. I wonder whether or not the semantic item of (b)

---

[44]In brief, "hot blood", "cool the blood", etc., are particular Chinese expressions of the essence causing unhealthy conditions of human body.

[45]Cf. *Preface of the editor and translator* by Li Beida. In *Oxford Advanced Learner's English-Chinese Dictionary*, Fourth Edition. Printed in Hong Kong, Oxford University Press, 1999.

here is derogative in the circle of English culture. If in their values the second item also conveys a normal desire, there would not be the parlance of two poles. The point is, nevertheless, why did the compilers of the *Oxford Dictionary*[46] as such separate the two items? Presumably, they also considered them as different mental acts, so I sort it to a two-pole word.

astute (adj.): clever and quick at seeing how to gain an advantage; shrewd. The "two-pole-ness" of such words is manifested in the opposition at the level of evaluation conception. Take "**He genuinely admired her astuteness at social climbing**" as an example, when a person is *astute* at social climbing, the third party would give completely different evaluations: some might consider it as *clever and quick* whereas some others might disdainfully attribute it to *shrewd*.

bribery (n.): giving or taking of bribes. As is known, giving bribes is opposite to taking them: one is outward, the other being inward.

dose (n.):…3 (fig. infml) (a) any experience of sth. unpleasant: a dose of boring conversation; (b) any experience of sth. enjoyable: What you need is a good dose of laughter. The former is "an unpleasant experience" whereas the latter "a pleasant" one.

collaborate (vi.): 1. (with sb.) (on sth.) work together (with sb.) esp. to create or produce sth.: She collaborated with her sister on a biography of their father. For another example: He and I collaborated in writing plays. 2. (with sb.) (*derog.*) help enemy forces occupying one's country. For another example: Frenchmen who collaborated with the Nazis. As a matter of fact, this word is typical on containing the distinction between approving and derogative meanings. The two meanings both refer to working together with sb. on sth., but the word means "cooperate" (*hezuo* 合作) at one level whereas "collude" (*goujie* 勾结) at the other. The point is, whereas in Chinese there are two words absolutely different on emotion (i.e., *hezuo* and *goujie*) for the expressions, in English only one phrase (i.e., collaborate with) is employed. The common information contained in the two poles is "work with."

identity (n.): The Chinese translation of this word once aroused debates. Is "cultural identity" "*wenhuagexing* 文化个性" (cultural individuality), "*wenhuatezhi* 文化特质" (cultural speciality), "*wenhuarentong* 文化认同" (cultural identification), or "*wenhuagongxing* 文化共性" (cultural universality)? Someone once published an essay on *Dushu*, contending that it was wrong that many people in domestic academia held that this word should be translated into "*rentong* 认同." His reason is that this word stresses individuality to which the translation of "*rentong*" exactly runs counter. This word is de facto a two-pole one: it stresses individuality and speciality, but it also stresses identity and universality. In terms of its first semantic item, namely, "who or what sb./sth. is," it indeed stresses the identity, the self, and who or what sb./sth. is. For instance, in "There is no clue to the *identity* of the thief," identity refers to the thief's identity and individuality. The second semantic item of the word however is: (state of) exact likeness or sameness. In this context, we can see the usage of "identity"

---

[46] *Oxford Advanced Learner's English-Chinese Dictionary*, Fourth Edition. The Commercial Press and Oxford University Press, 1997. Since the coming English words are all taken from this dictionary, I will not put particular notes on them any longer.

from the verb "identify" with the same root. For example, in "One can not *identify happiness with wealth*," identify means "confuse"; for another example, in "I found it hard to *identify with* any of the characters in the film," identify apparently refers to "*rentong*." In this connection, it is not that hard to decide whether "cultural identity" refers to *wenhuarentong* or *wenhuateyixing* 文化特异性 (cultural specificity). No matter upon which reference is the author or the utterer's original meaning directed, he/she will give a definite context for the reader or the hearer to make a judgment.

pious (adj.): 1. having or showing a deep devotion to religion; 2. (derog.) hypocritically virtuous. *He dismissed his critics as pious do-gooders who were afraid to face the facts*. To be sure, there are true and false pieties, so the second semantic item here is derogative. In this way, *pious do-gooders* can be translated into "*jiasharen* 假善人" (false do-gooders). As to the truly "pious," three more examples[47] are given as follows: *His parents were pious churchgoers*. (FWF) *The pious man attended Mass every day*. (MD) *Auntie is a pious lady*. (Neal).

spare (v.): … 2. refrain from using, giving, etc., (sth.); use as little as possible: *No trouble was spared to ensure our comfort*. 3. be able to afford to give (time, money, etc.): *I can't spare the time for a holiday at the moment*. In Chinese, the former semantic item can be paraphrased into "*linxi* 吝惜" (grudge), "*jieyue* 节约" (economize), or in a word "*bugeichu* 不给出" (refuse to give (sth.)); the latter one can be paraphrased into "*bochu* 拨出" (allocate), "*yunchu* 匀出" (set aside), or in a word "*geichu* 给出" (give (sth.)).

stuck (adj.): 1. not able to move or continue doing sth.: *Help! I'm stuck in the mud!*…5. **get stuck in** (to sth.) (infml.) start doing sth. enthusiastically: *Here's your food. Now get stuck in!* The first semantic item means "being unable to move" whereas the fifth one means "being able to move, and move in a great extent."

beg (v.): 1. ask for (money, food, clothes, etc.) as a gift or as charity; make a living in this way; 2. ask earnestly or humbly (for sth.). We can position this verb with "ask; implore, pray"; in the idiom of "**beg the question,**" nevertheless, "to beg" already becomes "not properly deal with the matter being discussed by assuming that a question needing an answer has been answered," which is usually employed to evade the essence of the question. That is to say, "to beg" means no longer "ask, pray" but "evade" (not properly deal…). For one more example: Your proposal begs the question whether a change is needed at all.

proud (adj.): 1. (approv.) feeling or showing justifiable pride: proud of her new car; 2. (derog.) self-important: He was too proud to join in our fun.

There are also two-pole words in Russian.

Some examples of Russian two-pole words cited by Wu Tieping in *Fuzzy Linguistics* are as follows:

разучить: to learn; make unlearnable

рубить: fell; erect (a wooden house)

славить: praise; slander

гордый: (approv.) feeling or showing justifiable pride; (derog.) self-important (identical to "proud")

---

[47]Zhang (1985, p. 3151).

учить (что): learn, read, recite; учить (кого чему): teach, lecture on

бесценный: invaluable; valueless

прослушать: hear (sth.); listen to but remain to hear (sth.)

презрителъный: (old use) disdained; (current use) disdainful

пучина: the rise of the land; abyss

просмотреть: peer at; glance at

…

Why can a word assemble two polar meanings?

In *Fuzzy Linguistics*, Wu Tieping contends first and foremost, "Everything whatsoever in the world is a unity of contradictions. The two contradictory poles will unexceptionally transform themselves into their opposite in certain conditions which, as a dialectic law, is manifested in many aspects in language," "There are various causes to this phenomenon (i.e., one word, two meanings) and one of them is language fuzziness."[48] "Antonymous fuzzy words all have certain relativity, which is the objective foundation on which the antonyms are very easily transformed into their opposite sides." "There are fairly abundant phenomenon of one word having two meanings which, presumably, is the reflection of the fact that in China, dialectic thought is developed from ancient times to the present." In the couple of theoretical explanations, he cites Lenin's ideas before noting, "The unity and mutual transformation of the contrarieties are manifested in a multiple fashion in language," "As to one word having two polar meanings, it is merely a special case of the fact that one word has many meanings. This is exactly where the secret of language being a perfect communicative tool is located, which is a merit rather than a fault of language," and "The idea that a word's meaning cannot be A and non-A at the same time is nothing else than a typical inference based on the traditional binomial logic and its characteristic law of excluded middle….Be that as it may, since fuzzy logic came into being, the phenomenon that something belongs but not completely to category A whereas simultaneously to category B, namely, being situated at the cross-border area of two categories, has been generally known to people now."[49] He further says, "That one word has two polar meanings is legitimate at the level of the clustering relationship amidst word meanings rather than at the fact that in some specific word combination, a word simultaneously has two polar semantic items (the pun excluded)." Undoubtedly, these elucidations are pertinent and correct.

How about we change a way of elucidation?

Halliday points out that a cline is a scale on which all the things gradually develop into other ones. The two poles of a scale are fairly different from one another, but it is hard to tell where their boundary is. The principle of "All things on the scale gradually develop into other ones" reveals to the full the holographic relationship between linguistic units on the same scale. As has been noted in the discussions of language fuzziness, "The indefiniteness of the category and the boundaries between the linguistic units on one scale is exactly due to the fact that **the category contains**

---

[48] Wu (1999, pp. 187–217).

[49] Wu (1999, pp. 222–242).

the information of both poles. In my view, this is the holographic phenomenon between linguistic units: the part embraces the whole, and the whole naturally embraces the parts." This is "one encompasses all." When it is acceptable that one encompasses all, it should not sound strange that one encompasses two polar points. Of the ten principles of the theory of cosmos holography, the pertinent ones to my discussions are: the first principle, namely, the part is holographic with the whole. This is the cornerstone of the whole edifice of the theory of cosmos holography, being the most fundamental and important principle; the fifth principle, namely, homogeneity surely leads to isomorphism, isomorphism to holographibility, holographibility to isomorphism, and isomorphism to homogeneity. The three are equal in value and are absolutely identical to one another.

When we observe the two-pole words, we will find that in between the two polar meanings, there is surely an intersecting or overlapping part, which is also called conjugation. "*Pi*" has two opposite semantic items of "cover" and "open" (clear away). "Cover" (or *da* 搭) and "open" (clear away) are two opposite conditions acting on the same object (thing or a part of human body): either it is all-inclusiveness (covering), or it is the elimination of the all-inclusiveness (making it all exclusive). The focus of the two overlapping meanings is situated at the distance between the covering and the covered. Their distinction merely lies in the fact that all-inclusiveness means the distance between them being zero whereas all-exclusiveness means the two being separated from each other, namely, considerable distance appears between them. The overlapping part of the two poles of "*jiu*" ("saving the object" and "avoiding, putting out, or eliminating the object") is to take rapid measures to deal with disasters or dangers. The distinction between them is merely on developing or evading the results. The conjugation of the two poles of "ambition" (strong desire and particular desire) is all the more clear: strong desire. The same holds to the overlapping part between the two poles of "pious" (true and false piety): a deep devotion to sth. The devotion as such is an expression, and the true/false is where the distinction rests. The overlapping part of the two poles of спавить (praise and slander) rests in воздовать, создовать, and распространять which mean to spread some fame. The distinction between them consists in what kind of fame —good or bad—is spread. Учить (что) and учить (кого чему) are two opposite processes, one referring to "learn," "read," and "recite" by oneself, the other to let others learn. They share "grasping and remembering": заниматься, усваивать, and запоминать, and the distinction between them rests in the causative direction—to learn and recite by oneself or to let others do so. There being many an example notwithstanding, we can all the time sense in the limited conjugation analyses such an idea: **there is always communicative information between the two polar meanings of a two-pole word, and the overlapping part is the common information as such. Only when there is a communicative part between the two poles can there be the possibility of their mutual transformation. Thus is formed the mutual containing, viz., holographic relationship, between the two polar meanings**. Singly seen, "end" can be understood as "farthest or last part or point of the length of sth."; when people give "end to end" and "make both ends meet," nevertheless, we will see that "end" can be both the end and the beginning the conjugation between which is "extreme limit." That is to say, each pole can be either the end or the beginning, and the distinction is merely the corresponding direction of the matter. It is because conjugate information is contained between the two poles that we can understand the holographibility of two-pole words.

References

Barthes. Roland, *Semiotic aesthetics*. Shenyang: Liaoning People's Publishing House, 1987, 3.

Chomsky, A. N., *Aspects of the theory of syntax*. Cambridge, MA: The MIT Press, 1965a.

Chomsky, A. N., *Linguistic theory and language learning, aspects of the theory of syntax*. The MIT Press, 1965b.

Gabelentz. Georg von der, *Die Sprachwissenschaft: Ihre Aufgaben, Methoden Und Bisherigen Ergebnisse*, 1891, S. f9.

Kant. Immanuel, *Collected works of the Critique of Historical Reason*. Trans. He Zhaowu. Beijing: The Commercial Press, 1991.

Li. Xiaoming, *Fuzziness: An enigma of man's cognition*. Beijing: People's Publishing House, 1987.

Qian. Guanlian, *Aesthetic linguistics*. Shenzhen: Haitian Publishing House, 1993.

Qian. Zhongshu, *Guanzhuipian*. Beijing: Zhong Hua Book Company, 1994.

Robins, R. H., *A short history of linguistic*. London and New York, 1982.

Schleicher. August, *Die Darwinsche Theorie und die Sprachwissenschaf*, 1873, S. f7.

von Bertalanffy. Ludwig, *General system theory: Foundations, development, applications*. New York: George Braziller, 1968.

Wang. Cunzhen & Yan. Chunyou, *The theory of cosmic holographic unity*, 1995.

William Pitt, America unconquerable. In *100 famous speeches*. Beijing: China Translation Cooperation, 1989.

Wu. Tieping, *Fuzzy linguistics*. Shanghai: Shanghai Foreign Language Education Press, 1999.

Xu. Guozhang, *Xu Guozhang on language*. Beijing: Foreign Language Teaching and Research Press, 1999.

Xu. Shenghuan, Language deviation and language system. In *Linguistics and Applied Linguistics*, 1991 (1).

Xu. Shirong, Origin tracing of enantiosemy. In *Studies of the Chinese Language*, 1980 (4).

Yao. Xiaoping, The historical relationship between languages and sciences. In *Foreign Languages in Fujian*, 1998 (4).

Ye. Xiaoqi, Going out of the dialectic metaphysics. In *Social Sciences Weekly*, March 26, 1998.

Yuan. Yulin, Comparison between the encoding of linguistic information and that of biological information. In *Contemporary Linguistics*, 1998 (2).

Zhang. Daozhen. *A dictionary of current english usage*. Shanghai: Shanghai Translation Publishing House, 1985.

Zhang. Jin, The hypothesis of thought module (abstract). In *Foreign Languages and Their Teaching*, 1998 (2).

Zhao. Nanyuan, *Cognitive sciences and general evolution theory*. Tsinghua University Press, 1994.

Zhou. Shuoyu, *Introduction to system science*. Beijing: Seismological Press, 1998.

Chapter 6
The Outer Rootstock of Different Theories of Language

Abstract Where do theories of language come from? They are summarized from language facts. Yes, they are. Nevertheless, why the same language fact can produce so many different theories? This is because people interpreting them have different viewpoints and perspectives. For instance, tagmemics compares language to the physical movement of the matter, and valence grammar compares language's inner structure to the combination of the atoms inside the matter, which are nothing but the viewpoints and perspectives of cosmic structure on the linguistic one. In this chapter, I aim to seek the outer rootstock of these theories of language, and the relevant endeavors would surely reach this conclusion: whether or not the presenters of the original theories are aware of this, these theories can all find their interpretative rootstock outside themselves: language structure is isomorphic and similar to, corresponds to, and is embedded in the cosmic one, namely, they are holographic with one another. All these can be seen as the state of the outer language holography.

Keywords Tagmemics · Ferdinand de Saussure · Systemic view-point of language · Cognitive grammar · Valence grammar · Systemic grammar · The integrity of language meaning

Modern theories of language are manifested in a pluralistic fashion: the stratification grammar founded by S. M. Lamb, the tagmemics by K. L. Pike, and the systematic grammar by M. A. K. Halliday have exerted great influences; the transformational generative grammar founded by Chomsky, the generative semantics by P. Postal and others, and the case grammar by D. J. Fillmore have once been renowned; other theories of grammar such as the Montague grammar founded by R. Montague, the generalized phrase structure grammar by G. Gazdar and others, the relational grammar by P. Perlmutter and others, and the lexical-functional grammar by J. Bresnan, also once led the trend, respectively.

Of the seven cases I employ to seek the outer rootstock, tagmemics and valence grammar are hardly the mainstream of current linguistics. To examine whether or not a theory is strongly interpretative and penetrating, we must let it be faced with objects as many as possible. After all, these two grammatical theories prevailed before. They can be said working to a certain extent in that they can offer different interpretive

G. Qian, *The Theory of Language Holography*,
https://doi.org/10.1007/978-981-16-2039-3_6

perspectives and support the theory of language holography from different aspects, and they do not occupy much room here, so I chose them.

In this chapter, I will use several cases to illustrate how the theory of language holography interprets the various theories of language. Each theory of language is a sort of viewpoint or perspective, but what is interesting is, you will eventually find that **many perspectives can find their rootstock in the structure of the world, and they will meet in the structure of the cosmos**. This is what I mean when I say that some theories of language can find their rootstock outside themselves. For instance, when comparing tagmemics with the law of cosmos holography, we can get a general mode to infer the relations between other theories of language and linguistic disciplines on the one hand and the law of cosmos holography on the other. We cannot compare one by one all the linguistic theories and disciplines with the law of cosmos holography insomuch as the workload is beyond the length of this book, it is impossible for me to make clear the broad and abundant contents one by one, and the redundant comparisons one after another might not be necessary or preferable to the readers also.

Necessary theoretical memorandum:

"The law of biology holography" holds, "The distributing results of all the parts with incompletely identical biological properties turn the holographic node into a microcosm of the whole to different extents, and the holographic nodes are similar to one another to different extents. We call this the law of biology holography."[1] That is to say, a single cell of the organism embraces all the information of the latter.

The fundamental thought of the law of cosmos holography is: any system whatsoever embraces all the information of the whole cosmos. Thus comes the "multum in parvo" of the theory of holography. In brief, the law of cosmos holography is: one is all, and all is one. Of the ten major principles of the theory of cosmos holography, the most fundamental part is: the first principle, namely, the part is holographic with the whole. This is the cornerstone of the whole edifice of the theory of cosmos holography, being the most fundamental and important; the fifth one, namely, homogeneity necessarily means isomorphism, isomorphism holography, holography isomorphism, and isomorphism homogeneity, the three being equivalent and absolutely identical to one another; the sixth one, namely, the infinite holographic recursive structure; the ninth one, namely, the law of holistic identity. The part is the whole, the whole the part, the two being absolute identical to one another.[2]

The fundamental state of the law of language holography is: in each level of language's morpheme-word-phrase-clause-sentence-discourse, the part is holographic with the whole; one part contains the same information as the others; each holographic node has its counterpart or similar information in the whole and other nodes, respectively, namely, each holographic node in the system becomes, to a different extent, a microcosm of the whole.

[1]Zhang (1980, 1985).

[2]Wang and Yan (1995, p. 306).

1 Tagmemics

Tagmeme is another viewpoint of observing language, another perspective of seeing the problem. People can observe the varying aspects of something which either heads for a nuclear peak of experience or content or leaves it. This mode tentatively focusing on variation is a wave view of the circumstances. As to the application of this "wave" theory, in tagmemics, we can observe that the vowel /o/ in *go* is articulated by means of rounding the lips before expanding them backward, and that the /g/ in *go* is articulated by the vocal organ at the front part whereas that in *give* by it in a flat state. In grammar, a wave component might be manifested in the fusion of the rapidly articulated words, say, when rapidly articulated, *come here* are fused into *kmere*. A field view is focused on the system or the subsystem rather than the segmentation of the units (The units are segmented due to the fact that human presumes that the units have certain borders at some point and that they do not change). The application of the theory of "field" can be thus assumed: in the field view of tagmemics, we can focus on the holistic curve process of a tagmeme. In grammar, the "filed" view is employed to record (trace) a set (or a matrix, i.e., mode) of clause types.

Considering the statements of the founder of tagmemic grammar, nevertheless, we have different ideas. Language form can correspond to the matter's particle, wave, or field. Doesn't it mean that the form of language structure is embedded in the forms of all other matters in the material world? This condition of originating from and being embedded in each other is certainly based on the common information. Reversely inferred, the conclusion is: **without the information pattern and structure similar to other material worlds, language could not share the form of movement with other matters. That they share the form of movement is certainly due to the fact that they share the information pattern and structure. This is the holographic state between language and the world**.

Let us start from tagmeme. Tagmeme is used to analyze language's basic units.

The first aspect of the holographic relationship between tagmemics and the law of cosmos holography is: **the particle property of language units is exactly the repetition of the cosmic structure**.

Pike contends that language is a behavior, a part of the whole human behavior. Human behavior and all things in the cosmos consist of units which appear in the fashion of being embedded in each other and which constitute the whole system of hierarchy. The behavior is composed of units, say, the three meals of the morning, afternoon, and evening are included in the behavioral activities in a day which again are included in those in a week which, still, are included in those in a month. The same holds to language units, namely, morpheme is included in word, word in phrase, phrase in clause, clause in sentence, and so on and so forth.

Here I would like to mention this by passing: as to the parlance that language is a behavior and human behavior consists of units, J. L. Austin (1961) holds the same view. He believes that the world is composed of objects with kinds of attributes. Human life is also composed of actions one after another.

Let us return to Pike. He holds that language unit is of the property of particle. De facto, language is a sort of language stream, and we cannot but separate it into isolated structure units for the sake of seeing it clearly when studying it (It is like seeing the close-ups in the film: it is originally a complete person which, nevertheless, is set aside tentatively to give way to the minute detail of the tip of the brow on the face. The detail of language is "particle"—the author). Phoneme is a particle, so is syllable, stressed group, rhythm group, or the like; similarly, morpheme is a particle, so is word, phrase, clause, or the like. That which is particularly noteworthy is, these particles, to wit., structure units, are in the state of the lower level being embedded in the higher one which is again embedded in the still higher one. As to a particle, there are bigger ones above it, and there are smaller ones below it. He says that this is observing language from the static perspective, and to put the words one by one into the dictionary and to analyze the sentences one by one are both the application of "particles."

Are the cosmos' structure units also the case?

All the systems and levels of the cosmos are mutually penetrated and embraced. "The macro cosmos embraces innumerable micro ones, the big system innumerable small ones, the high level innumerable low ones, and each microcosmos, low level, or small system is the microcosm of the macro, high, or big ones respectively. We call this "Chinese embedded box" structure the holographic recursive structure."[3] It cannot be more clearly elucidated here: the cosmos is characterized by the higher level embracing the lower ones, and it is a Chinese embedded box structure. It is my contention that this is the innermost source of the parlances with regard to language, namely, "Its structure units are always characterized by the lower level being embedded in the higher one" and "As to a particle, there are bigger ones above it, and there are smaller ones below it."

The second aspect of the holographic relationship between tagmemics and the cosmos is: **the wave property of language units is exactly the repetition of the cosmic wave**.

Pike regards language's structure units as a sort of "wave," contending that there are innumerable waves in language, and that the whole language is composed of waves, which is a method of considering problems in a dynamic fashion. This view comes from the fact that language stream cannot be separated into isolated parts. For instance, we cannot cut/bed/ into three isolated tones of /b/, /e/, and /d/ (In Chinese, we cannot articulate "*gou*狗" (dog) into "/g/ /ou/"——the author, the same below) but must combine the syllables. The combination per se indicates that these phonemes cannot be isolated from one another. Nor can syllables or words be articulated in isolation from one another, or else people could not get them. In daily life, if someone reads with this isolating method, he must have other fish to fry. I still remember that when I was young, I studied at Jingzhou Middle School in Hubei province. There once prevailed among my classmates a speech act virtually taken as a game: to articulate some word in isolation. Say, when one said "*Ni shi yi tiao /g //ou/*你是一条/g/ /ou/ (You are a dog)," the other would return by cursing "*Ni zhen bu shi ge /d/ /ong/ /x /*

[3]Wang and Yan (1995, p. 54).

/i/ 你真不是一个 /d/ /ong/ /x/ /i/ (You are really despicable)." The interpretation in pragmatics is this: in the pragmatic inference model, Stephen C. Levinson presented three quite influential principles——Quantity Principle (Q-principle), Information Principle (I-principle), and Manner Principle (M-principle). M-principle mentions "There must be a reason for weirdness." In normal language stream, it is usually not hard to differentiate how many syllables there are, but people have no idea definitely segmenting them one by one. It cannot be determined as to where each syllable's beginning or end is located, where the borderlines between adjacent syllables are, or the like. These situations make people regard language units as "waves" like the waves hitting the shore, namely, they can be counted on by one, the borderlines between them however fuse and overlap with one another, being indistinguishable. In English, when articulated rapidly, *Come here* will become *C' m' ere* (and *sons and daughters* will become *sonsan' daughters*. In Chinese, when it comes to the monosyllables ending the words, most of them are finals except for a few /n/s and /ng/s, so they can hardly form the "consonant-prior-to-vowel" combination between words like English. Contrariwise, there are too many English words ending with consonants so that they are easily combined with the successive words starting with a vowel). In normal articulation, it is usually that before a sound ends, another one already begins, namely, the vocal organs continuously move with no pause. The fusion and overlapping as such also occurs in grammatical structure. For instance, in *We saw him come*, *him* is the object of *saw*, but it is also the action subject of *come*, so the two "S + V" structures overlap with one another. (In Chinese, similar telescopic forms where the object is simultaneously the subject like "*Wo qing ta lai* 我请他来 [I invite him to come] are quite common. I contend that this phenomenon is one of the recursive structures of language, please see Sect. 2 of Chapter 5, the holographic observation of language recursiveness.) This phenomenon of vague borderline is visible everywhere in syntactic analysis, say, the *on* in *This depends on two factors*. Does *on* constitute the compound verb *depend on* with *depend* or constitute as a preposition the prepositional phrase *on two factors*?

Since it is hard to distinguish, why the factual language stream is speakable and audible?

Pike offers a great answer: the wave has its nucleus, i.e., the kernel part of the wave——the peak, and it also has its margin, i.e., the peripheral part——the edge. Being the center of the attentions of the utterer and the listener, the wave peak is easily determined; the wave edge on the other hand is easily fused or overlapped with other units, which bring about the vagueness of the borderline. In fact, so long as we can differentiate the wave peak, we can differentiate the units without definitely drawing the specific borderline peripheral to the units (the peripheries are nothing but the connected and overlapped parts when one sound slides to another). It can thus be seen that that which is produced by the utterer in practical language is wave whereas that which is heard by the listener is units one after another. On the whole, it is a consideration of problems from the dynamic perspective to regard language's structural units as "waves," and to think that there are innumerable waves in language and that the whole language consists of waves.

Is the fusing and overlapping phenomenon of the front wave and the back one cosmic? Is there the wave phenomenon in the cosmos?

"No matter is without the property of wave. Waves permeate the cosmos. Therefore, any piece (or particle or ball) of matter is different from others merely on the width of function distribution, and they principally permeate the whole cosmos."[4] Since waves permeate the whole cosmos, they must overlap with one another, being continuous without borderline. That we regard language units as waves comes from this property of the natural waves. Seen from the perspective of the theory of cosmos holography, there is no independent and stationary substance in the cosmos, and no system has an absolute borderline. It seems that this parlance obliterates the clearly existent, visible, and touchable substances. De facto, "Substances are nothing but the agglomerating or scattering relations, and things are merely the aggregates of the relations or a set of networks. Once these relations are cut off, this particular system would collapse. This is the nonlocality or omni-locality of the holographic node. Holographability is exactly the source of the vagueness of things in that it shows that things are characterized by being this and that simultaneously, you are in me and I am in you, and that things are merely aggregates of relations which, whereas, are changing all the time hence indeterminate. Indeterminateness is one of the properties of vagueness."[5] That is to say, the holographic node of the cosmos is characterized by nonlocality or omni-locality, and holographability is exactly the source of the vagueness of things. This recognition above regards language unit as the source of the wave, and of the field as is discussed in what follows.

The third aspect of the holographic relationship between tagmemics and the cosmos is: **the field property of language units is exactly the repetition of the cosmic field**.

Pike holds that in a language system, a language structural unit will always share something with other ones or differ from them in comparison. The case is so in horizontal or longitudinal comparisons, or in the flat or spacial relations. For instance, in English:

	Labial	Alveolar	Velar
Obstruent Voiceless	p	t	k
Obstruent Voiced	b	d	g
Nasal	m	n	

In this matrix, each sound is related to those before and after it, or left and right to it, forming together a network of relation. This network and the sum of the units in it constitute a "field." What is important here is, the whole field is itself also a unit, an expressing mode of language's structural unit. That which it stresses, nevertheless, is the status of each unit in the field, and the interconnections between the units, which differs from the conditions of particle or wave. Given that "field" is also a unit of

[4]Ibid., p. 169.

[5]Ibid., p. 54.

language structure, we can naturally understand that there might be smaller fields inside it, and bigger ones above it. (Chinese phonetic alphabet can also be processed into many such relationships between big and small fields. It is just that complete signs of Chinese phonetic alphabet cannot be found in the computer, so we suspend it.) The following is a field pertinent to phrase which, of course, can be embraced by a bigger one:

	Noun Phrase	Verb Phrase	Adjective Phrase	Adverb Phrase
Single subject phrase	an old gentleman	…	…	…
Multiple subject phrase	…and…	…	…	…

In the same vein, I can supplement it with such fields of which the prior one is embraced by the posterior one (in the following formula, < refers to "is embraced by"):

clause < compound sentence < sentence group < discourse

What is the condition of field in the cosmos?

In essence, **the cosmos consists of embedded networks of relation**. The network as such is field. As was stated afore, "Substances are nothing but the alliterating or scattering relations, and things are merely the aggregates of the relations or a set of networks. Once these relations are cut off, this certain system would collapse." The law of the cosmos' three-layer fields means: "All things even the cosmos as a whole have three layers of inside, middle, and outside fields which are interconnected and united with each other and constitute a unified three-dimensional typological network. This proves that field information always permeates the whole cosmos. The fields of all things and the cosmos as a whole like the field of main and collateral channels by no means merely exist in their figures but simultaneously exist in the internal emptiness and the external space of the whole, and constitute the changing and moving unified three-dimensional topological networks."[6] In the unified cosmic field, the change of any smaller one will directly or indirectly provoke the corresponding change of all the things, all the fields, even the cosmos as a whole, which can indeed be said "The pulling of one piece of hair will affect the whole body."

The field in the structural unit of language is merely a tiny constituent of the cosmic field. In other words, the field property of language units is nothing else than a microcosm of that of the cosmos.

Comprehensively seen, the particle, wave, and field properties of language are a rough metaphor of the structure of human language. By saying that language is of the particle, wave, and field properties, we in fact mean that they are the results of human beings' observation of language by virtue of the cosmos' structure. The observation as such proves in all respects the holographic relations between language and the cosmos. In addition, when speaking of language's particle, wave, and field properties, we may as well unite them into one field——the holographic unified field of the cosmos. "The information is material, and the cosmos is united into

[6]Ibid., p. 429.

information. The cosmic information exists in an infinite intensive fashion, namely, it exists in a state of infinitely approaching absolute or limitless continuity. The totality of this state is the unified field of cosmic information."[7]

2 The Theory of Ferdinand de Saussure

2.1 The Holographic Observation of Saussure's Differentiation Between Langue and Parole

Saussure thinks that we should put the foothold at two aspects from the very beginning: the execution of language and parole, the former being a regulation, the latter the expression of speeches.[8] "It is both a social product of the faculty of speech and a collection of necessary conventions that have been adopted by a social body to permit individuals to exercise that faculty,"[9] and parole is the individual's act when executing his own function, and the means he uses is the social convention, i.e., language.[10] He says that language is a grammatical system which does not show itself but hides in the brain of every one. Parole is the execution of language, the concrete expression of it. Language is abstract and steady whereas parole is concrete and changing.

Be that as it may, if the holographic nodes in the language system of everyone's brain do not correspond one by one to the spoken parole (language's substantial morpheme—word—phrase—clause—sentence—discourse), how can it prove that what he or she uses is language system? Albeit the words uttered each time by a person are a part of the grammatical system in his/her mind, the part is holographic with the whole. When his/her utterances remain to be isomorphic to and homogeneous with that which is reserved in his/her own brain or the brains of the other members in the language group, it would bring about an absurd phenomenon: one's utterances are incomprehensible to him/herself! Let alone to others. This is because your utterances are not isomorphic to that which is reserved in the brain of another one. If there is isomorphism, it necessarily means homogeneity. Isomorphism necessarily means holography.

---

[7]Ibid., p. 310.

[8]Cf. Liu (1997, pp. 87–92).

[9]Saussure (1959, p. 9).

[10]Cf. Liu (1997, pp. 87–92).

2.2 *The Holographic Observation of the Syntagmatic Relation Among Linguistic Signs*

The sign signifier (opposite to the signified) is a sort of sound in parole (uttered words), so they cannot but emerge one by one chronologically, and two elements cannot emerge simultaneously in a split second; in this connection, it is a time, a line, or a chain. Different from the visual sign, auditory sign can only take time as its foundation hence is unidimensional. By virtue of this property, Saussure differentiates two relations among language signs: one is syntagmatic relation, the other being associated relation. Associated relation is paradigmatic relation. **Syntagmatic relation means that each sign is opposed to the signs before and after it for the sake of obtaining its own value**.

What is syntagmatic relation? Analyzed by means of the inner state of language holography, for example, *If the weather is nice, we'll go out*, syntagmatic relation is holographic. Due to the constraint from the sign *whether* (singular form) before it, *to be*'s value is situated at the transitional part (to *nice*) of the "rheme," and can only become *is*. That is to say, *is* embraces the singular information of the language sign (*weather*) before it; otherwise, why *is* in lieu of *are* is used? Differently put, the singular form of *weather* and the information in *it* embrace one another. The *nice* still after it becomes the main part of the rheme. On this ground, the rheme value of *is nice* is determined in the opposite state to *weather* before it. In the same vein, we can determine reversely, according to *is nice*, that the *weather* before it is the value of theme. In the same vein, again, we can point out that *go* is *go* rather than *goes, went, going, gone*, or *have gone* insomuch as it is constrained by the language sign *will* before it and *we* still before. In other words, *go* forms a unified informational relation to the *we'll* before it.

As regards the holographic observation of language's linearity, please also see "Language linearity" in Chapter 5, "The outer rootstock of the different properties of language." These two parts can enlighten one another.

2.3 *The Holographic Observation of Synchronic and Diachronic Linguistics*

Another great contribution of Saussure is that he differentiates synchronic and diachronic linguistics. Synchronic linguistics studies the conditions of a language in some stage during its historical progression, i.e., linguistic state, rather than considering how this state evolves. Diachronic linguistics studies the variation of a language over a long period. As to this, Saussure gave a quite vivid metaphor: if language is compared to a tree trunk, when it is cut open longitudinally, the annual ring will present a complex design; when it is cut open horizontally, the annual ring will present another design. These two designs are drastically different but closely related to one another: the smaller designs on the cross section are the specific states of those on the longitudinal section, and the latter is the extension of the former. The designs on the cross section are like the state of language in some period, and those on the longitudinal section are like the long evolution process of language.

How do the two linguistic states embrace one another?

Without the longitudinal growth (of the tree), there would not be horizontal extension. The longitudinally growing tree trunk embraces all the biological information of any cross section whatsoever. Reversely, the biological information of a cross section is the start of the information and basis of the future trunk. If the biological information did not develop from a cross section, how would there be the tall trunk (the holistic information)? Insofar as English is concerned, without **some** parlance (namely the synchronic state at that time, e.g., fōti [There was a - above o]) in ancient times (the first stage), where could **this** present one (e.g., feet) come? To put it in another way, language's historical development and evolution embraces its static state and vice versa. The parlance of *fōti* exists in a state (I presume that it is cross section A) of ancient English (the first stage), whereas that of *feet* exists in a state (I presume that it is cross section B) of modern English. Albeit section A and B are not completely coincident with one another, they are surely generally so, or else section B would be a totally different language, which is apparently not the case. That literatures in ancient English can be translated into modern English is an evident proof. That is to say, section B has counterparts or similar information to section A in the holistic fashion——there are coincident or similar aspects between fōti and feet. Plainly, ancient and modern English are in such a condition: the parts embrace identical information; the individual holographic nodes in language system become the microcosms of the whole to different extents.

In Saussure, the holographic situation is reproduced in a wonderful metaphor——the rules of chess are like the grammar, chess pieces the language signs; the value of chess pieces are determined by the rules, that of language by the grammar. The importance of each chess piece is determined by its position at that time and, correspondingly, the value of each language sign is determined by its position in the sentence.

The importance of each chess piece is determined by its position at that time. When the red "pawn" is situated before the black "commander in chief," the former is of fatal killing power to the latter whatever their respective original "status" is; once the "pawn" goes so far that it is situated after the "commander in chief," whereas, it loses the fatal aggressiveness. Even the ever triumphant "chariot" will be killed when it is situated at the killing site of the "elephant" (i.e., 田) or the "horse" (i.e., 日) whatever their respective original power or status is. In this way, the positions of all the chess pieces constitute a system of relation. Once a system of relation is constituted by the dominant and the dominated, the eating and the eaten, the attacking and the defending, and the like, you are in me and I am in you. At this time, the mutual embracement of the part and other parts, or the part and the whole, cannot become more obvious.

The value of each language sign is determined by its position in the sentence. For example, once a noun is situated at the subject, it can dominate the changes of the number of the verb as the predicate: *There* ***was*** *a man named Lazarus* ***who had***

***fallen** ill*. In the main clause, *a man* dominates *was*; in the subordinate clause, *who* dominates *had fallen*. For another example, an adverb or a phrase indicating time will influence the variations of time and tense of the predicate verb after it: in *After this, he said to his disciples...*, *After this* determines the past indefinite tense of *said*. Sometimes, there is no adverbial indicating time or state in a sentence, and so long as there are sufficient cognitive conditions in the context, they will replace the language units as the adverbial to constrain the following sentence from changing greatly. For instance, in the *Gospel of John* of the *New Testament* of The Bible, there was a Lazarus who had been dead for four days, but Jesus decided to revive him. On seeing Jesus, the younger sister of the dead, Mary, knelt at his feet, saying, "O sir, if you *had* only *been* here my brother *would* not *have* died."[11] In this sentence with a virtual context, *had* in the front and *would have* in the back are both language units without meanings. The seemingly redundant language units attached to the predicate verb are the results of the fact that the predicate is dominated by the previous adverbial or the context substitutable for it.

Looking back at the corroboration afore, we can see that the importance of each chess piece is determined by its position at that time, and, correspondingly, the value of each language sign is determined by its position in the sentence. Playing chess is a game of sign, and language application is also a "game" of sign, both being, respectively, a holographic node in the cosmos. **The two seemingly irrelevant holographic nodes however have apparent corresponding states, namely isomorphic and homogeneous states. Isn't this their holography**?

3 The Systemic View-Point of Language

The man who first presented "Language is a system" is certainly the renowned Saussure. (Nevertheless, he remains to demonstrate why language is a system. In Sect. 5 of Chapter 3 of this book, I demonstrate, by virtue of the properties of modern system, why language is a system.) My view is, "Language is first and foremost a system of signs, so we must appeal to semiotic science. Isn't that an obvious thing?" Please note, I put stress on **sign** rather than **system**.

Notwithstanding that, I consider language signs as a **system of relation**. It is my contention that "Language is not a substance but a form", and "It is a system of relation."

I compare the rule of chess to grammar, the chess piece to language sign, arguing that the importance of each chess piece is determined by its position at the time, which is one of the proofs. I also say in several other places that language is a distinctive system, a system of relation in which each component is defined according to its relation to other ones.

[11] All the examples in this part are from *The Gideons International "The Holy Bible" (The Authorized King James Version)*, National Publishing Company, Nashville, Tennessee, 1975.

Someone notes that in language, there are also constituents depending on no contradictory relation. It is my contention that this case cannot change the mainstream of the relation system of language. This mainstream is manifested in these: (1) The binarity on which Saussure puts particular stress exists in a universal fashion in language system, say, voiced/voiceless, vowel/consonant, singular/plural, and so on; (2) linkage relation (see the second question in the last section); (3) choice relation (ibid.); (4) particularly, "Each component is defined according to its relation to other ones." "Each component" is a part, so is "other components," If "each" part and "other" ones fail to embrace each other's information, how can "each" be defined by "other"? The simplest example is: $4 = 1 + 1 + 1 + 1$; $4 = 1 + 3$; $4 = 2 + 2$; $4 = 3 + 1$… If, in these equations, the left is not equal to the right and they do not embrace one another, how can the equation be tenable?

Later, the Prague School (also called Functionalists or School of Functionalist Grammar, they hold structural-functional language view) inherited and developed Saussure's view that language is a system. Of the fundamental views of the Prague School (with Vilem Mathesius, Nikolai Trubetskoi, Roman Jacobson, Vachek J. as the representatives), the second one is "Language is a system of value rather than the convergence of thousands and thousands of irrelevant isolated phenomena." On this, Trubetskoi and Jacobson made the greatest contributions. Jacobson believes that no component in language system can be studied in isolation. To correctly assess a linguistic component, we must make clear of its relation to other co-existent components. To correctly understand language's evolution, we must regard it as the holistic evolution of the whole. During the process of evolution, the relation between components is often changed or replaced by other relations; the change as such is mainly aimed at maintaining or recovering the balance and the steadiness of language system.

In the statement above, the most important is, I think, "To correctly assess a linguistic component, we must make clear of its relation to other co-existent components." In *Children make a room beautiful*, for instance, the predicate verb *make* leads three actants (namely, one subject, one object, and one objective complement. According to valent grammar, *make* is a trivalent verb). To correctly assess *children*, *room*, or *beautiful*, we must be clear about their respective relation to *make*; to correctly assess *make*, we must be clear about its relations to *children*, *room*, or *beautiful*; to correctly assess *a*, we must be clear about its relation to *room*. **The foundation of such intertwined elucidations is deeply hidden in the holographic state**. We have discussed in detail this state in Sect. 4 of Chapter 3, "The argument for the state of the inner language holography in terms of the theory of system." This holographic state means that the parts are holographic with the whole; the parts share the same information with one another; each holographic node in language system has its counterpart or similar information, respectively, in the whole and other nodes. That is to say, each holographic node of the system becomes, to a different extent, a microcosm of the whole.

After the 1950s, scholars of the Neo-Prague School inherited the fundamental principles of their forerunners, and developed as well as replenished the latter's language theories. An important notion of this school is, language is not an absolutely unified and closed system; but rather, it is an open and incompletely balanced system, being composed of many interdependent subsystems. These subsystems are usually called levels of language, phoneme, syntax, and the like. **Due to the fact that these subsystems depend on one another and cannot be separated, changes in one subsystem might provoke those in one or two other subsystems**. For instance, changes in lexicon will necessarily influence the level of syntax. Changes in the phonemic system might also provoke those in other systems. Changes in phonemes might also be provoked by those in other systems, particularly those at the levels of morphology and lexicon.

One of the typical traits of holography is that one holographic node (equivalent to a subsystem in a system) is inseparable from other ones, and changes in one holographic node might provoke those in one or two other nodes. This situation happens to correspond to that in language system, namely, "Changes in one subsystem might provoke those in one or two other subsystems." The corresponding as such is holographic relation. May I ask: if the information in these subsystems did not embrace one another (like a person's kidneys and urinary system embrace one another), how could it change from one situation to another (like nephritis would provoke the pathological changes of the urinary system)? How can changes in other systems be provoked?

Lous Hjelmslev, a representative (with *Prolegomena to a Theory of Language* (1943) as his magnum opus) of Copenhagen School, discovers via discourse analysis that the existence of the whole and the part completely depends on their interdependence; the whole is determined by the sum of its parts; each part is determined by the sum of the interdependences between other parts, between it and the whole, it and the smaller parts, and between the smaller parts. That is to say, a whole is composed of many relations rather than many independent substances; it is not the single substance but the relationship between the inside and the outside of the substance that has scientific reality. On this point, Hjelmslev's views are coincident in toto with Saussure's, namely, "Language is a form rather than a substance," and "It is a system of relations."

"The existence of the whole and the part completely depends on their interdependence; the whole is determined by the sum of its parts; each part is determined by the sum of the interdependences between other parts, between it and the whole, it and the smaller parts, and between the smaller parts." It is amazing that the relation description discovered in linguistic discourse is identical to the description of the holographic relation of any system in the cosmos. For an example of holographic analysis, let us have a look at a passage by means of the description of relation:

Cleanest airport[12]

Shenzhen Airpot, on May 25, was rated the cleanest airport all over China by two specialists from World Health Organization, after a very strict examination and inspection tour. The airport spent nearly 30 million yuan, over the last thresh years, on upgrading the medical and sanitary facilities, on improving the grounds by planting trees and renovating the lawns and restructuring the food and eating areas.

---

[12] *Guangzhou Morning Post*, June 2, 2000, p. 1.

The whole's information is determined by the sum of its parts' information (i.e., Hjelmslev's "The whole is determined by the sum of its parts"): after reading this passage, the reader might draw a conclusion that Shenzhen airport is the cleanest of all the airports in China. How does this total information, *cleanest airport*, come from? It is determined by the sum of the information offered by each part, say, (1) spent nearly 30 million yuan + (2) upgrading the medical and sanitary facilities + (3) planting trees + (4) renovating the lawns + (5) restructuring the food and eating areas. That is to say, the information of *cleanest airport* is embraced in the five pieces, and so on.

The mutual embracement of information between parts (i.e., Hjelmslev's "the interdependence between parts"): in the English news above, *May* is not that in *May I come in* but the expression of the month May. That is to say, the "25" (and the whole situation) after May determines that the signified of May is not "may" but "May the fifth month"; the signified of examination is not "the test that students take" but "the check and evaluation of administrative affairs," and this definite information is determined by two other pieces of information, namely, *specialists from World Health Organization* before it and *inspection tour* after it; and the meaning of facility is "an equipment" rather than "a department or college of a university." The information as such is embraced in the two parts of *Shenzhen Airport* and *medical and sanitary* before it; in the same vein, the information that *areas* does not refer to "a region" but to "a hotel, a bar, or a snack bar" is embraced in that of *food and eating* before it.

Hjelmslev finds that this relation of interdependence is not single but multiple. If the existence of A takes that of B as the premise, and the existence of B also takes that of A as the premise, the relation between A and B is called interdependence; if the existence of A takes that of B as the premise, whereas the existence of B does not take that of A as the premise, the relation between A and B is called determination; if A and B do not take each other's existence as the premise of theirs, but they can still coexist harmoniously in the same system, the relation between them is constellation. In a process, the interdependence between two units is called solidarity, in a system, complementarity; the determination in a process is called selection, that in a system specification; the constellation in a process is called combination, that in a system autonomy. That which can help to make these relations clearer is the form below:

	interdependence	determination	constellation
process:	solidarity	selection	combination
system:	complementarity	specification	autonomy

In language system, such complicated relations in process and system show the state of the inner language holography.

Till the era of Halliday, the system of relation developed into systemic linguistics, and he became an outstanding representative of the latter. The first fundamental principle of systemic linguistics is, importance is attached to language's sociological traits; the second one is, language is considered as a form of "doing" rather than a form of "knowing"; the third one is, importance is attached to the descriptions of individual languages and individual variants; the fourth one is, the concept of "cline" is employed to interpret many linguistic facts. There is a phenomenon of fuzziness in language, so the concept "cline" is created. A cline is a "scale" in which everything gradually turns into something else; the two poles of a "scale" are quite different, it is very hard however to judge where the borderline between them is. Some languages belong to category A, some others to B, and still others are located between clines A and B.

Why does everything in the "scale" gradually turn into something else? Why is it that the two poles of a "scale" are quite different but it is hard to judge where the borderline between them is? According to the theory of language holography, the information between the parts of a cline embraces one another. If so, when "some things" do not embrace "some other things," how can the former turn into the latter? The embracement of holographic information is infiltrative and pervasive, so it is very hard to tell their borderline.

In Halliday's view, the system is a set of choices. Every language has many systems. For instance, number system: singular and plural; person system: the first person, the second person, and the third person; tense system: past tense, present tense, and future tense. He holds that language system is a network for people to make choices. When choices (e.g., person, number, transitivity, mood, tense, etc.) are made one by one in relevant systems, the sentence structure can be generated. The following sentence is a product of a series of choices: *here is your king, who comes to you in gentleness, riding on an ass, riding on the foal of a beast of burden.*[13] In terms of number, according to *your king*, *is* and *comes* are chosen before and after it, respectively. That is to say, *your king* (singular) in the subjective position has early potentially embraced the information of *is* and *comes*; in terms of transitivity, according to that of *comes*, *to* is chosen and added before *you*. In other words, the necessity of the appearance of this *to* is potentially embraced in the action verb *to come*; in terms of tense, *is* + *comes* + *riding* + *riding* are coincident with each other, and their tense forms are determined by the scene in which the utterer speaks: these four parts are coincident and harmonious at the level of information; when choices are made in at least the five systems of person, number, transitivity, mood, and tense, the sentence structure is generated. The choice of these five systems sufficiently expresses the network state in Halliday's terminology, namely, the state of the inner language holography in which the systems restrict and coordinate with each other.

[13]The Gideons International "The Holy Bible": New Testament: Matthew: Entering Jerusalem on a Donkey (The Authorized King James Version). National Publishing Company, Nashville, Tennessee, 1975.

4 Cognitive Grammar

The following discussions as regards cognitive grammar comes from the two literatures of Langacker R. W's *Foundations of Cognitive Grammar* (1987) and *Cognitive Grammar* (1995).[14]

The foundation of cognitive grammar is the three fundamental hypotheses as follows:

(1) Language is not a self-sufficient cognitive system; the description of language must take human's general cognitive law for reference. This article is directed upon a fundamental hypothesis of generative grammar: language is a self-sufficient system, and linguistic competence is independent of other cognitive abilities of human beings.

(2) Syntax is not a self-sufficient formal system; like lexicon, syntax and morphology are in essence a symbolic system established by people through long social practices; syntactic analysis cannot digress from meaning. This article is directed upon another fundamental hypothesis of generative grammar: syntax is a self-sufficient formal system, being independent of the lexical and semantic parts of language structure.

(3) The formal logic based on truth conditions is insufficient to describe meaning in that semantic description must take an open and unlimited knowledge system for reference. The meaning of a word is not merely a "situation" it forms in human brain, but also a specific mode of the formation as such, which is called imagery. This article is directed upon still another fundamental hypothesis of generative grammar: the means by which meaning is described is a formal logic based on truth conditions.

In this connection, there are three inseparable relations: linguistic cognitive abilities cannot digress from the general ones of human beings, and they embrace one another, which is the state of the inner language holography——this is the theme of Chapter 4 of this book; syntactic formal system cannot digress from language structure and meaning, and syntax and language structure embrace one another, which is also the state of the inner language holography; semantic description cannot digress from human's knowledge system which totally comes from the cultural accumulation of the society in which he/she is located, and semantic description and cultural accumulation form the state of the outer language holography (Chapter 8, "The holographic relation between language and culture," is particularly directed to this topic). These three inseparable relations are so to speak nothing but the states of the inner and the outer language holography.

Later, when introducing his cognitive grammar, Langacker (1995) noted that it was an overall unified theory of language structure. In his mind's eye, "The gist of cognitive grammar is that the latter can well be simplified to a series of symbolic structures." These symbolic structures are embedded in one after another.

[14]Cf. Shen (1994).

Cognitive grammar's view of meaning emphasizes "the process of conceptualization." Concept refers to perception, emotion, conception, recognition, and the like. The assignment of semantics is to describe the conceptual structure. Conceptual structure is a product of cognitive precess, so the ultimate goal of semantics is to elucidate the specific cognitive process. In the network of verbal meaning, different nodes or relations are different at the level of "prominence," and the most prominent meaning is in general the prototype of a word. For instance, the prototype meaning of *ring* is a piece of jewelry that one wears on one's finger, and the meaning furthest from the prototype but remaining in the same category is its marginal meaning. When describing the meanings of words, cognitive grammar refuses "semantic properties" in favor of "cognitive domains." Cognitive domain is defined as the conceptual area concerned when some semantic structure is described. It may be a simple perception or concept, but it may also be a considerably complicated knowledge system. Semantic description needs encyclopedic knowledge, and there is no definite borderline between linguistic and non-linguistic knowledge.

When we describe the meanings of a word, it is not enough to merely reach the cognitive field, we need to describe the conventionalized imagery of the word, namely, we need to form a specific mode of concept or of conceptual structure.

Cognitive grammar holds that there are only three kinds of unit in language: phonetic unit, semantic unit, and symbolic unit, and nothing else. Phonetic and semantic units are the two poles constituting symbolic unit, namely, symbolic unit is bipolar and can be manifested in ([meaning]/[speech]). For instance, *pencil* as a symbolic unit is ([PENCIL]/[pencil]) in which the capital letters represent the semantic pole, the lower-case letters the phonetic pole. "Symbolic" means that a certain form represents certain meanings, and that the representation as such is conventional. An important view of cognitive grammar is, the big or small units and various grammatical categories and structures in traditional grammatical analysis are all symbolic units.

In cognitive grammar, categorical relation is also a symbolic unit. Cognitive grammar breaks the boundaries between lexicon, morphology, and syntax, contending that this demarcation is also artificial, and that there is merely the difference as regards the degree of abstraction and concreteness between lexicon (morphology) and syntax. For instance, both the word *pencil* and "a noun expression" are symbolic units, just that one is concrete, the other being abstract. This also means that syntax is not a self-sufficient system.

Grammatical constructions are also symbolic units. Cognitive grammar aims to elucidate from the perspective of cognition how grammatical constructions are formed, and what the connections between the component structures, and between them and the compound structures, look like. Langacker believes that the formation of any grammatical construction is always concerned with the correspondence between two component structures, and that compound construction is the result of the congruence of two corresponding component structures.

In terms of research method, cognitive grammar's essential property is, it does not intentionally pursue formalization, nor does it interpret form via form; rather, it starts from meaning and concept to investigate the collocation between them and form, and to explore language categories and the conceptual foundation of language structure.[15]

Seen from the overall situation of cognitive grammar, semantic description is more than that with regard to the objective truth conditions, but it is also that of the subjectively formed "imageries." Syntax is no longer a self-sufficient system or the center of grammar; a certain form represents certain meanings, as is established through long social practices, and the same holds to lexicon and syntax. Language is no longer an independent cognitive system, and human's linguistic competence is inseparable from his/her general cognitive ability.

This fundamental principle coincides with the theory of language holography. Language is no longer an independent cognitive system but a system embracing, and being embraced by, other cognitive abilities. As to this, there are detailed analyses in section one, "Cognitive linguistics and the theory of language holography," of Chapter 4, which can be taken for reference by you.

The inner communication between language and cognitive mode forms a relation of correspondence. Cognitive processes and results will be reflected on language forms. This state is nothing but the manifestation of the communication between them at the level of information. The corresponding communication as such is manifested in at least two points as follows:

First, the metaphor of cognitive mode corresponds to that in words. Metaphor is more than the general law of language form; rather, it is first and foremost the fundamental law of cognition. Exactly because cognition is performed in the mode of metaphor, there are large quantities of metaphoric responses at the level of language unit. In a dictionary, if a word has many meanings, most of them are usually given in the form of metaphoric extension in accordance with the prototype (i.e., the central meaning). For instance, the prototype meaning of *late* is *after the proper or usual time*, so a result of its metaphoric extension is *no longer alive*. The process of metaphoric extension from the former meaning (after the proper or usual time) to the latter one (no longer alive) is temporal.

Secondly, **the modularity generation in cognitive law corresponds to the movement of linguistic modularity.**

The movement and dissection of language form are usually manifested in segments, which can be called the movement of linguistic modularity. As to this, I believe that it surely appertains to the state of modularity in cognition.

An example of linguistic modularity is the duality-oriented discourse of Chinese. For instance, people might fail to understand, even might misunderstand, a single sentence (the former or the latter sentence, e.g., when either sentence of "One baby, install the contraceptive ring" and "Two babies, receive the ligation operation" emerges singly), and only the contrast between two sentences can form a discourse with apparent meanings. Orientation is the minimal information, so we couldn't understand a sentence with less information than it. It is of no problem to correctly understand the slogan of family planning written on the wall, say, "One baby, install the contraceptive ring; two babies, receive the ligation operation," since

[15]Zhang (1998, p. 9).

the two components coexist. In Sect. 3 of Chapter 8 of this book, I thus interpret this structure: "In language structure is condensed cultural vision." It is another approach to understand this according to cognitive law. It is related to human cognitive modularity. What kind of genetic state of modularity is it? Presumably, the conceptual process of the slogan-maker thus goes: "In the rural area, when a couple give birth to **one babe**, the wife is supposed to **install the contraceptive ring**; after **two babies**[16] were born, the husband is supposed to **receive ligation operation**." **The genesis of modularity might have a process of selection and elimination in accordance with needs**. Which one, of a series of concepts generations, is the most important, prominent, striking, and needed? We need to put them in order first, which is the selection and elimination. **The most important, prominent, striking, and needed modularities automatically come out and put themselves in order, and other ones automatically go ignored, which is both the genetic law of cognitive modularity and, it happens, the law of movement of linguistic modularity**. It does not matter when the former modularity is unclear, and we may just wait for the supplement or notation of the next one. It is my contention that the movement and dissection of language is necessarily a product of the selection and elimination of modularities in accordance with needs. The duality-oriented discourse of Chinese can perfectly interpret many phenomena of binary structure of Chinese (I will not unfold this here in that it will be discussed in another place).

From the analyses in this section, we see the inner communication and the correspondence between language and cognitive mode. This state is exactly the manifestation of their interconnection at the level of information. The correspondence between the metaphor of cognitive mode and that in words, and the correspondence between the generation of cognitive modularity and the movement of linguistic modularity (Chinese duality-oriented discourse) are nothing other than the evidence of the holography between language structure and cognitive process.

5 Valence Grammar

The collocation between the verb and the noun phrase (and the adjective phrase, adverbial phrase, verbal phrase, another clause, and so on) in a clause is strikingly similar to the combination among atoms in the matter. **If it is really the case, valence (or valency) grammar describing this state so to speak reflects the holographic state between language structure and the material one of the world, namely, the state of the outer language holography**.

Rudi Gebruers (1995) contends that valence grammar interprets the complicated language structure by means of the repeatedly emerging potentials combining the governors of language structure and some certain dependents. The structural potential of a governor cannot be inferred from the members in its lexical hierarchy. In this

[16]In this condition, the only one baby is usually a boy; as to the two babies, the first one is usually a girl—the translator.

situation, the governor is considered as owning a subclass-specific "valency" (not a chemical one in the true sense of the word), which resembles the capacity to combine chemical elements and some certain atoms. In this connection, when words like *rise*, *resemble*, *put*, etc., act as the valency-bearers and own the position of the verb, they are supposed to be considered as having different valency modes insomuch as they cannot be interchanged in the following context (say, *put* and *resemble* cannot be interchanged with *rise* in the first sentence in that they have different valency modes):

(1) Prices continue to rise.
(2) Twins often resemble each other.
(3) The secretary will put the papers on the desk.

Rudi Gebruers (1995) believes that there are two sorts of valency mode. One is "quantitative valency," the other being "qualitative valency." We must find the source of the lack of interchangeability and reveal the relationships between the different potentials of the forms with identical valency capacities. For instance, in the above context, the verb *drop* is a form having the same valency capacity as *rise*, and hence it can be interchanged with the latter. That with which valency is particularly concerned is the number of the needed dependents (This is "quantitative valency," namely, *rise* only needs one dependent, i.e., *prices*, *resemble* two, i.e., *twins* and *each other*, and *put* three, i.e., *the secretary*, *the paper*, and *on the desk*), and the innate properties of these dependents and their "roles" in the structures surrounding the valency maker (This is "qualitative valency," e.g., *the secretary* plays the role of the subject, *the papers* the object, and *on the desk* the adverbial).

Valence grammar is a sort of dependency grammar which analyzes the relationship between sentence components from their mutual dependence or subordinate relationship. Starting from this point alone, it already lays the foundation of holographic analysis: mutual dependence is a property of the system, and a system is necessarily holographic inside. The renowned French linguist, Lucien Tesniere, the founder of valence grammar, regards sentence as a whole, contending that the constituents of a sentence are more than the superficially seen words, but rather the relationships between them, and that this syntactic connection sets up the subordinate relationship between the governing and the subordinate words. Predicate verb is of the function of governing the noun or adverbial phrase, and in this relationship, the noun phrase constitutes the "actant," the adverbial phrase the "circontant." The number of the circontant might be infinite (theoretically) whereas that of the actant cannot be more than three: the subject and one or two objects. There are two actants in *The girl* ***is reading*** *the book*, three in *The girl* ***gave*** *him the book*. The number of the actant determines the "valency" of the verb (like the atom is of valencies), and the number of the verb's valency follows that of the actant. To this connection, the *read* in the first sentence above is a two-valency verb, and the *give* in the second a three-valency verb. The actant is the core and quintessence of the theory of valence grammar.[17] It can also be called "verb argument." It is plausible to interpret argument (i.e., the actants and circontants) from the perspective of meaning. For instance, Radford contends

[17]Cf. Zhi and Liu (2000).

that arguments are the "expressions which typically denote the participants to the activity or event described by a verb."[18]

Valence is understood in the broad sense as "A language sign is combined with other languages' so as to constitute the holistically evolutionary capacity with broader contents."[19] According to the strength of the valence function of the word, valence can be divided into the active and passive ones. The former refers to the word's capacity to govern its subordinate components (e.g., the *read* in the example sentence above governs *the girl* and *the book*), the latter its potential to depend on its governing word. At the level of syntactic form, valence can be divided into the necessary and non-essential ones. To most action verbs, the subject-object relational item is necessary as well as essential, which produces at least two valences. Situational factors (manifested in adverbials in a sentence) are secondary to the action verb. Notional words are all of the property of valence and the most complicated is verb valence. The verb having one actant (subject) is mostly intransitive, say, in *he stood here*, *to stand* is a monovalent verb. The intransitive verbs meaning existence, expression, etc., have two actants. The verbs having three actants are usually action verbs, e.g., *you will bear witness for me*. In some languages, the verb can have four or five actants. Compared with the verb, the noun has simpler valences. Words necessarily carrying valences include first of all verbs expressing action, and then property nouns, relational nouns, categorial nouns, and so on.

As regards the valence requirement of the verb, we can also give some Chinese examples.[20] For instance, in "张三的头发脱了不少" (A lot of **hair** of Tom falls out) or "张三脱了不少头发" (Tom loses a lot of **hair**), the requirement on valence of the verb "脱" (fall out; lose) is, the noun acting as the subject can also be an object; in "张三把大衣脱了下来" (Tom **took off** his trench coat) or "在昏迷中张三的大衣被人脱了下来" (The trench coat of the fainting Tom **was took off**), the valence situation of the "脱" (take off) is, both "把" and "被" are permitted to "be chemically combined"; how about the requirement on valence of the "脱" (miss) in "这一行脱了三个字" (Three characters are missing **in this line**)? It will choose the subject, namely, it does not accept a person as the subject, e.g., we cannot say "张三脱了三个字" (Three characters are missing **in Tom**); in "张三偷了些钱" (Tom stole some **money**) or "张三偷了李四一些钱" (Tom stole some money from **Dick**), the requirement on valence of the verb "偷" (steal) is, two objects are permitted to coexist; in "歹徒又抢了乘客" (The gangsters robbed the **passengers** again) or "歹徒又抢了银行" (The gangsters robbed the **bank** again), the item of meaning of "抢" is rob, and the requirement on valence of it is, the object can be both human and non-human (e.g., horse or habitation); in "张三终于把论文抢出来了" (Tom became the first one to finish the essay **at last**), or "你们必须抢在他们之前" (You **must** make it before them), the "抢" (being the first) presents a strict requirement on

[18]Radford (1997, p. 142).

[19]Лосев (1981).

[20]The several Chinese sentences are borrowed from Mr. Zheng Dingou's speech, "Lexical grammar and the compilation of the digital dictionary," on June 14, 2000, in Guangdong University of Foreign Studies.

"circonstant" or "modal-ant," namely, they cannot be omitted. We can see from these two example sentences that the valence of "抢" is, the circonstant (at last; must) is indispensable; in "张三摔了一跤,膝盖抢破了皮" (Tom fell and broke the skin on his **knees**), the requirement on valence is that the subject is indispensable, namely, we cannot change this sentence into "张三摔了一跤,抢破了皮" (Tom fell and broke the skin).

During the course of comparing the combinations of atoms and of sentence components, we can find many interesting similarities. At the level of matter, the combination of atoms constitutes molecules, but what would happen when a molecule loses an atom of it? A possible result is that it will no longer exist, and another one is that it might turn into a new molecule. When it comes to the collocation of sentence components, what would happen to the sentence (or a clause of it) when a component (here we call it "valence") in it is lost? A possible result is that it will no longer conform to grammar——corresponding to the fact that a molecule no longer exists, and another one is that it might still conform to grammar but its original meaning will change——corresponding to the fact that a molecule converts into a new one. What an interesting comparison it is! Let me give more examples. In *The ants died*, if you use *Died* instead, it is like a molecule loses an atom in it hence no longer exists, as a result of which the sentence will no longer exist, either. For another example, *I gave you the argument* is a normal sentence, but if an actant is lost, it will turn into, say, *I gave the argument*, which is just like a molecule loses an atom and turns into a new one. Albeit the new sentence is readable, its original meaning changes and it turns into another one. For still another example, *I do so very much wish for a little child!*[21] which, if changed into *A little child does so very much wish for me*, will have a completely reverse meaning, just like a molecule changes into another matter when the atoms in the former are reversely ordered.

That in which I am interested is, valence grammar provokes a question: from which perspective do people categorize and conceptualize language? The clarification of this question will make it clear how the combination in the clause greatly resembles the chemical one in the material world.

The generation of valence grammar is due to the fact that the founder of it found the similarities between language structure and the worldly matters. The term "valence/y" (valentia, валентность) is broadly used in chemistry, meaning the relationship and correspondence between the number of one atom and that of other ones in the chemical combination, namely, the combining capacity of one atom and a number of other ones. Take water as an example, since O is negatively bivalent, it entails two Hs for collaboration during the process of chemical combination with the positively univalent H. The steady water molecule is H_2O_1, abbreviated as H_2O. The combination of language signs (say, the verbs, nouns, etc., in the clause) are similar to the chemical combination of atoms, and that is why "valence" is borrowed and transplanted into linguistics from chemical sphere with the aim to indicate what

[21]Cited from A complete Andersen (English translation by W. A. & J. K. Craigie) Thumbelina. Also cf. *Complete Works of Andersen's Fairy Tales* (2nd Edition). Beijing: Tsinghua University Press, 2000, p. 32.

items are needed when a word is to refer to a certain situation. Valence grammar holds that each sentence embraces a subjective item and some subordinate ones, just like a matter embraces some major elements and some minor ones. The combination of the major and minor elements is mainly determined by the valence of the former; likewise, the combination of the verb and other sentence components is determined by the valence of the verb. For instance, in *Barbara will man the telephone switch-board*, the major elements *to man* requires a subject and an object, just like an O atom entails two H atoms for collaboration to form a steady H_2O molecule. The collaborative situation between the components of language structure is turned by some grammarians into valence grammar, which **exactly reflects the isomorphic holographic state between language structure and the cosmic matters**. We can see therefrom that valence grammar is by no means obtained by chance by some grammarian out of fantastic imagination. If there were not the structure (chemical valence) as such innate in the matter, no brain, however phantastic it is, would think of valence grammar. The Modestae School in the Middle Ages held that "If we can prove that there are certain connections between nature's laws and the inner ones of language, we can interpret the linguistic phenomena."[22] Undoubtedly, the founder of valence grammar found the certain connections as such, say, the collaboration between the verb and the noun in the clause resembles the chemical combination between two or three atoms in the matter. That is to say, the language system in human society and the material (chemical combination) system in nature are nothing but two nodes in mutual holography. On this account, **valence grammar can be regarded as a grammar interpreting linguistic phenomena, just like the theory of language holography is a theory interpreting language**.

6 Systemic Grammar

Systemic grammar is a theory of language analysis presented by Halliday (1964a, 1964b, 1966) on the basis of his development of J. R. Firth's theories. This theory establishes a set of levels and categories elucidating language form. The three fundamental levels are: form (the meaningful items namely grammar and lexicon composed of substances), substance (speech sounds and textual materials), and context (the relations between form and the environment, i.e., meaning). The four fundamental categories are: unit (carrying the modes of bracketing elements at any level, e.g., sentence, clause, tone group), structure (the arrangement of the structural segment of the mode, e.g., the subject—predicate—complement—modifier of "clause structure"), class (the aggregation of the items playing some role in a higher-level structure, e.g., noun phrase, syllable), and **system** (**arranging the classes longitudinally for people to choose**). In addition, he also sets up three "scales" to explicate the relations between the categories in this theory and the observed speech acts, and so on.

[22] Qtd. Liu (1997, p. 25).

Merely knowing the fundamental levels and categories will not make us immediately understand the essence of systemic grammar. The most important knowledge on understanding systemic grammar is, at the same time when Halliday analyzes the horizontal linear sequence relations of the structure, he pays particular attention to **the longitudinal systematic paradigmatic relations**, which is the key point of systemic grammar. It is by reason of this that Firth calls syntagmatic relations structure, and **paradigmatic relations** system.

The naming of systemic grammar reminds people of paying more attention to the system of paradigmatic relation. This analyzing theory holds that grammatical analysis should be based on a series of systems. Each system has many items and when people speak, they can choose one in relevant position. For instance, there are singular and plural systems of number, so people can choose one; there are past, present, and future in the system of time, so people can choose one; there are declarative, imperative, and interrogative systems of mood, so people can choose one, and so on and so forth. So long as you say a word, you must make many times of choice. …That which is chosen is in essence meaning which is expressed via nothing but tone, lexicon, and grammatical structure.[23] This means that **so long as you say a word, you must come in and go out of many systems.** Never think that *He came* is simple in that *he* alone requires you must come in and go out of three subsystems: you will choose the third person in person system, masculine in gender system, and singular in number system. In this connection, language is a network in which many semantic choices must be made. When all the items in relevant systems are chosen one by one, appropriate horizontal structure—language stream——would be produced.

Halliday contends that language is a multiple rather than single level system. Hence we must make multiple choices. Language is hierarchic, including at least semantic, lexical, and phonetic levels. There is the relation of embodiment between the levels. In addition, language is also a code system of multiple levels, namely, a system is plugged in another one, and further in still another one. Semantic level is de facto the embodiment of context or the level of social signs (behavioral level) in language system.

On the whole, systemic grammar is a theory of language analysis describing language's horizontal linear sequence relations, notably longitudinal systematic paradigmatic relations, by means of the system network as metalanguage. What, then, is the relationship between systemic grammar and the theory of language holography? How can systemic grammar look for its source from outside, from the properties of system (any open system rather than the linguistic one), even from the holographic state of the cosmos?

For instance, the verb has a subsystem of time. In this subsystem, there are three items for choice: present tense, past tense, and future tense. This sort of system is called disjunctive system (Only one of the systems is selected after they are analyzed), and the logical relation between the chosen items is "either/or." For instance, in *I saw it yesterday*, the utterer chose the past tense of *see*. In addition to the "either/or"

[23]Cf. Wang (1988, p. 381).

relation of the disjunctive system, there is also the relation of "both…and" between the chosen items in a system, namely, all the items are selected at the same time. This sort of system is called conjunctive system (one in which all the items are used simultaneously), and the logical relation between the chosen items is "both/and." For instance, the tense and aspect of the verb are in the relation of conjunction or both/and, namely, the verb requires both tense and aspect. Say, in *I have been waiting for you*, as to *wait*, the utterer chose both the present tense and the perfect progressive aspect. That is to say, the holographic node of *wait* is located at the intersection point, being of the information of present tense and that of perfect progressive aspect. This is a property of one point (component) manifesting two subsystems, i.e., one is two, two one.

Now we come to the property of one point manifesting three subsystems. For instance, *he* in *He came* chooses the third person in person subsystem, masculine in gender subsystem, and singular in number subsystem. For another example, in Я читаю эту книгу (I read this book), эту книгу chooses the fourth case, viz., the objective case in the case subsystem, feminine in gender subsystem, and singular in number subsystem. One component simultaneously contains the properties of three subsystems, that is to say, one is three, three one. What does it mean that the choices from more than two subsystems coincide?

The above situation of one being two even three shows at least the following characteristics of an open system:

The organic connection of the system. The wholeness of a system is guaranteed by its organicity. The elements (e.g., the tense and aspect of the verb, or the gender, number, and case of the noun) of a system correlate and interact with each other. The connection between the elements in any whole system is organic (If a verb contains two or three choices, or if the connection between more choices is not organic, the coincidence will not occur). The elements correlate and interact with one another, and co-constitute the whole of the system (For instance, the tense and aspect of the verb should be fused and organized into other subsystems so as to form a word or a discourse).

The dynamicity of the system. The system's organic connection is not static but dynamic, being related to time. Bertalanffy (1973) contends that the system changes along with time (the tense and aspect of the verb happens to be embodied in the flowing of time).

The orderliness of the system. The structure and hierarchy shown by the system's organic connection and the gradually changing directness shown by its dynamicity both enable the system to have orderliness. For instance, confusion between the subject and the object does not occur in Я читаю эту книгу. This is because according to the restricted choice between the suspect and the object, Я is the subject, and читаю эту книгу must choose the objective case in the case system, or else the orderliness of the sentence would become a big problem. In this sentence, the foundation of the orderliness also depends on the verb's conjugation: the читаю after Я must choose the first person читаю in the case system, and it is prohibited after ты, он, она, мы, вы, они. This longitudinal paradigmatic relation becomes the foundation of the correct horizontal syntagmatic one, i.e., orderliness; in addition, these syntagmatic and paradigmatic relations are ultimately embodied in the property that meaning conforms to context. Bertalanffy believes that the system's change from disorder to order marks the increase of its organizational nature or degree, and its organizational nature (e.g., that between the verb's tense, aspect, and conjugation, etc., on the one hand and the noun's gender, number, and case on the other is very delicate) appertains to both the organic connection between the internal elements of the system (for instance, each ultimately uttered word containing the proper connection between the verb's tense, aspect, and conjugation on the one hand and the noun's gender, number, and case on the other is always organic), and the dynamic process of them (the verb's tense and aspect are themselves a sort of movement within time).

On this ground, we say, systemic grammar repeats some properties of the open system at evolutional level.

The previous situation of one being two even three shows at least the following properties of the theory of cosmos holography: of the levels of the cosmos, one part contains the same information as the others; each holographic node (subsystem) in the cosmic system has its counterpart or similar information in the whole and other nodes, respectively, namely, each holographic node in the system becomes, to a different extent, a microcosm of the whole. The specific analyses are as follows:

One part contains the same information as the others: as is stated afore, some segment or point in the tense coincides with some kind of aspect in a verb; some kind of gender coincides with some kind of number and some class in the case in a noun. For instance, in *he* the substance of coincidence in *He came*, the information of the third person (this is one part) is identical to that of singular (this is another part) and masculine (this is still another part). Given that these three parts can coincide with one another on a substance, they are compatible and identical with each other. The same holds to came, читаю, and эту книгу. The coincidence of the points from different subsystems (the relation between parts) indicates that the parts communicate the same information to one another.

Each holographic node (subsystem) in the cosmic system has its counterpart or similar information in the whole and other nodes, respectively, which is easier to understand: if some point (e.g., now) in the tense of a verb (e.g., wait) cannot find its counterpart or similar information in some kind of aspect/tense, why can they coincide with one another and produce *have been waiting* in present perfect continuous tense? If a kind of gender (e.g., feminine) cannot find its counterpart or similar information in the number (e.g., singular) or case (e.g., the fourth or objective case), how can they coincide with one another and produce книгу?

Each holographic node in the system becomes, to a different extent, a microcosm of the whole: even a word can embrace all the information of the language in which it belongs (which has been demonstrated in Sects. 4 and 5 of Chapter 3), let alone a Russian sentence Я читаю эту книгу or an English word *I have been waiting for you.* Three subsystems are involved in *he (came)*, two in *(I) have been waiting (for you)*, and three in (Я читаю эту) книгу. Isn't this the manifestation that three subsystems are condensed to *he*, two to *have been waiting*, and three to книгу? Let us have a look at a slightly more complicated sentence, *That is the essence of science: ask an impertinent question, and you are on the way to the pertinent answer*.[24] When we regard it as a point or a holographic node, we can make choices in the English subsystems as follows: morpheme, word, phrase, clause, subject-verb concord, sentence pattern transformation, possessive case of the noun, determiner, reference, anaphora, the tense and aspect of the verb, voice, mood, infinitive, the finite form of the verb, clause relations, and the like. Just imagine, according to the operation of systemic grammar, how many times of choice must we make in terms of longitudinal paradigmatic relations before saying a word? Hundreds of times are conservative, and thousands even tens of thousands of times are completely proper in theory (Human brain is indeed very great for so many choices can be accomplished in a split second!). In this vein, this holographic node can be, to a certain extent, a microcosm of the whole English.

What, we would like to ask, does systemic grammar mean? It means that the law of cosmos holography is repeated by it at evolutional level.

7 The Principle of Integrity of Language Meaning

Modern Western philosophers, notably those philosophers of language[25] strongly upholding the linguistic turn of philosophy, hold the stance of holism. What is the carrier unit of language meaning? Is it the word, the sentence, or the whole language system? G. Frege, the founder of the philosophy of language, first presented the integrity principle of meaning. In the "Introduction" to *The Foundations of Arithmetic: A logico-mathematical enquiry into the concept of number*, he says that as to the study of philosophical logic, he has kept to three fundamental principles: (1) always to separate sharply the psychological from the logical, the subjective from the objective; (2) never to ask for the meaning of a word in isolation, but only in the context of a proposition; (3) never to lose sight of the distinction between concept and object.[26] Philosophers of language usually believe that Frege's second principle (also called "the principle of context") sets a precedent for the holism of language meaning. Early L. Wittgenstein contended that only the proposition was of meaning, and the name was meaningful only in a propositional context. He upheld in his later stage that to understand a sentence was to understand a language. D. Davidson says, "[then] we can give the meaning of any sentence (or word) only by giving the meaning of every sentence (and word) in the language."[27]

"Never seek the meaning of a word in isolation, and we can only do so in a propositional context." This is of the same sense as "No context, no text." The meaning of a word can only be determined in a sentential context. Such a view, namely, the information of a part (e.g., text) should be found in the whole (e.g., context), coincides, so to speak, with the theory of holography——"The part is of

[24]Bronowski (1973, p. 153).

[25]Martinichi (1990).

[26]Frege (1953, p. xxii).

[27]Davidson (1967, p. 308). Also cf. Martinichi (1990, pp. 70–90).

the same information as the whole." Davidson's assertion, i.e., "give the meaning of 'any'...only by giving the meaning of 'every'...," means in effect that the information of the parts should be sought in the whole's, which resembles the previous two views, being coincident with the law of cosmos holography: "The same information is shared by the part (subsystem) and other parts or by the part and the whole; the part embraces all the information of the whole." When we regard a single word as a part, the context of the proposition (the language form expressing a judgment in logics: subject—predicate—object, namely, a sentence at the level of syntax) is a whole; as to a language on a higher level, it is all the more a whole to a word or a sentence in it. The phenomenon that in language the part embraces all the information of the whole is nothing but the repetition, at the evolutional level, of the law of cosmos holography.

As to this point, I spared a whole chapter (Chapter 3: The inner language holography) to demonstrate it: "The same information is shared by the part (subsystem) and other parts or by the part and the whole; the part embraces all the information of the whole." The two examples I gave therein are, the English *vicissitude* can be interpreted with all the words in the whole English lexicon, and the "*leizhui*累赘" in Chinese is in the same case. This case is virtually coincident with Davidson's expression afore——"[then] we can give the meaning of any sentence (or word) only by giving the meaning of every sentence (and word) in the language." On this account, Frege, Wittgenstein, and Davidson's elucidations as regards the principle of integrity of language meaning are supposed to be demonstrable in Chapter 3, and I will not repeat them here.

References

Bronowski. J., *The ascent of man*. Boston/Toronto: Little, Brown & Co., 1973.

Davidson. Donald, Truth and meaning. In *Synthese*, 1967.

Frege. Gottlob, *The foundations of arithmetic: A logico-mathematical enquiry into the concept of number* (2nd edition). Trans. J. L. Austin. New York: Harpers & Brothers, 1953.

Liu. Runqing (ed.), *Schools of linguistics*. Beijing: Foreign Language Teaching and Research Press, 1997.

Martinichi. A. P., *The philosophy of language* (2nd edition). Oxford: Oxford University Press, 1990.

Radford. Andrew, *Syntactic theory and the structure of English: A minimalist approach*. Cambridge: Cambridge University Press, 1997.

Saussure, F. de, *Course in general linguistics*. Etds. Charles Bally and Albert Sechehaye in collaboration with Albert Reidlinger. Trans. Wade Baskin. New York: The Philosophical Library, 1959.

Shen. Jiaxuan, R. W. Langacker's "cognitive grammar." In *Linguistics Abroad*, 1994 (1).

Wang. Cunzhen &Yan. Chunyou, *The theory of cosmic holographic unity*. Jinan: Shandong People's Publishing House, 1995.

Wang. Zongyan, *An English-Chinese dictionary of applied linguistics*. Changsha: Hunan Education Press, 1988.

Zhang. Min, *Cognitive linguistics and chinese Noun phrases*. Beijing: China Social Sciences Publishing House, 1998.

Zhang. Yingqing, The law of biology holography. In *Potential Science*, 1980(2).

Zhang. Yingqing, The theory of biology holography and holographic biology. In *Potential Science*, 1985(5).
Zhi. Youchang & Liu. Wanyi, Valence grammar and valence semantic underspecification. In *Journal of PLA University of Foreign Languages*, 2000(3).
Лосев, А. Ф. *О понямии языковой волемносми*, Серия летературы и языка, 1981.

Chapter 7
Linguistic Evidence for the Law of Cosmos Holography

Abstract In this chapter, I will continue to discuss the state of the outer language holography. Another rationale of the theory of language holography is: the law of cosmos holography is corroborated in language. The more this corroboration is derived in an all-round fashion, the more astounding we will be on the coincidence between the cosmos and language, and the more clearly we will recognize how far-reaching and insightful the second task of linguistics presented by Saussure is——it thus notes, "To determine the forces that are permanently and universally at work in all languages, and to deduce the general laws to which all specific historical phenomena can be reduced" (cf. Chapter 2, "The overall frame of the theory of language holography"). What on earth is "the forces that are permanently and universally at work in all languages"? The force of the system is its self-organizational movement. Nevertheless, the force of the system is also a system existing in the material world. The whole world, the whole cosmos, is also a huge system. So to speak, the force eternally and universally functioning in all languages is the cosmic system. In this section, I will use the definition of the law of cosmos holography, so my dear readers, please read by yourselves Chapter 2, "The overall frame of the theory of language holography," and I will not repeat it here. Now let us look, one by one, at the corroborations of the law of cosmos holography in language.

Keywords Up-down-containment · Monstrous-circle · Self-intertwining discourse · Cosmos prototype · Language modularity

1 The Up-Down-Containment of Cosmos and Language Respectively

Dialectics acknowledges that all things can contain and convert into one another, and the higher form develops from the lower ones. Not merely mathematics as a pure science is in the case, the same also holds to all things, e.g., biology, physics, chemistry, and the like, in the material world.

The containment in each level of language cannot be clearer, so no laborious demonstration is needed (say, to select a Ganodorma lucidum from a weedy place). Discourse contains sentences, sentence clauses, clause phrases, phrase words, words

G. Qian, *The Theory of Language Holography*,
https://doi.org/10.1007/978-981-16-2039-3_7

morphemes, and vice versa. This coincides with Engel's remark of the relationship between any number and 1. The cosmos is holographically repeated at evolutional level, so is language. Like the word contains syllables, the phrase contains words. The repetition as such goes on one level after another until that of the discourse containing sentences, and vice versa.

2 Biology and Language: The Higher Hierarchy Having Attributes of the Lower Hierarchy

The law of biological repetition tells us that in addition to their own attributes, the higher creatures also contain some attributes of the lower ones. Human beings will go through the plant stage when they remain embryos, characteristics of monkey might emerge on human body (e.g., such atavism phenomena like a person has a monkey-like head, a person is covered with hairs all over his body, or the like), and the frog cannot throw off its tail until after becoming mature, which are three of the many proofs.

The discourse also contains the attributes of the sentence in addition to its own. This phenomenon of the upper level containing the attributes of the lower one keeps effective until the level of morpheme. The situation of "the upper containing the attributes of the lower" is the best explanation of the state of the inner state of language holography.

There are more examples that can indicate the holographic relations between language structure and the biological one. For instance, the most famous historical linguist August Schleicher (1868–1921) in the nineteenth century believes that language has its own law of development identical to that of the biological evolution process. He studied language's historical kinship by the means of taxonomy with which biology classifies the plants, and adopted Sweden naturalist Carl von Linné's nomenclature. He classified the then languages, according to their common points (like the coincidence of lexicon, their conformance to the law of phonetic change, and so on), into different language families, branches, and subfamilies. He found a "mother" of each language system or branch, say, Latin as the "mother" of Romance languages, and then traced to the source language. At last, he drew the genealogy tree of Indo-European language family. For another example, Schleicher's theory of language history is closely related to the prevailing Darwinism at that time. In 1863, his essay, "Darwin's theory and linguistics," was published, publicly confessing his view that language theory conformed to evolutionism, and that Darwin's method of taxonomy on animals and plants were fundamentally suitable for the study of language history. He contended that like all the life forms, language also had its processes of development, growing-up, and decline; animals and plants maintained the fine breed via natural selection, and "advantageous varieties are usually easy to retain, whereas disadvantageous ones to vanish"; the connection and contrarieties, and the mutual influences and interpenetration between languages were just like the life-or-death struggles among animals, and the languages in advantageous positions were preserved while those in disadvantageous ones gradually vanish.[1]

At the level of detail, these demonstrations of Schleicher might not stand the examination of modern sciences, many aspects of them however are correct. Take the genealogy tree of Indo-European language family as an example, albeit his taxonomy has been modified by later generations, most common genealogy trees still follow his methods.

In addition, Schleicher's view that language theory conforms to the theory of evolution generally coincides with language's factual history of development. It would not go too far to say that Darwin's method of taxonomy on animals and plants is fundamentally suitable for the study of language history. Apropos his contention that language has its processes of development, growing-up, and decline as all the other life forms, it has also been proved by the decline and fall of some languages: Latin, etc. are no longer suitable for communication, and some indigenous and minority languages have also fallen and cannot be rescued. By my estimation, if our country performs a survey after decades or a hundred of years, not a few minority languages would become unsuitable for communication. For instance, according to my knowledge, few people now can speak the Tujia dialect of Tujia nationality in the southwest of Hubei province. When all the current old people pass away, what else can we describe this dialect except as "fallen"? The mutual influences and interpenetrations between different languages occur at any time, which resembles more or less the struggles among animals, namely, the languages in advantageous position are preserved whereas those in disadvantageous position gradually decline and fall.

3 Godel's the Monstrous-Circle of Mathematics and the Monstrous-Circle of Sentences

> In language, logic, lawsuit, artificial intelligence, CD, computer, etc., the 'monstrous-circle-like' phenomenon of holographic repetition appears. … 'Monstrous-circle' refers to this phenomenon, namely, when gradually upgrading (or downgrading) in some hierarchical system, we find unexpectedly that we return to the initial situation. We can use 'self-intertwining hierarchy' to describe the systems containing monstrous-circles. …More than a circle, it is also a process manifesting the infinity by means of finite methods. This chimes in with Kurt Gödel's mathematical circles. …What is the mechanism of the profound similarity among the monstrous-circles? It is holographic repetition. …The law of holographic repetition broadly exists in scientific world; many self-intertwining circles of holographic repetition generally exist in each discipline, and multi-hierarchical self-intertwining 'monstrous-circles' of holographic repetition even exist amidst disciplines and the whole scientific world.[2]

David Hilbert, a German mathematician, once had a very ambitious plan, that is, once the axioms and procedures were given, all the truths could be deduced. The

[1]Cf. Liu (1997, pp. 60–64).

[2]Wang and Yan (1995, pp. 206–207).

truth is, nevertheless, Gödel incompleteness theorem terminated this great plan. This theorem indicates that the means to obtain truth via algorithm is very limited in that in any formal system, there are always correct propositions that cannot be verified or falsified by axioms or laws of procedure. In a word, the world's kaleidoscopic complexity cannot be exhausted by countable formulae.[3] The monstrousness of many "monstrous-circles" lies not merely in the self-intertwining but also in the fact that "There are always correct propositions that cannot be verified or falsified by axioms or laws of procedure." That which is correct cannot be demonstrated by axioms!

The reader might still remember (in Chapter 5, "The outer rootstock of the different characteristics of language") that I previously employed a word game of an infinite long sentence to explicate recursiveness:

> This is a cat that can be defined as a small, domestic, fur-covered animal often kept as a pet, to catch mice which are sorts of small rodent (house-one, field-one, harvest-one) e.g., a rat, rabbit, squirrel, or beaver, which gnaws things with its strong teeth specially adapted for this ***purpose*** which one means to do, get, be, etc.; plan; design; intention which can be explained as intending; thing intended; aim which can be paraphrased as ***purpose***; object which can be defined as person or thing to whom action or feeling or thought is directed; thing aimed at; end…

Now let us deal with this infinite long sentence remaining to be ended. When the second *purpose* emerges, it follows *which one means to do*… rather than *object which can be defined*…. Doesn't this return to the *which one means to do* after the first *purpose*? A monstrous-circle is finished when the returning as such occurs. Now, *which also means purpose* follows *end*, and we immediately meet the third purpose. Isn't this the second monstrous-circle? It's indeed "When gradually upgrading (or downgrading) in some hierarchical system, we find unexpectedly that we return to the initial situation"! It's indeed "self-intertwining"!

The situation of monstrous-circles in Chinese is a bit different from that in English. In English, the attributive clause can immediately follow the noun by way of which/that-clause, and hence the English sentence is in theory infinitely long needing only one full stop. In Chinese, whereas, the objective clause must be situated before the noun, which makes it hard to be extended. In the following intertwining sentence, I make a slight modification by putting the objective clause after the noun for the sake of extending it. If the reader has interest, let us choose randomly the Chinese word "宇宙" (*yuzhou*, cosmos) and interpret it continuously, to wit., linger on it continuously. This time, my interest is not in recursiveness but in examining how many monstrous-circles there are. Then, we have:

> "宇宙是包括地球及其他一切天体的无限空间, 而 "包括" 是……; "地球" 是……; "及" 是……; "一切" 是……; "天体" 是太阳、地球、月亮和其他恒星、行星、卫星,以及彗星、流星、宇宙尘、星云、星团等的统称; "无限" 是……; "空间" 是……; 而……; 而……; ……而 "宇宙尘" 里的 "宇宙" 是 "包括地球及其他一切天体的无限空间。"
>
> ("**<u>The cosmos</u>**" refers to an infinite space containing the earth and all the other celestial bodies, and "contain" refers to…; "the earth" refers to…; "and" refers to…; "all" refers to…; "celestial body" refers to the overall name of the sun, the earth, the moon, and other

[3] Cf. Hua (1996).

stars, planets, satellites, and comets, meteors, **cosmic** dust, nebulas, star clusters, and so on; "infinite" refers to…; "space" refers to…; and…; and…; … and the "cosmos" in "**cosmic** dust" refers to "the infinite space containing the earth and all the other celestial bodies.")

Look, the sentence ends at its beginning ("the cosmos")!

In the above sentence, when "the cosmic dust" is met in "the celestial body," only the second level of "the cosmos" is interpreted, and we must interpret what "the cosmos" in "the cosmic dust" is. Isn't this the returning to the starting point namely "the cosmos"? This is again a monstrous-circle. In addition, in the second level, to save the length of this book, I perform large amount of ellipsis in which the solar system and the sun are employed to interpret "the earth." "The sun" is again employed when I interpret "the celestial body," and I am supposed to interpret later what "the sun" is. This is still another monstrous-circle. This apart, "the earth" is employed in the interpretation at the first level, and it is used again when "the celestial body" is interpreted at the second level, and I am supposed to interpret later what "the earth" is. This is yet another monstrous-circle. This is to say that when "the cosmos" is interpreted, three monstrous-circles will be met merely at the second level. How many monstrous-circles would be met if the interpretation were to go on ad infinitum?

4 The Law of Cosmos-Return-into-Itself and the Self-Intertwining Discourse

4.1 The Self-Intertwining Discourse

The ancient Greek philosopher Euclid presented a famous paradox, "This statement is false," which has been arousing people's interest. A paradox is a proposition that can provoke an ambivalent conclusion: from the assertion that it is true, people can infer that it is false, and from the assertion that it is false, people can infer that it is true. The ambivalent conclusion provoked by this paradox is: if what he says is true and reflects the reality, then, it contradicts the literal meaning of "This statement is false." If his word is false (a lie), it happens to coincide with what he himself admits (the literal meaning of "This statement is false"), and the coincidence itself indicates that his word is true. If so, how can we say that his word is a lie? This is again a paradox, and it is never eliminable.

This paradox is de facto a special case of the law of cosmos self-returning.

The law of cosmos self-returning and paradox are also a monstrous-circle, being of the same source with, and interrelated to, the corroboration (Gödel's mathematical circle and the sentence circle) in last section.

"People start from some point or level, proceed for a long time, but at last find that they have returned unwittingly to the original point. The case is so to all things in the cosmos. We call this the law of cosmos self-returning." "Self-returning is a necessary conclusion of holography. In other words, the holographic is necessarily self-returning, the self-returning holographic, and they are inseparable from each other. …Circulation exists due to the fact that things embrace themselves during the progression, …The circulation or monstrous circle revealed by the law of cosmos self-returning is of another portrait, viz., being self-intertwining or self-related."[4] In my view, the previous definition (i.e., starting from some point and returning to it at last) remains to be correct in that it fails to reveal what the law of self-returning is but merely describes the phenomenon. Comparatively, the latter corroboration gives more essential ideas: circulation exists due to the fact that things embrace themselves during the progression, viz., being self-intertwining or self-related.

There is another similar paradox: I am always a liar.[5] It is also a proposition that can provoke an ambivalent conclusion. If what the speaker says is true, then at least this time he does not lie, which runs counter to the *always* in the sentence; if what the speaker says is false (i.e., he is lying), then it exactly coincides with what he himself confesses (i.e., I am always a liar), which per se indicates that he is telling the truth. If so, how can we say that he is lying? This is again a contradiction.

In daily life, there is also another sort of self-intertwining and self-related speech act. Luckily, in my childhood, I once unintentionally performed a self-intertwining and self-related speech event. I wrote on the white wall several characters with a brush dipped in read ink, "是用红笔写的(I write this in red)," so my elder sister immediately told my father about this. My father was in anger and asked my sister something. The following is their dialogues:

Father: What did he write?
Sister: "[I] write this in red."
Father: I know this. I mean what did he write?
Sister: "[I] write this in red."
Father: Idiot! I ask what did he write?
Sister: That's it: "[I] write this in red."
Father: (in a rage) You are an idiot!

In the dialogues above, they return twice to the original point, "[I] write this in red." What my father asked is the content or object of the writing (What is written) and hence he thought that my sister's answer was merely a description of the writing instrument, which is why he blamed her for giving an irrelevant answer. In fact, what my sister gave is nothing but the content or object of the writing, and she did give a relevant answer. Given that they stuck to their respective logic, the seemingly funny communication failed. My father did not know the reason until he saw the characters on the wall. Afterwards, he remained to put his thoughts on solving this monstrous-circle. As to me, albeit I read in my youth the patiently guiding *The Analects*, the persuasively eloquent *Mencius*, the amazingly mysterious *Zhuangzi*, and the wisely

[4]Wang and Yan (1995, pp. 297–298).
[5]Cf. Lu (1991).

instigating inaugural addresses of the successive presidents of America, I remained to solve this twining knot planting "idiot" on my sister![6]

The example above is a special form of expression with respect to the law of cosmos self-returning. The word on the wall creates a self-related and self-intertwining trap. First of all, the writing tool is a brush dipped in red ink, a fortiori, the third party will use "[I] write this in red" to describe the tool and process. Coincidentally, the content namely the object of the writing is also "[I] write it in red." Thus is formed the overlap between interpretative language or metalanguage——the language describing **how** to speak, listen, read, and write—and the content of the language (object language, namely, that which reveals what is spoken, heard, read, or written). This is also the source of trouble. When interpretative language overlaps with object language, a self-intertwining discourse is generated. This is a case of self-related-ness in point! Such a discourse can be called "self-intertwining discourse." This notwithstanding, the self-intertwining discourse is a bit different from paradox (like "This statement is false") in that it is not concerned with whether the sentence per se is true or false.

In Xu Youyu's *Spirit Generates Language*, there is the following passage: "Russell contends that paradox emerges due to the fact that in ordinary language, people can make self-referential assertions. For instance, one can say, 'Someone lies' which, when used to judge other's words or any word of his own, will be of no problem. Nevertheless, when it is used to judge itself, paradox will arise. Russell's solution is to present the 'theory of types', that is, to classify a language into different levels of which the language at the upper level can make assertions as regards that at the lower but not the same one. To be sure, Russell's theory of types can eliminate paradoxes, it however provokes other technical problems. Later, people tried to eliminate paradoxes by means of distinguishing object language from the interpretative one. Interpretative language is a basic language, and the language it asserts is object language."[7] This passage contains three layers of meaning: how paradox comes; Russell's method of solving paradoxes; later people's method of eliminating the paradox. Here, I notice "to eliminate the paradox by means of distinguishing object language from the interpretative one." Inferred from the previous remark, namely, **"When interpretative language overlaps with object language, a self-intertwining discourse is generated,"** the method of eliminating the paradox shares the same source with the generation of the self-intertwining discourse.

We should also notice that Russell's "self-referential assertion" is coincident in toto with "The circulation or monstrous circle revealed by the law of cosmos self-returning is of another portrait, viz., being self-intertwining or self-related."

If the reader has interest, he/she can try to generate a self-intertwining discourse by means of creating the overlap between interpretative language (that which describes how to speak, listen, read, and write) and object language (that which reveals what is

[6]To further understand the phenomenon of paradox (or antinomy), the reader is supposed to probe into Tarski. A., The semantic conception of truth and the foundations of semantics. In *Modern Philosophy of Language*. Ed. Maria. B., Counterpoint, Washington, DC, 1999.

[7]Xu (1997, p. 56).

spoken, heard, read, and written). This is not without benefit to the corroboration of the law of cosmos self-returning and to the recognition of the essence of language. For instance, in recent years, some comic sketches provided some jokes by this means, so, can some new ones be created for similar compositions along this path? For the sake of articulation, in what follows, I will give one more example of self-intertwining discourse that is by no means elaborately designed.

Context: A said to B, "His word is in too poor taste" (This is an interpretative language remaining to become an object one).
C asks B: What did A say?
B: "His word is in too poor taste." (At this time, the interpretative language overlaps with the object one)
C: That is another question. I mean what he said.
B: That's it, "His word is in too poor taste."
C: (Still puzzled) I ask what he said.
B: "His word is in too poor taste." (Now we return to the original point again)
C: (Angry) He word is indeed in too poor taste, but you are also too muddled to be cured!

If this passage of dialogue were not given for the sake of creation but indeed occurred in daily life, if C were a linguistic scholar, he should have realized suddenly that B is not that stupid, and that all-possibly there occurs the overlap and intertwining between interpretative language and the object one.

4.2 The System of Self-Expression and Self-Intertwining Discourse

The concept of "self-expression" comes from Douglas Richard Hofstadter's *Gödel, Escher, Bach: An Eternal Golden Braid* (1979). Apropos of the system of self-expression, Zhao Nanyuan once mentioned it when he set up the model of general theory of evolution. He thus said, "If we could leave the earth even an inch by clutching our own hair, we might be able to lift ourselves to the moon."[8] According to him, in the terminology more conforming to law of physics, we should study a device like the rocket, namely, that capable of blasting off by itself without relying on other supports, so as to promote the creative recognition of cognitive subject like human beings. In the sphere of engineering, there is a concept of "bootstrap" corresponding to this. The starting process of the computer is also a process of bootstrap. During this process, a read-in program can read other ones including itself. "Bootstrap" can be said a primary form of "self-expression."

[8]Zhao (1994, pp. 113–117).

On the ground of "self-expression," the objects of scientific research can be divided into two types: one is the object of "self-expression," the other being that of "non-self-expression." Physics is a case in point of the non-self-expressed object, say, the establishment of Newtonian mechanics does not change the orbit of the planet (It is human rather than the planet that is describing the orbit). Society on the other hand is of the obvious property of self-expression, say, the research results of social sciences will always exert more or less influences on itself (otherwise, what is the usage of ethics and law?). The cognitive process of human brain is also a typical system of self-expression and the result of human's each consideration will influence his/her later thinking mode. Compared with the object of "non-self-expression," that of self-expression is harder to study. To begin, **the object of self-expression is varied with poor steadiness, so it often cannot meet the repeatability that science requires. When the shallow recognition can hardly be steady, the deep one would lose its foundation**. On this account, it is very difficult to set up profound theories like Newtonian mechanics. It is by reason of this that to date we are still lack of a research paradigm directed upon the system of self-expression, one resembling Euclidean paradigm employed to establish Newtonian mechanics in the sphere of non-self-expression.

Zhao Nanyuan aims to offer a paradigm, a general model, to the study of the system of self-expression for the sake of studying the process rich in creativity. The process as such includes the evolution of social structure, the evolution of culture, the cognitive process of human brain, biological evolution, the developing process of biological individuals, and so on. By saying that the system of self-expression is complex, Zhao Nanyuan means that the complexity is most prominently manifested in the fact that **during the working process, the system can change its structure even working principles**. To grasp this system, we need a deeper model that can keep identical when the shallow one varies. This is the soft-hard structural model presented by him. The fundamental operating mechanism of the soft-hard structural model is the variation and selection in the theory of evolution. According to Darwin's view of evolution, variation occurs at random and can be realized in a simple fashion by means of introducing into the system random factors. Selection on the other hand is more complex insomuch as it must rely on some view or system of values. **To establish the evaluation criteria is the crux of the evolution progress**, so **evaluation is the nub problem** of the complex system as such. This is also why we must set up the system of good-reason centering at evaluation at the level of philosophy. When the soft-hard structural model and the concept of self-expression are introduced into Darwin's theory of evolution, general theory of evolution is constituted.

Now let us return to the previous "the self-intertwining discourse is generated when interpretative language overlaps with the object one."

By extension, when we study language and linguistics, we are situated in a system of self-expression. The self-intertwining phenomenon occurring this time is more severe than the self-intertwining discourse. We can guarantee the accuracy when researching the language of bees or animals in that it belongs to the system of non-self-expression. The object in that system does not vary much and it does not matter even if it is the other way round. This is because the communication of bees or animals is steady as an act which can often meet the scientific requirement for repeatability. What is particularly important is, the evaluation system is not established by bees but by human beings researching the former's "language." Therefore, the most crucial link is of objectivity. Nevertheless, when human beings research their own language, they set the evaluation criteria by themselves. To evaluate one's results of research according to the evaluation criteria set by oneself will lead to the overlap between interpretative language (language used for research) and the object one (the researcher's own language)! The phenomenon of self-intertwining at this time is inevitable. This is the difficulty in doing research on oneself. What is commonly seen is, a skilled doctor cannot diagnose his/her own disease, which is also an evasion from self-intertwining and from the non-objectivity of treatment.

Comprehensively seen, today's linguistics, particularly the Western one, is characterized by unprecedented novelty and diversity. This notwithstanding, we had better not give complete acknowledgment as regards the objectivity and profoundness of every theory, including the theory of language holography upheld in this book. This is because human beings have gotten enmeshed in the system of self-expression as the result of doing research on themselves. This system is of its inherent defect, namely, "When the shallow recognition can hardly be steady, the deep one would lose its foundation." He who can jump even half a step out this system and look outward would usually be clear-minded and profound. Being wedded to one's system is as a rule the beginning of superficiality and corruption.

5 Cosmos Prototype and Language Modularity

Needless to say, to design itself with the cosmos as the prototype is language's corroboration of the cosmic structure (they two are isomorphic with one another).

When discussing the categories in universal grammar in his *The Problem of Meaning in Primitive Language* (1923), Bronislaw Malinowski notes that universal categories are "factual categories" that reflect people's universal attitude toward life. He says, "Language structure reflects the real categories deviated from children and the primitive humans' practical attitude toward the surrounding world. These grammatical categories reflect … practical world-views." In terms of the practical attitude here, he believes that it is inherent in children rather than being acquired. He also contends that universal grammar "exists in all the human languages, no matter how different they are at surface." The first type of category in universal grammar is noun substance. At a very early stage, children begin to play material objects, particularly the separable and holdable ones, and they always take apart the complex objects to play.

It is my contention that what is described above as to children indicate that they construct their own language according to the reality. This can explain why nominal concepts are formed earlier than other words.

Malinowski says that verbs appear relatively late in children's mind's eye. Verbs appertain to action, body gesture, mood, temporal variation, etc., and are more often used in order, description, and interpretation. They appear due to the fact that human beings are particularly interested in their changes, the types of their activity, the state of their bodies, their thought and mood, and so forth.

I argue that the sequence of the noun and the verb exactly reflects the general situation of "Language is constructed according to the reality.". The correspondence is by no means contingent. The only interpretable reason is: language structure corresponds to the real world.

It is an age-old view that language reflects the reality. A prominent achievement of the medieval linguistics is speculative grammar presented under the influences of scholasticism. *Speculative* comes from the Latin *speculum*, meaning "the mirror reflecting the reality." That is to say, grammar is a mirror reflecting the reality.[9]

Speculative grammarians believe that human beings can recognize the world by means of language in that the "sign" of word is related to their mind on the one hand, and to the thing it represents on the other. This is a fundamental principle, and a universal one also. They think that all things in the world have several different modes of existence (modi essendi), say, the eternal one and the temporal one. People are supposed to distinguish and induce things by virtue of the eternal mode, and to observe things' changes and development by virtue of the temporal one. In this connection, the language reflecting objective things does not immediately express a person or a thing but the particular mode of existence of things (e.g., reality, action, quality) instead.[10]

From the passage above, we obtain the inspiration as such: the sign is related to the mind on the one hand, and to an outside thing on the other. Under such circumstances, the only interpretable reason for one thing connecting two poles is: the sign embraces the information of both the mind and the outside thing. In this vein, the sign, the mind, and the outside thing are in a holographic state.

What is the situation in nature? Particularly, how is nature's movement reflected on human language? On this question, there was once a heated debate between Syrian-Pergamenian school and Alexandrian School in the third century B. C. Pergamenian scholars believed that there was no principle or law in the movement of nature; contrariwise, Alexandrian scholars insisted that the movement of heavenly bodies and the variation of seasons were by no means disordered. In addition, they believed that both the movement of nature and the structure of language were dominated by laws the models of which could be discovered and described by people. Only in this way, could grammar exist, or else we could merely list the expressing modes but could not elucidate their interrelations.[11] In fact, given that people can discover, and can describe in particular, the model of language, this indicates that there are laws apropos of language structure to be followed. In the eyes of today's people, these descriptions are beyond reproach; at the end of the third century B.C., whereas, this debate was quite uneasy. That is to say, people have early sensed something as to

---

[9]Cf. Liu (1997, p. 20).

[10]Ibid., p. 21.

[11]Qtd. Ibid., pp. 12–13.

whether or not the information of nature's structure and that of language structure embrace and correspond to one another.

Zhang Jin says, "(According to the materials offered by Shen Jiaxuan) Language designs its model with reality as the prototype."[12] If the infinite space is "*yu*宇" (Space), the infinite time "*zhou*宙" (Time),[13] doesn't "with reality as the prototype" mean that the cosmos is taken as the prototype?

The previously mentioned materials mainly encompass four situations as follows:

In the first situation, the arrangement sequence of sentence components coincides with the chronological order of events.

E.g.: He got up, got washed, had the breakfast, and then went to work.

In the second situation, when the substances are adjacent to one another in objective reality, the linguistic components expressing them are also adjacent to each other.

E.g.:

my mother 我妈妈 (inalienable subordination)

a book of mine 我的书(alienable subordination)

The author remains to interpret how the adjacent or nonadjacent substances in objective reality influence the arrangement of linguistic components. According to the examples, it seems that we can understand them in this way: in the "inalienable subordination," my mother is mine and inalienable to others, and hence "my" overlaps with "mother." The case is so in both English and Chinese; in the "alienable subordination," whereas, a book is alienable to others, and hence there is an "of" (的) between "a book" and "mine." In terms of this, English is more demanding than Chinese.

In the third situation, the separable substances and qualities in objective reality are also separable in language, and vice versa.

E.g.:

(1) Xiao Wang's schoolbag → This schoolbag is Xiao Wang's. (The sentence after the arrow is acceptable in that Xiao Wang is separable from the schoolbag.)
(2) plastic slippers → This pair of slippers is plastic.
(3) a rabbit's hole → This hole is a rabbit's.
(4) Xiao Wang's dad → This dad is Xiang Wang's. (?) (The sentence after the arrow is unacceptable in that "Xiao Wang's dad" refers to one person hence is integral and inseparable.)
(5) the plastics' elasticity → The elasticity as such is plastic. (?) (Plastic(s) and elasticity are inseparable.)

In the fourth situation, it is linguistically reasonable that the mouth shape is big when words expressing big are pronounced, and small when words expressing small are pronounced.

E.g.:

*da*大 (big mouth shape) *xiao*小 (small mouth shape)

---

[12]Zhang (1997, p. 8).

[13]In Chinese, "*yuzhou*宇宙" (Space and Time) is used to express the cosmos——the translator.

large (big mouth shape) little (small mouth shape)
dark (big mouth shape) small (small mouth shape)
big (The mouth shape is not big but the corners of the mouth are extended to both sides.)

To the materials above, I would like to supplement an interesting linguistic event: it was around the early 1980s. I once attended in Wuhan University a lecture given by Prof. Xu Youlan a Chinese-American. The old lady was aged but energetic. When she pronounced "large," her mouth shape was big and the tone was long, and her two hands also tried to spread to both sides, which is impressive to me even now. It can be seen that the generation and development of language tries to approach the prototype and imitate the cosmic one.

Zhang Jin employs the previous materials in order to show that the starting point of his research on linguistics is dialectic system theory and prototype-model theory. I employ these materials in order to enunciate the holographic unity of language and the cosmos.

The previous materials show this: the various laws of language are the logical forms of things——language shares the logical form with the reality due to the fact that thought is the logical form of the latter. Why is our grammar manifested in this rather than that way? It is because the logic of things in the cosmos is in the case. "The logic of grammar comes from that of life. That which is given to us by language is not merely a pile of facts; rather, it gives us the facts together with the reason (the logic of reason)."[14]

The school of Anglo-American analytic philosophy upholds the study of thought and the world via language with a reason that language is isomorphic with the world, and the world's structure can be deduced from the study of language's. "In their views, the development of Western philosophy experienced a trilogy from ancient times to the present day: in ancient times, it pivoted around ontology, studying what Being is and what the essence of the world is; in modern times, it pivoted around epistemology, studying the relationship between thinking and Being, and the sources, paths, capacities, and limits of human cognition; in the twentieth century, it pivoted around the meaning of language, studying their communication and conveyance between subjects. Some of these philosophers held that thought and the world could not be studied unless language was studied first. Russell and early Wittgenstein believed that language was identical to the world on structure, and the world's structure could be deduced by virtue of studying language's."[15] Why is it the case? Hegel's view can offer the answer: human brain embraces the logical structure identical to the movement of the cosmos.

Russell and Wittgenstein "presented a mode in which language rigidly corresponds to the world in the logical atomism during their early stage. Their logical atomism failed to be accepted by later philosophers of language, their view of the rigid correspondence between language and the world, nevertheless, was inherited

---

[14]Xu et al. (1996, p. 290).

[15]Xu (1997, p. 38).

by not a few philosophers of language as their rationale that language must be the outset to corroborate and study philosophy."[16]

As to the previous point, Xu Youyu thus comments:

> Why is there the correspondence of isomorphism between language and the world? Russell and Wittgenstein answer in their logical atomism that this isomorphic relation is apriori. This answer remaining to offer detailed elucidations leads to the negative attitude of many philosophers toward them. In fact, there might be two sorts of answer to a question. One is ontological: there is an undefended objective world irrelevant to human cognition, and when people reflect this world via language, they enable language to have the properties identical to the world at the level of structure. If this is the answer, there would be no meaning to study the world's structure by dint of language's. This is like one studies a city, draws its map, and then says that the city can be understood via the map. On the other hand, some philosophers contend that the so-called world is meaningful only to human beings, namely, it is a world graspable by human recognition, and that it is human beings' conceptual frame that manages to turn the integral and chaotic experiential world into distinctive things (like matters, qualities, relations, etc.) for them to understand it, and to make it exist for them. In the eyes of philosophers of language, the so-called conceptual frame…can only be the apriori one of language. …Words are more distinctive, operable, and easy to be arranged into a system than concepts, and the constituents in the former are in more precise relations to one another. According to this **anti-realism understanding of the world**, it is human beings' linguistic means that divide and integrate a distinctive world 'existing for human beings'. In this connection, it is fairly meaningful to study the world's structure via language's.[17]

Why does "the realist answer" have little meaning whereas "the anti-realist understanding of the world" have much when it comes to studying the world's structure via language's? Xu remains to answer this question. The question as such however is the right one to the theory of language holography. Following the objective world irrelevant to recognition, human beings "enable language to have the properties identical to the world on structure," probe into the world, and get enmeshed into a circle. This is really like drawing a city's map before studying the city according to the map. To study the non-substances in favor of the substances, viz., to attend to trifles in favor of the essence, might facilitate the modification of non-substantial texts but would bring no novel discoveries to the study of the city itself. When it is understood in an anti-realist fashion, the world divided and integrated by language does not directly come from the real things (the objective world) but is merely an apriori frame of language. If the structure obtained from this apriori frame comes through verification and is justified to be identical to the objective world's structure, the fact that language's apriori frame matches the objective world would exactly indicate this: language structure is holographic with the cosmic one.

It is less possible for people to create language according to the world's structure after they understand thoroughly, become familiar with, and grasp the essence of the latter. This is because according to this logic, language would remain to be created till now: after all, we can hardly say that human beings have understood thoroughly, become familiar with, and grasped the essence of the world. On this account, the fact that **language has early been here** demonstrates by itself that language's frame

---

[16]Ibid., p. 38.

[17]Ibid.. p. 74.

is apriori. How to corroborate the world's frame by means of language's apriori one? We may as well borrow the philosophers' (of language) train of thought of seeking from language solutions to philosophical problems (they refer to "being." As regards this train of thought, I have performed meticulous elucidations in Sect. 2 of Chapter 2, "The different directions of Western and Chinese philosophies," of my *Language: the Last Homestead of Human Beings*. As a consequence, to avoid repetition, I will only make a brief review of my train of thought during the process of demonstration: "Many philosophers have held that language is a reflection of reality, so, if one could understand the structure of language, one could understand the structure of reality."[18] Here, the real structure is supposed to be understood as the structure of the real world. This view pertinent to "language-the real world" could be confirmed by Plato and Socrates. Plato says that if he tries to figure out the structure of reality by studying reality directly, he is afraid that he might get puzzled intellectually. Therefore, he decides to employ language as a real situation: "I decide to take refuge in language and study the truth of things by means of it" (Phaedo, 99E). How to understand the structure of the reality namely the real world by virtue of understanding language's structure? "People generally think that the fundamental structure of language is the subject plus the predicate. This appertains to the fundamental structure of the reality (i.e., being): particularity plus universality. If people think that the fundamental structure of the reality can be understood by means of that of language, it is very important to understand the distinction between the subject and the predicate."[19] Well, let us set out from the subject and the predicate. The fundamental structure of language is that of the subject plus the predicate, and it happens that the dichotomy of the world is a universal phenomenon. **To this connection, language's apriori structure verifies the world's structure**.

Moreover, the great significance of this verification (namely, language's apriori structure matches the objective world) is: language is the product of the spirit, and the spirit's product is also of the same structure as the material things (from the cosmic bodies to the biological ones). That is to say, the law of material-spiritual holography in the theory of cosmos holography is again (this time in language) verified!

The law of material-spiritual holography (see Sect. 3 of Chapter 3) holds that the subject (human beings) contains all the information of the object (the practical or recognitive object of human beings), and vice versa. This is the fundamental connotation of the law of subject-object holography. Given that human beings capable of thinking are generated from the material world, this indicates that the subject in the narrow sense——human beings——already latently exists in the object. Recognition is the self-aware information of the object, the reconstruction of the objective world, and the self-aware objective world. Every artificial thing is nothing but a material sign expressing the spirit. The subject-object holography is first of all due to the homogeneity of the subject and the object, namely, they are the different states of development, coming from the same thing, and the homogeneity as such essentially determines the holography between them. At the level of evolution, the spirit and

[18]Martinich (1996, p. 3).

[19]Ibid.

the materials are holographically synchronous and isomorphic with one another. The spirit is the highly specialized material memory while material memory is the primitive state of the spirit. The fact that the spirit is capable of recognizing the material world demonstrates by itself the identity of the spirit and the material, namely, the two are isomorphic and homogeneous, viz., holographic, with each other.[20]

Are the results of the respective verification of language and the world's structures the same, then? The answer is Yes. So to speak, from Chapters 3 to 8, I have been verifying this result. I verify the inner state of language holography before doing so to the outer state of it.

The demonstration as such is of great significance. Language is both a spiritual phenomenon, a product of the spirit, and a material one (i.e., sound). If there were no identity between the materials and the spirit, namely, if they were not isomorphic with each other, it means that there would appear something quite alien to the cosmos! As a matter of fact, this alien relationship does not exist at all; as a matter of fact, language structure and the cosmic one are holographically isomorphic. The rationale that language can recognize and describe the material world is also here.

6 Cosmos Clarified by Language

How does the cosmos enunciate itself to human beings? The fact that the cosmos per se is revealed as what it is already gives a voiceless enunciation. In this situation, it enunciates itself.

Be that as it may, human beings are not dumb, and they want to pursue a meaningful life, so that they endlessly interpret this or that with various signs. As a result, the cosmos cannot but be interpreted by many sign systems one of which is language. Language can interpret the cosmos, which alone indicates that language is isomorphic with the cosmos insomuch as the heteromorphic things cannot communicate with or interpret one another. "Human beings are an epitome of the cosmos, the most perfect microcosmos. After the cosmic spirit externalizes itself into nature during its own progression of development, it manifests itself in human mind in the fullest fashion. Therefore, the development of nature must be understood via human beings' mental activities in that the latter will necessarily reflect the former. Rudolf Eucken vividly writes, 'Man is a complete embodiment of God. Man is the summit of nature's development, so he must embrace all the previous happenings, just like the fruit embraces all its developing phases.'"[21] Here I merely say that human beings are the concentrate of nature. I already demonstrated the isomorphism between language the product of human beings and the latter (Cf. Chapter 1, "Introduction: The harmony of cosmos, human body and language," of this book, or *Aesthetic Linguistics*). On this ground, the fact that language can elucidate the cosmos indicates by itself the former's verification of the latter.

[20]Wang and Yan (1995, pp. 174–183).

[21]Qtd. Ibid., p. 31.

References

Hua. Lei, Does computer have consciousness? In *Dushu*, 1996(7).

Liu. Runqing (Ed.), *Schools of linguistics*. Beijing: Foreign Language Teaching and Research Press, 1997.

Lu. Gusun (Ed.), Item "paradox" in *The English-Chinese Dictionary*. Shanghai: Shanghai Translation Publishing House, 1991.

Martinich. A. P. (Ed.), *The philosophy of language*. Oxford: Oxford University Press, 1996.

Wang. Cunzhen & Yan. Chunyou, *The theory of cosmic holographic unity*. Jinan: Shandong People's Publishing House, 1995.

Xu. Youyu, *Spirit generates language*. Chengdu: Sichuan People's Publishing House, 1997.

Xu. Youyu, Zhou. Guoping, Chen. Jiaying & Shang. Jie, *Language and philosophy——Comparative studies between modern anglo-American and traditional German-French ones*. Beijing: SDX Joint Publishing Company, 1996.

Zhang. Jin, *Hypothesis of thinking module——My view of language generation*. Zhengzhou: Henan University Press, 1997.

Zhao. Nanyuan, *Cognitive science and the general theory of evolution*. Beijing: Tsing Hua University Press, 1994.

Chapter 8
The Holographic Relation Between Language and Culture

Abstract In this chapter, I will go on demonstrating the outer state of language holography. The holographic relation between language and culture is the outer state of language holography. The two holographic nodes (as parts) that will be discussed in Sect. 1 and the cosmos (as the whole) embrace and are telegraphic with each other. The two nodes are both the microcosms of the world's information also. Section 2 will discuss the coevolution of language with culture. Section 3 will discuss the cultural elements condensed in language structure.

Keywords Cultural reality · Coevolution of language with culture · Cultural perspective · Condense

1 Language and Cultural Reality

1.1 Introduction: Language and Culture Are Respectively the Microcosm of the World's Information

In Chapter 4, we regarded the relation between language and cognition as the inner state (language is a tool to cognize the objective world, and it can also be a cognitive object. Meanwhile, cognitive process and language genesis embrace and react to each other, and cognition and language must be attached to human body) and **that between language and culture as the outer state of language holography with this reason: culture (particularly the part of material cultivation) can exist relatively independent of human body**. In my opinion, this argument holds water. Insofar as the hierarchy of cognition is concerned, the layer above the linguistic one (language, symbol, technique, behavior) is the layer of logic, i.e., the level of culture: logic, science, religion, art, and that below it is the layer of consciousness: perception, consciousness, emotion, feeling.[1] In the following three sections, I will discuss in brief the holographic relation between language and culture.

The definition of "culture" here follows Kroeber's theory: (1) culture includes the mode of behavior and that guiding the behavior; (2) whether it is extrinsic or intrinsic,

[1] For the detailed demarcation, see Sect. 2 of Chapter 4.

G. Qian, *The Theory of Language Holography*,
https://doi.org/10.1007/978-981-16-2039-3_8

the mode is acquired via learning by way of the artificially constructed system of signs; (3) the materialization of the mode of behavior and that guiding the behavior is manifested in artificial products which, in this connection, also belong to culture; (4) the values formed in history are the core of culture, and heterogeneous cultures can be distinguished according to different values; (5) cultural system is both the cause to the constraints of the mode of human activities and the product and result of the latter.[2] The first and the fourth items above exactly explicate the spiritual characters of culture, the third one the material characters.

Are language and culture (as parts) respectively the microcosm of the world's (as the whole) information?

The question of language being the microcosm of the world's information is discussed and answered from Chapters 3 to 8 of this book.

Now, I will discuss why culture is the microcosm of the world's information.

To be sure, culture is inherently human beings' mode of behavior and values, and it comes from interpersonal constraints; scientifically speaking, nevertheless, human behavior is not a purely interpersonal one characteristic of mutual generation and restriction. A part of cultural behaviors of human beings comes from their **physiological and psychological aspects which, whereas, are nothing but the adaptation to the cosmos, the acceptation of the telegraphy for it, and the identification with the cosmic constraints**. That is to say, **some cultural behaviors are the results of the mutual generation and restriction between human beings and the cosmos, and the telepathy of human beings for the cosmos**. Are there proofs? Yes, there are too many to enumerate them. The changes of sunspots appertain to some human diseases; all the big movements on the earth——magnetic storms, volcano eruptions, floods, Nino phenomena, and so on, influence human emotions, minds, and bodies; the rainy weather influences the arthritis patients; the moon phases influence women's menstrual cycles; some cultural behaviors of a nation are all the more relevant to the local environment of nature, namely, they are caused by natural factors. **The environmental factors of nature obstinately reproduce their tempers in the nations' characters**——the vast grasslands raise and train the enthusiastic, passionate, and tough minds; the deep mountains and forests cultivate thoughtful, self-sustaining, and honest minds; the tropical areas might cause the habitants emotionally unsteady even violent, and so forth. Indeed, the environment of nature amounts to some characters of human beings which, in the end, are manifested in cultural characters. **The cosmos brings up human beings, and the latter's modes of behavior imitate all things in the cosmos and are mutually telepathic with them**. That is all.

Hitherto, each of human beings' own material products, from the first stone ax to the spacecraft, was made on the basis of tracing the world or human beings themselves (when they consider themselves as a sort of being in the world). The house is the imitation of the cave which can shelter people from rain and wind and accommodate them; the table, chairs, stools, and the bed are the imitations of the flat stones on which utensils can be laid; the umbrella is made via comparison to the tree with a big

[2]Cf. Hu and Gao (1997, p. 4).

crown which can shelter people from rain; the pot and the bowl are the imitations of the puddle and the lake whose shapes are suitable for retaining water; the chopper is the imitation of the sharp stone; the man-made satellite and the spacecraft are the imitations of the meteor in the sky; the various tools are the imitations of human beings' own hands, and so on and so forth. Hitherto, each of human beings' spiritual products, from the first folksong or love song to religion, epic, art, music, sculpture, was made on the basis of copying or tracing the world or human beings themselves. Cultural accumulation, be it material or spiritual, is the accumulation performed by human beings with respect to their impressions of the world or to their own feelings of life. On this account, culture is the microcosm of the world (the cosmos) and, a fortiori, it embraces all the information of the latter.

In addition, seen from the explicit state, the cosmos is a universally interconnected body in which all things are connected with, interact with, and constrain one another in a full-scale fashion. As a consequence, everything or each locus in the cosmos owns all the mutually connecting, interacting, and constraining information of any other one, and hence each locus becomes an information microcosm of the cosmos. Language and culture are respectively a locus in, hence an information microcosm of, the cosmos.

1.2 The Coevolution of Language with Culture

When people make the following judgments, it indicates that they have early admitted of the fact that language and culture indeed contain each other's information:

> Language is the carrier of culture.
> Language is a key to a national culture. (By Franz Boas the anthropologist)
> Language is a product of culture, and the understanding of it is restricted by certain cultural experiences.
> Language also reacts to culture, and they are the results of each other. (By Porter the communication scientist)
> Language is a part of spiritual culture. Language is inseparable from culture. Pronunciation emerges together with other modes of behavior (e.g., the physical one). The learning of language is also that of culture. The maturity of language is also that of human beings in their social and cultural statuses. (Malinowski the anthropologist)
> Language is a cultural model. It is a key for human beings to recognize the world, but it is also a shackle of them. (Edward Sapir the anthropologist)
> Each language contains a particular world view. (Wilhelm von Humboldt the European linguist and philosopher)[3]

It is my contention that both language and culture are the spiritual materialization or solidification created by human beings.

---

[3]The last three citations are quoted from Hu and Gao (1997, pp. 16–18).

Language is a sort of human behavior, to wit., doing things with words. Culture is also one of the modes of behavior of human beings to express their idea of values. The two behaviors are both produced by human beings, being in a state of "You are in me and I am in you." **There is never a pure language without any cultural flesh and blood. If language and culture were split or isolated from one another, there would be a split human mind**. As is known, a normal human mind cannot be split. Language and culture are two behaviors released by human beings with the same mind and soul, so how can there be one spiritual commander-in-chief when people use language while another when they are engaged in cultural activities?

Language is a primary means on which people rely to live their social lives. Once language enters into the communicative context, it is bound with culture, the two being embedded in and intermingled with one another.

According to Claire Kramsch (1998), there are three sorts of relationship between language and the cultural reality.

The words uttered by people are directed upon the same experiences. These words express communicable facts, ideas, and events, mobilizing people's common knowledge reserve with respect to the world. Words also reflect the utterer's own attitude toward, belief in, and views about others. Seen from these aspects, **language expresses the cultural reality**.

Be that as it may, it is impossible that the members of a language league or a social group only express their experiences; but rather, they also create experiences via language. People bestow meaning on language and communicate with each other by means of the media they choose, say, talking on the phone, performing face-to-face conversations, writing letters, sending emails, making charts, or the like. People employ the modes of oral language, written language, and visible media, which per se creates the various meanings understandable to the social groups to which they belong. During the course of meaning creation, people use tones, accents, conversation styles, gestures, countenances, and so on. By virtue of these verbal and non-verbal aspects, **language embodies the cultural reality**.

Furthermore, language is a sign system with cultural values. The utterers can differentiate themselves from others via the conditions in which people use language: identification or differentiation; they regard their own languages as a sign of social identification. The prohibition to use some language (Language disputes once occurred in many places of the world. For instance, in a certain language area, or on a certain occasion, a foreign language was prohibited.) is often believed to be a refusal of some people to join in some social group and their culture (which is more than shutting the door but is discrimination in toto). In this connection, we can say that **language marks the cultural reality**.

Language and culture embrace and contain one another in roughly the three ways mentioned afore. "Language expresses the cultural reality" is the first sort of relationship between them. One of the mostly used statements by scholars in China, namely, "Language is the carrier of culture," is generally pertinent to this. "Language embodies the cultural reality" reveals the holographic relation between language and culture. Nonetheless, insofar as the differentiation of categories is concerned, I cannot see the essential difference between Kramsch's "Language expresses the cultural reality" and "Language embodies the cultural reality" (Of course, I notice that his "People created experiences via language" is meaningful). As to "Language marks the cultural reality" (with this main rationale: language is a sign of social identification), in terms of the relation between language and culture, this discovery is important and meaningful. When it comes to the degree of relevance to the theory of language holography, nevertheless, I contend that "Language marks the cultural reality" remains to be the most relevant. The most relevant, profound, and typical information fusion of culture and language is: the cultural perspective is condensed in language structure (see the upcoming Sect. 3 of this chapter).

2 The Coevolution of Language with Culture

The thesis of coevolution refers to such a theory which holds that cultural replication and genetic replication became intertwined, each providing the context for the evolution of the other.[4] Nevertheless, what is the rationale of this theory? Durham (1991) believes that language provides the best evidence for the thesis of coevolution. This question arouses my interest in that it is meaningful to the explication of the holographic relation between language and culture.

It can be seen from language how cultural and genetic replications provide the context for the evolution of each other. In our discussion, when we tentatively suspend the parameter of genetic replication, we will have this: it can be seen from language how culture evolves.

It is an indisputable fact that in language we can see the evolution of culture. When you read the literatures through the ages in every country with a long history and a developed culture (e.g., China, Greece, Egypt, India, France, Russia, and the Great Britain), you will find that none of the languages (historical literatures are the crystals of the diachronic language state) therein does not rely on or is not bound with the country's developed-ness of productivity and the state of spiritual cultivation through the ages——manifested in logic, science, religion, and art. The degree to which a culture evolves determines the degree to which its language changes. De facto, to study the evolution or the state of culture in a country's languages through the ages already becomes a most important means to study the cultural evolution, another means is to study the unearthed relics, and the third one is to trace back from the accumulation of existent material civilization. To study the literatures through the ages is to study the language as such. In this relationship, we can thus see: **the information of cultural evolution is read in that of language evolution. This is the holographic relation between language and culture**.

Languages differ in fundamental ways: their phoneme inventories vary from 11 to 141. There are an estimated 7000 or more distinct languages in the world, each a cultural tradition of (generally) thousands of years in the making (please cf. the

[4] Wilson and Keil (1999, p. 441).

following Sect. 3). Each [language] is adapted to a unique cultural and social environment, with striking differences in usage patterns (Bauman and Sherzer 1974). This cultural adaptation constitutes the cultural capital of language, and language differences are perhaps the most perduring of all aspects of culture. In fact, language provides the best evidence for the thesis of coevolution, whereby cultural replication and genetic replication became intertwined, each providing the context for the evolution of the other.[5]

We thus further infer that not only cultural and genetic replications coevolve, the same also holds to linguistic and cultural evolutions. **Why can they coevolve? Could the coevolution as such be realized if they were not in a state of "You are in me and I am in you" at the level of information?** As was previously mentioned, there are three methods to study the evolution of a culture, namely, to study the historical literature, unearthed relics, and existent material civilization, which offer references to, are compared with, and are traced back (in both directions) to one another. For instance, the comparison and tracing back between existent material civilization and the unearthed relics, the comparison between the unearthed relics and ancient linguistic literatures, and the comparison between ancient literatures and existent material civilization (by means of tracing back in both directions) will help people see the evolution of culture. What, then, does the study of historical literatures mean? In historical literatures, diachronic linguistic state is solidified. To study historical literatures is to study the languages through the ages. To observe the evolution of language is the most convenient way to observe the evolution of culture. In this relationship, we can see this: **the information of cultural evolution is read in that of language evolution. This is one of the holographic relations between language and culture**.

3 The Cultural Perspective Condensed in Language

According to Robert A. Wilson and Frank C. Keil, through language, and to a lesser extent other semiotic systems, individuals have access to the large accumulation of cultural ideas, practices, and technology that instantiate a distinct cultural tradition. The question then arises as to what extent these ideas and practices are actually embodied in the language in lexical and grammatical distinctions. Humboldt, and later Sapir and Whorf, are associated with the theory that a language encapsulates a cultural perspective and actually creates conceptual categories.[6]

"Each [language is] a cultural tradition of (generally) thousands of years in the making" and "Each is adapted to a unique cultural and social environment, with

[5]Maddieson (1984).

[6]Wilson and Keil (1999, p. 441).

striking differences in usage patterns"[7] are assertions of great profoundness, which echos the fact that the cultural perspective is condensed in language structure.

Insofar as the cultural perspective is condensed in language structure, I will also cite many phenomena found in Chinese as evidences.

The first evidence. In English, there is a sentence pattern with *it* as the formal subject or object. In this sentence pattern, the actual subject or object is supplemented by the successive components (that-clause, to do sth., or some other component equivalent to a noun). There is not such a situation in Chinese, nor is there the inflection of form. This difference is the solidification and accumulation of the respective cultural views and qualities of the two nations. Specifically speaking, it is my contention that the difference as such in language structure **is very likely the solidification and accumulation of the philosophical ideas of the people speaking these two languages at the level of sentence structure**. This is because philosophical ideas are located at the innermost level of a culture, and it surely has its manifestations in language structure. On the part of English nations, such a rigorous requirement on form corresponds to the nations' philosophical ideas. There is not a corresponding requirement on form in Chinese, which might be attributed to Chinese philosophical ideas.

Let us have a look at whether or not this is the case. To begin, insofar as Chinese philosophy is concerned, it never makes deductions via logical forms. The language of Chinese philosophy riches in hints but is not very clear, namely, it contains no concept of deduction or inference at all. With regard to the language barrier in philosophy, Feng Youlan notes that if one cannot read the original philosophical works, it will be very hard for him/her to understand and appreciate them in toto. The case is so to all the philosophical works. This is due to the fact that the language barrier plus the property of Chinese philosophical works, viz., rich in hints, keeps people away. In Chinese philosophical remarks and works, the places rich in hints are virtually untranslatable. He/She who merely read the translations of them would lose their hints, which means that he/she would lose much.[8] Feng Youlan further notes that Chinese philosophy starts from the immediate eidetic understanding of things, which can interpret why its language riches in hints but is not very clear. The unclarity as such results from the fact that it does not express any concept in deduction or reference. The philosopher does nothing but tell us what is in his/her eyes, and just because of this, his/her words rich in hints and it is unnecessary for them to be definite.[9] At the theoretical level, when a language is not very definite while people intend to find definitely the exact thoughts in it, to strengthen the analysis is supposed to conform to logic, so why Chinese philosophy refuses to appeal to language analysis but let this "not very clear" go? Isn't this a little strange? In my view, this is exactly the mystery of the relationship between Chinese philosophy and the language. To uncover this mystery, one must observe the doings of the School of Logicians, sophists, logicians, and

[7]Bauman and Sherzer (1974).

[8]Feng (1996, p. 13).

[9]Feng (1996, pp. 22–23).

dialectic philosophers in the history of Chinese philosophy, particularly the fundamental spirit of it. Limited to the length of this book, I cannot unfold much, so please cf. Sect. 2 (“Different linguistic directions of Chinese and Western philosophies”) of Chapter 2 (“Prospect: Philosophical inquiries into language) of my *Language: the Last Homestead of Human Beings*. Chinese philosophy “emphasizes society, ethics and morals, and the present life,” and seeks the top spiritual state. “This state is located in but simultaneously rises over the mundane world.” In terms of philosophical appeal, “The East is inward-oriented.” For instance, Chinese philosophy notes that human beings “need inner peace and happiness,” and “it regards human life as nothing other than a natural fact and tries to improve it spiritually,” which are all manifestations of the inward-oriented-ness.” The inward-oriented spiritual sought needs no signal expressions; just the opposite, it needs long-term introspections. “In Chinese philosophy, the method of logical analysis has never been fully developed,” which tells us very clearly that a research method not that concerned with logic may not necessarily need signal expressions. “Traditional Chinese philosophy is a sort of human-centered ‘theory of humankind’.” Does a philosophy developing by virtue of intuition and experiences need rigorous signal or linguistic expressions? Chinese philosophy has gone deep into *Xin-Xing*心性(Mind-Nature) that is like a huge labyrinth in which philosophy is enthralled and is reluctant to go out. Neither mind nor humanism desperately needs the help of signal statements, so they need not head toward language analysis. **Chinese philosophy is characterized by high conceptualization, spiritualization, and self-examination, and by the stress on the individual’s eidetic understanding. A philosophy as such does not necessarily appeal to language analysis** (cf. *Language: The Last Homestead of Human Beings*), and it will not perform much inflections of language form. Next, let us have a look at the situation of Western philosophy. Being constrained by formal logic, Western philosophy is guided by mathematical and scientific knowledge. Logic, mathematics, etc., cannot but rely on the help of signs, then, a fortiori, Western philosophy employs language analysis. **Western philosophy is characterized by high signification, logicalization, and rigorous formal demonstration, which plants the seed of it heading toward language analysis** (cf. *Language: the Last Homestead of Human Beings*) **and attaching importance to formal variation**.

The second evidence. The duality-oriented text structure (see Sect. 4, “Cognitive grammar” of Chapter 6) is a typical paragon which condenses the cultural perspective of Chinese. The Chinese people show special preference to duality-oriented discourse, having long since chosen and brewed the aesthetic taste of “in pair.” Presumably, this is closely related to the Chinese nation’s philosophy and religion, say, the calculation and prediction of the eight *gua*卦 in *Zhouyi*周易 (*The Book of Changes*) is performed in pair, the *yin*阴 and *yang*阳 fishes in the *taiji*太极 diagram are in pair, and so are the antithetical couplets that every family will patch on their doors to welcome the coming Lunar New Year. These cases prove that the cultural perspective of the Chinese nation is condensed in language structure. I even assume that the “你说什么，我信什么” (Whatever you say, I believe it) in Chinese is also of this structure albeit some think that the relationship between the two sentences belongs to bare condition. I am against this view insomuch as this is not a relationship of condition, and condition is not necessary at all. What, then, is the relationship as such? Is this relationship temporal, cause-and-effect, progressive, or adversative? None of them is. Is the latter sentence the object of the former one (namely, it is a simple sentence with a fronted object)? Neither is it. This is because the latter sentence itself has had its own object of "what." Overall, this is a sentence having no meaning until it is expressed in pair, a discourse integrating two parts. Can it be that, which is also another interpretation of the duality-oriented discourse, such a discourse appertains to the cognitive modules of human beings? As to this point, I have discussed it in Sect. 4 of Chapter 6.

The third evidence. Variations of perspective or focus can be seen in the sentence structures of different languages. There is the remark of "我头疼" (My head aches.) (subject-predicate predication) in Chinese, and "我头疼得厉害" (My head aches badly.) is also a common saying. If one wants to highlight the part of "头" (head) and merely say "我的头疼" (My head, aches.) (where "头" becomes the subject and "疼" (ache) becomes the predicate, forming together a subject-predicate collocation), it would sound a little unnatural, and hence there is supposed to be, as a rule, an adverbial like "很" (very) after "头," or "得要命" (very badly) after "头疼" as a complement, which results in "我的头很疼" or "我的头痛得要命." In this situation, it is more natural that "头" acts as an independent subject. Of these two remarks, the more often said is "我头疼." Originally, at the level of logic, the subject of ache is "头" rather than the whole "I," in Chinese however, the remark of "我头疼" sounds very normal to people and cannot be more natural. In Russian, logically speaking, the subject of ache is "head": Голова (head) болит (aches). So where is the whole person? The word signifying the person is not allowed to be the subject but is constrained by a preposition: Голова ***у*** меня болит. Что ***у*** тебя болит? Где ***у*** тебя болит? Of them, Голова is the subject, the leading role; у меня or у тебя are the adverbial, the supporting roles. Болит **под** ложечкой (Aches on the stomach) and Болит **б** ухе (Aches at the ears) are straightforwardly impersonal sentences in which the word signifying the whole person is prohibited. There is an idiom as another proof: **У** кого что болит, тот о том и говорит (Tell where you are concerned) (Tell the place of the ache). In English, the similar remarks are differently expressed. Unlike Chinese or Russian, in English, there is not a corresponding structure that separates out a "head" as the subject capable of sending the feeling of pain, so "headache" is used instead. The word of *I have a splitting headache* generally corresponds to "我头疼得要命" in Chinese; that of *I suffer* ***from*** *headaches* is also a common remark; that of *I have a continuous pain* ***in*** *the head*, whereas, sounds a little bookish. Of these three sorts of remark, the subjects of the ache are all the whole person (including I, she, he…), which differs from the Russian expression but is similar to "我头疼" in Chinese; in English, there is no need of a preposition to introduce or indicate *head*, though. How to analyze the cultural perspective contained in these three sorts of language structure? Can we say this: Russian native speakers are the most logical and can tell that what is aching is the head (as a part) rather than the body (as the whole); Chinese native speakers sometimes are logical but sometimes else forget it; English native speakers, whereas, are not logical? That would greatly wrong the English native speakers. The Anglo-American philosophy is immersed in logic, and they are virtually bundled together.

Now let us come to the point at issue: what kind of cultural perspective is contained in language structure? In my view, the three aforementioned language structures reflect different variations of perspective or focus. The Russians have two sorts of perspectives in these remarks (Голова ***у*** меня болит and Болит **п*о*д** ложечкой): (1) The regard is put on the part before the whole (body) or, in other words, the part is highlighted (Голова is the subject) while the whole is subordinate (a preposition is used to constrain the word signifying the person, e.g., ***у*** меня). (2) The noun signifying the person is prohibited, and the regard is put on the more delicate part (e.g., **п*о*д** ложечкой), and the focus is on the part rather than the whole. Chinese native speakers fundamentally focus on the part. "我的头很疼" or "我的头疼得要命" is a paragon as such. Moreover, even in the remark "我头疼(得要命)," it is still the head that is aching and people do not say "我疼, 且仅在头部疼 (I ache, and only in the head)" or "我疼在头部 (I ache in the head)" (unless when answering the particular question from the third party: "你疼在哪儿 (Where is the ache)?" So to speak, the situation of perspective or focus variation when Chinese native speakers say such words is: from the part to the whole. Differently put, they highlight the part in favor of the whole. In terms of English, take *I have a splitting headache* and *I suffer* ***from*** *headaches* as an example, their perspectives go for the whole before concerning the part, so the variation of their focuses is: from the whole to the part. More cases are: *Pat a dog*. (The whole dog rather than the patted part of it is mentioned); *Pat a child* ***on*** *the head*. (The child being patted is mentioned first, and then it is told that the specific patted part is the head); *She hit him* ***on*** *the head with a book*. (The sentence first mentions that a whole person is hit, and then tells that the specific hit part is the head); *I was bit by a falling stone*. (The sentence does not tell the specific hit part but merely says that the whole is hit); *The car was hit by a grenade*. (The part is again ignored and the sentence merely says the whole is hit); *He has been hit* ***in*** *the leg by a sniper's bullet* (The sentence first says that the whole is hit, and then focuses on the part—the leg). Are there exceptional cases? Of course there are. For instance, *Pat sb's hand* takes the part as the center. Moreover, we can see or hear similar sentences, e.g., *My legs ached*. I believe that the readers can find more counter-examples. In this vein, as to whether or not "variations of perspective or focus" can interpret such sentences in English or Russian, it is a question deserving further discussions.

An interpretation different from the variations of perspective or focus is: different attitudes of analysis. Let's have a look at English first: the whole (I, she, he…) to which the feeling of pain belongs is first given, and then prepositions (from, in, on…) are used to introduce smaller parts——logically speaking, to demonstrate them. It should be said that this is an attitude of detailed analysis layer by layer which starts from the whole and performs the analysis on the parts. Russian uses the same attitude of detailed analysis, just that the detailed spots of analysis are different. There are two sorts of placement in Russian with respect to the detailed analysis of the feeling of pain, i.e., two demonstrating (introducing) methods: (1) in the personal sentence, the part acts as the subject, and the analysis is placed on the whole person, e.g., Голова

у меня болит. (2) In the impersonal sentence, say, in Болит ***под***ложечкой and Болит б ухе, the whole qua the feeling of pain does not show itself, so the analysis is placed on the part, e.g., ***под***ложечкой and **б** ухе. In Chinese, remarks such as "我头疼" fundamentally refuse to take an analytic attitude toward the feeling of pain, and hence they do not use prepositions to analyze the details. This is because the feeling of pain is de facto inseparable from the whole human body, all the less from the part, and as to which part is the place of the detailed analysis, the listener would understand it without the recourse to the introductions from the prepositions. This is the manifestation of Chinese's trait of supplementing the formal analysis by means of intellectual interference. Different attitudes of analysis are of course different, and more profound, cultural perspectives. This apart, the "starting from the whole and focusing, namely, performing the analysis, on the parts" in English exactly originates from the rigorous attitude of analysis in its philosophies; the "refusing to take an analytic attitude toward the feeling of pain, and hence using no preposition to analyze the details," whereas, exactly originates from the property of Chinese philosophy of emphasizing eidetic understanding (as to this view, please cf. the analyses of the examples in the first evidence).

The fourth evidence/example. When it comes to the answering words in phone calls, or those of the person who knocks at the door, an English native speaker usually introduces him/herself with the third person, e.g., *It's me... It's John....* A Chinese native speaker whereas usually introduces him/herself with the first person, e.g., "我是张三呀" (I am Tom) or "是我呀" (Me). The former situation can be said a mentality of objective introduction while the latter one of subjective answering. Presumably, this is related to the fact that Western philosophies and scientific studies attach importance to form and the external world whereas Chinese philosophy pays more attention to the eidetic understanding, human beings, and humanism.

I believe, firmly, there are more evidences to prove that the cultural perspective is condensed in language structure, and Robert A. Wilson and Frank C. Keil's argumentation pertinent to the relation between culture and cognition is a paragon. Say, "There are many aspects of the cultural patterning of language that may be fundamental to its role in cognition," "Natural languages are learned in and through social interaction and constitute probably the most complex cognitive task that humans routinely undertake (and quite plausibly the major pressure for brain evolution in our specie)," "Fundamental variation in semantic parameters makes the interface between language and general cognition look much more problematic than is commonly assumed,"[10] and so on and so forth.

From the discussions in the three sections above, namely, **the relationship between language and cultural reality, the coevolution of language with culture, and the cultural perspective condensed in language, the conclusion that language structure is holographic with the cosmic one can be derived**. This view (i.e., the theory of language holography) offers an inspiration to us: when you are aware that the cosmos is holographic with language on structure, you can infer the minor structure from the major one, and vice versa. When you find in the vast

[10]Wilson and Keil (1999, pp. 441–442).

sky a structure (similar to or imagined as) of right triangle, you need not at all really go to the distant outer space (you cannot achieve this at all) like a moron to measure it; rather, you merely need to draw a right triangle on the paper on your desk, and then perform the calculation and operation. What is the rationale? The rationale is, the little right triangle on the paper is similar to, viz., holographic with, the (similar or imagined) one in the distant sky. It can thus be seen that when I give the following judgment, you need not regard it as nonsense: given that the astrophysicists can calculate the various cosmic structures by means of telescopes and mathematical formulae, the linguists are entirely capable of inferring via language structure the situation in which the major frames in the cosmos are embedded in each other. The rationale of this judgment is, given that the two sorts of structure are similar, we can infer the major from the minor. In this vein, we can reach another assertion: **the cosmic information is condensed in language structure**. "The capacity to grasp language is relevant to the hardwares, and it relies on the major center for language in the cerebral cortex and the motor center operating the vocal organs; on the other hand, which kind of language is spoken is determined by the cultural environment. On this account, whereas language capacity is biogenetic, the specific language structure results from cultural evolution."[11]

Now you can see that this chapter being short notwithstanding, it is very important.

References

Bauman, R., & Sherzer, J., *Explorations in the ethnography of speaking*. Cambridge: Cambridge University Press, 1974.

Feng. Youlan, *A short history of Chinese philosophy*. Beijing: Peking University Press, 1996.

Hu. Wenzhong & Gao. Yihong, *Foreign languages teaching and culture*. Changsha: Hunan Education Publishing House, 1997.

Kramsch, C., *Language and culture*, Oxford, Oxford University Press, 1998.

Maddieson, I., *Patterns of sounds*. Cambridge: Cambridge University Press, 1984.

Wilson, Robert A., & Frank C. Keil (Eds.), *The MIT encyclopedia of the cognitive sciences*, Second printing. Cambridge: The MIT Press, 1999.

Zhao. Nanyuan, *Cognitive science and the general theory of evolution*. Beijing: Tsing Hua University Press, 1994.

[11]Zhao (1994, p. 188).

Part IV
Prediction

Chapter 9
Two Speculations About Language

Abstract The two speculations about language are the appropriation of the theory of language holography. The appropriation might not be successful, though.

Keywords Activation of the sense of sound · Foregone generations · Innate language acquisition device · Robot · Artificial intelligence

Speculations and predictions are the conventions of scientific research. Strictly speaking, the research on the basis of which no further speculations or predictions can be presented is not scientific in the true sense of the word, and it can even be said a discounted one. Qian Xuesen once said, "Seen from the perspective of the science of thinking, a scientific work always starts from a speculation and then performs the scientific argumentation."

Speculations and predictions indicate that the objects of them are non-real, namely, inaudible, invisible, and untouchable. Due to this, they impress people with illusion even fantasy. Be that as it may, if a speculation or a prediction is scientific, it will be demonstrated sooner or later in the long history.

Speculations and predictions must have a certain amount of scientific support which might not necessarily be large on amount but must be scientific on quality and be authentic——of course, it is not necessarily acceptable to every one now (Speculations and predictions never take pride in being supercilious and particular insomuch as they risk much).

Therefore, the reader might doubt some speculation (say, the speculation presented here), and he/she might even present scientific refutations against it. In this line, he/she would not only eliminate an error, but also save a soul talking nonsense; if he/she could not present scientific refutations, my response is nothing but this: please read the speculation again.

The positive significance of speculations and predictions is more than seeking their realization, but it also lies in the fact that relevant scientific debates and discussions might be provoked therefrom. In the history of science, this situation often occurred: the obtainment from relevant debates and discussions were far more than the object's realization itself, and the former's significance was also far greater than the latter's. For instance, Jacques Derrida's critiques of traditional philosophy, from the ideological structure to the linguistic one, subverted the traditional structure by means of his

G. Qian, *The Theory of Language Holography*,
https://doi.org/10.1007/978-981-16-2039-3_9

particular philological theory and suspected all the metaphysical thinking methods and structures. As is said, "Derrida's theory provoked endless debates because of its radicalness, but this is exactly where its values lie."[1]

It is based on the recognition above that I present the following two speculations.

1 Activation of the Sense of Sound Transmitted from the Foregone Generations

1.1 Introduction: About "Innate Language Acquisition Device"

Chomsky's discussions about "innate language acquisition device (LAD)" are mainly these:

> "Human language seems to be a unique particular instinct of human beings."[2]
> "We can regard the universal grammar as a part of the initial state of human beings, that is, children's **mental state prior to experiences**."[3]
> "The situation of universal grammar or process mode is similar to this. In this way, albeit we are ignorant of the fact that human mind discovers this genetic device of language under suitable circumstances, we are not as ignorant of the brains with drastically different modes of construction. We are convinced that there is such a genetic device."[4]
> "The 'language faculty' is understood to be a particular component of the human mind,…this theory is now often called universal grammar (UG)."[5] "The grammar of a particular language, then, is to be supplemented by a universal grammar."[6]

As to whether or not this genetic device exists, there are various views and debates in the academia. Of Chomsky's demonstrations, a relatively persuasive point is children's acquisition of their native language. Why can children generally grasp their native language (albeit not very smoothly or fluently) within a very short period of time and show amazing creativity when they remain to receive systematic and regular education? The children who were born in their mother country but breed in a foreign one can also grasp the foreign language very soon, what is the reason? Why do children all over the world have so much in common on the process of native language acquisition? These questions oblige people to believe that there is a universal grammar, and that language device can be inherited.

[1]Xu et al. (1996, p. 215).
[2]Cf. Foreign Language Research (1982, p. 44).
[3]Foreign Language Research (1982, p. 5).
[4]Foreign Language Research (1982, p. 44).
[5]Chomsky (1986, p. 3).
[6]Chomsky (1965, p. 6).

The ultimate solution to these questions relies on the complete clarification of the black box of human brain. At present, no one can definitely give a conclusion universally acceptable. Be that as it may, psychology, linguistics, and anthropology are disciplines approaching the top layer of cognitive science. What is the "discipline approaching the top layer"? According to Zhao Nanyuan's "general evolutionism", the concepts relevant to cognition can be roughly divided into seven layers, namely, from the bottom to the top: the layers of biological physics, biological chemistry, neuron, neural network, groups of neural network, consciousness, language, and logic. We can see that language is located at the sixth layer approaching the top one. When human brain is considered as a black box, language layer can offer the box's input and output relations to us. If the black box were simple enough, its inner function and structure would be easily inferred from the relations as such. Alas, the black box is extremely complicated, so much so that it goes beyond the reach of inference. Another difficulty is, there are congenital and acquired differences among human brains, which obliges the afore-mentioned disciplines to employ statistical methods in research. Such a method, whereas, often brings subjective, arbitrary, and one-sided factors. If we had grasped the brain's cognitive mechanism, these upper-layer disciplines could offer very good methods of verification to it; otherwise, it would be hardly successful to infer the brain's mechanism from the psychological phenomena. This appertains to the exponential explosion (please see the first note in the first question, "The hierarchy of human brain's cognitive and thinking process", in Sect. 2, "The hierarchy of cognition and that of language" of Chapter 4).

Nonetheless, the theory of cosmos holography adds weight to the existence of LAD.

Before acquiring language, the baby needs, first and foremost, the innate capacity for meaning-understanding. Is there such an innate capacity? The baby is in fact really capable of understanding the meanings of the actions of people around. For instance, when it is ravenous, it will stop crying as soon as it sees the mother open the forepart of her upper garment, which indicates that it knows that this action means she will nurse it. The biologist interprets this as an instinct. What is instinct? It is an innate capacity inherited from the parents. The baby can understand the meaning of the actions, which has been corroborated, but how can it understand that which cannot be expressed via actions? Since many things are inexpressible, how does the baby manage to understand their meanings and how does it obtain this capacity? In other words, how do the parents pass on the capacity for and the knowledge of meaning-understanding to next generation? I argue that there is probably **an innate structure of meaning-understanding** in human brain. As is contended, "…It develops on the basis of the information resonance being everywhere in the material world, being the internalization of the law of holographic resonance of information on the organism. …Long-term experiences of some environment will leave traces on the organism, be gradually internalized into the genes, form a holographic structure coincident with this environment hence enable the organism to recognize this environment."[7] Language acquisition is possible, which is first due to the fact that the baby has

[7]Wang and Yan (1995, pp. 150–151).

an innate holographic structure of meaning-understanding. This structure is a latent cognitive capacity rather than knowledge itself. To get knowledge, the baby also needs the triggering, shaping, improving, and reinforcing of its acquired experiences in Chomsky's terminology, that is, education.

There is a counter evidence of the existence of the innate holographic structure of meaning-understanding: in the child's acquired education, albeit he/she is faced with colorful and diversified environmental stimuli, his/her acceptance of knowledge refuses to be blindly guided but follows the due order. "This indicates that in the brain, even in the DNA, there must be an innate holographic structure controlling the acceptance of the external information. If human consciousness were merely a result of the acquired education, children would be supposed to accept any information we teach them but would not show this orderliness. If the holographic structure of meaning-understanding of human beings were not inherited, the baby would be incapable of discerning the information in human society, let alone learning human language. If human beings did not have innate holographic structure of meaning-understanding, the knowledge they obtain in practices would not be delivered or communicated, and human culture would barely evolve."[8] Why would it barely evolve? This is because if so, the new-born babies would have to start from zero after the forerunners die. The fact is, nevertheless, starting from zero is not necessary. For instance, a merely four or five-year-old talented child can understand, triggered by his/her parents' education, the classic melodies centuries old without spending centuries again in learning them. If there were not the innate holographic structure of meaning-understanding, this would absolutely not come true. The later generation need not learn everything from the beginning but will rapidly grasp the knowledge handed down through millenniums, which proves that there is the innate structure of meaning-understanding. Memory is heritable, and the same holds to knowledge. It can be asserted that without these two heredities, there would not be the accumulation or evolution of culture.

That which co-exists with the innate holographic structure of meaning-understanding is supposed to be the innate language acquisition device. This is a necessary conclusion.

Regeneration necessarily leads to repetition. This is the second rationale provided by the law of cosmos holography to the theory of innate language acquisition device. If every new-born human being did not repeat namely condense the linguistic competence of the older generations, he/she should start from grasping the language knowledge created tens of thousands of years ago, but this is of course not the case. The repetition of language knowledge is the inheritance of linguistic competence of one generation after another. Inheritance amounts to today's amazing speed and quality of the baby on language learning: a child might even have a tone or manner indistinguishable from his/her parents. What is "Regeneration necessarily leads to repetition"? Insofar as all things are concerned, "From the second generation on, later generations will holographically repeat the progressions of the former ones in a

[8]Wang and Yan (1995, p. 152).

successive fashion. The 'seeds' of the later generations always condense the evolutionary sequences into themselves."[9] Here, to understand "condense" is of vital importance. "Condense" means to repeat rapidly and briefly, namely, to inherit as well as memorize the capacities (here they are manifested in linguistic competence) of the former generations. That is to say, "When a system evolves into a higher stage, it does not abandon the obtained results in the former stage but deposit them in itself in an unnoticed fashion, which makes the system show an increasing complexity and order."[10] Human beings do not abandon the periodical fruits of the past generations but deposit them generation after generation and gradually internalize them into the inheritance of language device, which is the innateness for posterity.

As a matter of fact, Chomsky is not the only one who believes that language is an innate talent of human beings. Based on the studies of A. von Haller (the author of *Physiological Elements of the Human Body*) and Johannes Muller (a German physiologist, the author of *Elements of Physiology*), F. J. Gall an Austrian doctor probed into the brain nervous tissue's control over language, and inferred that in the brain region, there are two nerve centers respectively controlling the capacity to speak and to store and memorize words. In 1861 and 1874, P. Broca a doctor and C. Wernicke a physiologist of France followed this train of thought and confirmed as well as discovered that there are the regions of speech generation and speech reception in the cerebral cortex. The second half of the nineteenth century witnessed the emergence of many works investigating the positioning of language in human brain and the phenomenon of aphasia. Humboldt also thought that language was a part of the biological capacity of human beings. He firmly believed that language should be regarded as a gifted belonging of human beings. Early in the 1960s, people noticed, from the studies of Lenneberg and others, that linguistic competence was independent of other cognitive capacities, and hence they primarily confirmed the existence of language gene and the idea that language was controlled by genes. Does language gene exist or not? Large quantities of reports in recent years indicate that there has been a significant development in the biological deciphering of genetic code. It can be predicted that the deciphering of language gene is a very definite possibility in next century.

"The innate language acquisition device" will be ultimately found via scientific (physical, chemical, or biological?) means. I am certainly not the man who presents "innate language acquisition device"; I merely infer by virtue of the theory of language holography that it is supposed to exist. This offers a warm-up for the speculation of the activation of the sense of sound transmitted from the foregone generations.

---

[9]Wang and Yan (1995, p. 221).

[10]Wang and Yan (1995, p. 222).

1.2 The Speculation of the Activation of the Sense of Sound Transmitted from the Foregone Generations

The activation of the sense of sound transmitted from the foregone generations has two meanings as follows: first, originally, the linguistic competence (including foreign linguistic competence) of the older one or several generations exists latently, in the form of the sense of sound, in the mind of the future one or several (consanguineous or non-consanguineous) generations. Secondly, it means to actively look for the scientific methods by virtue of which the latent linguistic competence (the sense of sound) can be manifested (activate or induced).

This hypothesis appertains to the existence of the innate language acquisition device.

In the passage above, I stressed that "the foreign linguistic competence exists latently" with a purpose relevant to practicability. This is because native language is acquired hence needs few efforts from children whereas the acquisition of a foreign language will cost virtually the lifelong energy of a person. On the part of a country, the investment in foreign language education is considerable. According to a survey, China's investment in foreign language education occupies two-fifths of the total education investment. What's more, this huge investment failed to obtain the expected result which, in China, has drawn the attention all around, including the worry from the former vice premier, Li Lanqing. He thus said,

"Some might ask, why does a vice premier of the State Council concern himself with the teaching methods of a discipline——foreign language? In fact, I have been thinking about this in the past many years. ... Due to the insufficient popularization of foreign languages including English, our country suffered a lot, say, the scale and efficiency of foreign exchanges were influenced, the international communications and cooperations of our many excellent cultural and scientific results were also severely constrained and, in particular, some economically underdeveloped areas even constrained the progression of the opening-up. Therefore, in a certain sense, to popularize foreign languages and to train foreign language talents, to improve foreign language teaching methods, and to improve foreign language teaching are already not an ordinary teaching problem but a great one that can influence the better implementation of our opening-up policy and promote our economic and social development. In terms of the present foreign language teaching levels and methods in our country, the problem of "**much time, low efficacy**" is a common phenomenon, so it needs studying and improving. ...The course of foreign language started rather early and occupied not a few class hours. For example, many students experienced 8–12 years of foreign language learning from the secondary school (some even from the primary school) till the sophomore year, but most of them are **incapable of skillfully reading foreign original works**. **Particularly, many of them are incapable of understanding what they hear or expressing what is in their mind, and hence they have difficulty in communicating with foreigners directly**, which indicates that **the effect of foreign language teaching in our country remains**

to be sufficient to meet the needs of the economic and social development, notably the needs of reform and opening-up, and the enlargement of international communications. Therefore, we should attach more importance to the study and reform of foreign language teaching methods. Our aim is, on the premise of adding no burden to students' study, to improve the teaching efficiency by means of reforming the teaching methods, and to spend relatively little time in helping students to grasp more foreign knowledge and improve their foreign language learning. In foreign language teaching, teaching materials, teachers, and language environment are all important, but the most important thing might still be teaching methods. I always imagine, **when we can find a more effective method of learning foreign language that is suitable for Chinese, that would be great**."[11]

In this lecture, that which merits most heed is the following two points: first, his conclusion about the foreign language teaching in our country is: much time, low efficacy. Secondly, his question is: When can we find a more effective method of learning foreign language that is suitable for Chinese? This in fact gives a mobilization order to all the foreign language teachers and researchers in China, namely, to solve a problem that has been unsettled for many years and that cannot be left unsettled any longer. So to speak, the importance of this mobilization order resembles an ancient method of solving problems——offering a reward. What is the value of this problem? What is the price to settle this problem? My answer is: it is priceless, namely, it is more than a price anybody asked. Here I would like to raise a small question by passing: Li Lanqing believes that "the most important thing might still be teaching methods", is this the case? If "teaching methods" is not understood as a pedagogical school (e.g., communicative approach), this judgment is correct. This is because we have tried the existent teaching methods one by one but failed to settle some big problems. **It is exactly after people tried these teaching methods** that Li Lanqing affirmed that "The effect of foreign language teaching in our country remains to be sufficient". Some regard the status quo of foreign language teaching as a kettle of water that can never be boiled. This metaphor has its legitimacy on describing the vicious circle state (namely, to cool the water before it is boiled and boil it after it is cool, and, again, to cool it before it is boiled) of foreign language teaching in China. Nonetheless, the country's investment in the project of foreign language teaching is a great thing, and it goes far beyond the reach of "water". The state of our foreign language teaching is like walking into a marshland. Walking forward, you will get down in deeper and deeper; stopping the moving, you will never be able to get out of it.

Well, do you think I will tender for this "royal assignment"? In my views, to any claim that "**I have successfully found a more effective method for Chinese people to learn foreign languages**", we should take a relatively circumspect attitude. I merely want to show that there are more than one sort of flying mode, so is seeking mode, and all the more so is advancing mode. We are supposed to look for solutions to problems in different ways. If we could find the scientific methods to activate the sense of sound transmitted from the foregone generations (the older one or several

[11] July 5, 2002. See http://news.sohu.com/38/65/news202016538.shtml.

generations), in what kind of speed and efficiency would a foreign language be grasped?——By inserting this previous passage, I intend to note that this speculation is more than a merely theoretical issue.

This speculation contains two parts. **First, the foreign linguistic competence acquired by older generation(s) originally hides latently, in the form of the sense of sound, in the brains of the next (consanguineous or non-consanguineous) generation(s)**.

Readers might say: it is already hard to imagine that "The sense of sound of foreign languages originally hides latently in the brains of the next consanguineous generation(s)", it is all the more so to imagine that "It hides latently in the brains of the next non-consanguineous generation(s)". Given that this problem will be discussed later, I will not linger on it here.

Secondly, we should actively look for the scientific methods to manifest (i.e., activate or provoke) the latent foreign linguistic competence (sense of sound). This is more important and significant. In this line, albeit children still need educating and training to learn a foreign language, **they would grasp it in an unconceivable efficiency with the aid of the scientific methods of activating the sense of sound**.

People now remain to seize upon the capacity for the sense of sound of the older (consanguineous or on-consanguineous) generation(s) at the level of foreign languages, which is merely due to the fact that they remain to find a scientific method to retrieve and trigger the originally existent inherence and memory of the sense of sound as regards foreign languages. The retrieving and triggering method is the method of manifestation. The moment this method is found, a creation of vital significance would occur, which might need the common efforts of the future biologists, geneticists, and linguists. This creation would be a great biological project of human beings. The method as such can greatly save a nation's investment on foreign language education, and everyone's limited as well as treasurable energy of life. What's more, **this would be a step of most substantive significance insofar as the whole planet becomes a factual global village**.

There are eight rationales for my hypothesis above:

1. The hypothesis of innate language acquisition device;
2. The apriori holographic structure of meaning-understanding;
3. The repetition law of the cosmos at evolutional level (Reproduction necessarily leads to resonance).

These three items have been discussed in the "Introduction: about 'innate language acquisition device'", so here I will not go into that.

4. **The calling-out and preservation of the sense of sound**. Here I would first say something about the phenomenon of calling out the sense of sound.[12] What is the calling-out of the sense of sound? For instance, someone spoke a dialect or grasped a foreign language many years ago but has long suspended it out of some reason. Once he/she needs to reuse it, nevertheless, say, when he/she opens a book, listens to the radio, or chats with someone else from his/her hometown,

[12] Qian (1990).

the familiar syllables will pop out and the memories many years ago will be aroused one after another. I call this phenomenon the calling-out of the sense of sound. Every normal person has this capacity with merely different extents of expression, most being considerably active, only few very weak. **When the internal sound impression is stimulated by the external language, it will call out the corresponding concepts to form a combination of speech sound and meaning. This process is called the calling-out of the sense of sound**. The calling-out of the sense of sound is the foundation of the capacity to blurt, and that of fluent reading. There must be the preservation of the sense of sound before the calling-out of it. Can the sense of speech sound be stored in human brain? The answer is yes. The environmental information can be deposited and internalized into the individual organisms. "The subject evolves gradually from the lower levels. It accumulates the levels in the previous evolving process which is also a process whence the environmental information is gradually deposited and internalized. …During the evolving process, the environmental information is gradually internalized into the organisms."[13] Here, the environmental information refers to the education and context of foreign languages, and to the objective existence of the sense of sound, say, the speech sounds, the sounds retransmitted via media. **These speech sounds will be gradually deposited and internalized into human brain, which is the preservation of the sense of sound**. As regards the fact that the impression of the sense of sound is stored in human memory, there is the latest evidence. Morris Halle (1985) drew this conclusion via experiments: "The information about the phonic shape of the words is stored in a fluent speaker's memory in the form of a three-dimensional object".[14] Everyone has already heard his/her native language for a long time (from his/her embryo period) before he/she learned it. He/she has stored quite rich and articulate senses of sound, and is ready at all times to accept the assignment of language stimulation, namely, once he/she has the intention to speak, his sense of sound will immediately reflect off successive meaningful syllables. Given that language is a social product of the combination of sound impressions and concepts, linguistic activity would not be realized without the calling-out of the sense of sound. The calling-out of the sense of sound is an all-encompassing media from listening to reading, speaking, and writing respectively, and from reading to writing.

The point is, is the sense of sound genetic? The following several points are the well-directed answers.

5. **The information of the genes of the sense of sound is immortal**. This de facto means that the sense of speech sound can be reproduced as well as stored. What, then, is the rationale? "We can make a bold inference: human is mortal, but the information of human consciousness is immortal. This is just like an astral body remote from the earth might have disappeared but its light still exists. What's

[13]Wang and Yan (1995, p. 181).

[14]Halle (1985).

> more, the information qua the starlight will never disappear in the cosmos but merely be transmitted or transcribed. In this vein, along with the progression of sciences, human beings can find the genetic information and, a fortiori, the genes of consciousness of ancient people."[15]

This inference is really "bold"! If the information of human consciousness is immortal and can be transcribed, and if the genetic information of ancient people can be found, then another inference would be: the genes of the sense of sound of the past generations can also be found. The memory of the sense of sound is also immortal. Albeit a person dies, the information of the sense of sound of the foreign language that he/she accumulated in his/her lifetime is stored in the cosmos on which human beings survive. In a word, **the information of this gene of the sense of sound is immortal, and it can be passed down in the form of transcription**.

Well, then, can the information of human consciousness be really immortal? It seems that many years would be needed to corroborate this inference. Luckily, the discovery of "ancestral brain" makes possible this inference abruptly.

Haruyama Shigeo a Japanese doctor found after many years of researches a new function of the right or left hemisphere of the brain, and called the right brain "ancestral brain",[16] which is also a great support for the assumption that the sense of sound is genetic. Please pay particular attention to the parlance of "ancestral brain"! Haruyama Shigeo contends that in addition to the perceptual functions such as intuition, image thinking, space, image recognition, etc., the right brain also has a deeply hidden function: to store all the information that the ancestors passed down to later generations via genetic factors. This is why he calls it the "ancestral brain". He also contends that the left brain is "self brain" whose fundamental activities and information storage can be determined by its reason and perception, and hence it has consciousness. Comparatively, the right brain is the "ancestral brain", being apriori and refusing to be dominated by emotions, and hence it has no consciousness. The information of the ancestors' genetic factors stored in the right brain shows directions to later generations whenever and wherever possible, telling them what they should do and what they should not. Due to the fact that the right brain is characterized by image memory and it does not deal with language, except that it can order some instinctive unconditioned reflexes, most of its guiding information is conveyed to the left brain before being implemented; on the other hand, the left brain sometimes tries to convey the most valuable information, after strictly screening the acquired information and determining that it is inheritable by later generations, into the information bank of the "ancestral brain" for storage.

In this vein, the right brain becomes the storage-transfer station of information between generations.

Here I would like to discuss a question. Since the right brain is characterized by image memory and it does not deal with language, the sense of sound is stored in the left brain in which language is handled. As was stated afore, the right brain is the "ancestral brain", and the ancestors' sound heredity is merely conveyed to it

---

[15]Wang and Yan (1995, p. 338).

[16]Zhang et al. (1988).

which, nevertheless, cannot give speech sounds. Won't this come to a dead end? It will not. Also as was stated afore, in terms of the inherited information obtained by the right brain, "Most of its guiding information is conveyed to the left brain before being implemented". Due to the fact that the left brain exactly handles language, the ancestor's heredity of speech sounds is accomplished.

To be sure, the aforementioned discovery remains to definitely note that the "ancestral brain" can pass down speech sounds, it however does not exclude this, either. As is said, "to store all the information that the ancestors passed down to later generations via genetic factors", since it is "all the information", it is supposed to encompass the information of speech sounds.

Does language have biological properties? Furthermore, does language have linguistic genes? The existence of the former makes possible that of the latter. Lenneberg (1964) studied the biological foundation of language from which it can be seen that **language has biological properties, which offers biological support to the discovery of linguistic genes**. Based on the fact that Lenneberg early believed that linguistic competence has the properties independent of other cognitive capacities, there are linguistic genes, and that language is controlled by genes, Chomsky presented a presumption that linguistics is ultimately a branch of psychology and biology. The two disciplines both aim to study the linguistic factors relevant to human body, but there is still a long way before they reach the genuine biological study of linguistics due to the limitations of present research means and conditions. Seen from the survey of current scientific fruits (notably around 2000), the deciphering of genetic codes in the sphere of biology has accomplished much (say, some smart businessmen have begun to sell "genetic medicines"). In this connection, then, it is not a dream to finish the deciphering of linguistic genes at the end of the twenty-first century. According to some literatures, there are astounding similarities between linguistic and biological codings both of which form a set of delicate structural systems by means of some numerable elements and a series of complex combinations.[17] Niels Kaj Jerne the biologist who won the Nobel Prize called his theory "generative grammar", which means that biological and linguistic phenomena are controlled by similar rules. The similarity between linguistic and biological phenomena indeed exists.

6. **The memory and reproducibility of DNA**. All the matters in the cosmos have memory: the photo remembers human images, the annual rings of the tree remember its age, the livestock's teeth record its age, the geological levels remember the earth's age, the artificial products record human thoughts, the computer remembers the signals input by human beings, and so on and so forth. "The memorization of matters contributes to cosmos holography."[18] "Without the memorizing structure as such, any occasionally happening complexity (complex things?) would disappear as occasionally."[19] Some diseases such as myopia, mental disorder, etc., might appear in foregone generations so long as the next generation remembers them, so, why can't the memory of the sense

[17]Yuan (1998).

[18]Wang and Yan (1995, p. 170).

[19]Balandin (1982, p. 22). Also cf. Wang and Yan (1995, p. 224).

of sound as a physiological phenomenon as well? A fortiori, DNA having high memorizing and self-replicating capacities can remember the sense of (foreign) sound. This is the internal foundation for the next generation to activate the speech sounds. Memory without reproduction is not sufficient. DNA has fairly strong reproducing capacity, which is manifested first and foremost in its capacity to continuously replicate itself. "Human embryo repeats the history of biological evolution exactly because human DNA records the information of the history as such hence reproduces it during the developing process of the embryo. This memory is exactly the cause to the development and evolution of all things."[20] **DNA's capacity to record and reproduce information is exactly the internal evidence that the senses of sound (including the foreign one) are stored and appear in foregone generations**.

7. **The law of holographic repetition of recognition**. This law means: "The progression of each sound individual's recognition is a microcosm of the evolving history of human recognition, a rapid and brief repetition of it. Since all the information of the latter is condensed into the former, we call this the law of holographic repetition of recognition."[21] Its physiological foundation is this: in human brain, the history of human beings is also accumulated, and the holographic repetition of recognition is produced on the basis of human brain's repetition of its history. In this vein, the accumulation of the sense of sound of the older generation will be reproduced in the brain of a sound younger generation, namely, the younger generation condenses and repeats the sense of sound of the older one.

That which supports the law of holographic repetition of recognition is **the conservation law of cosmic information**. This law indicates, "All the information in a system will not disappear by reason of the collapse of the latter; but rather, it will merely jump in terms of the energy level. That is to say, when a system collapses, its information will jump, in the form of holographic quanta, to a latent state of information and will exist in a new fashion in a new system or spacial locus. Even if the new system collapses also, the holographic quanta will not disappear but will jump again, according to its laws, to another system. The information is conserved, just that the original of the information might jump implicitly or explicitly in terms of energy level."[22] The conservation law of information definitely proves that the sense of sound will not disappear along with the death of its host: when a person dies (i.e., "a system collapses"), the information of the sense of sound will hide in the form of holographic quanta in the brains of his younger generation; even when the younger generation die also (i.e., "a new system collapses"), the holographic quanta of the sense of sound will not disappear but will hide again in the brains of the still younger generation (i.e., "jump into another system again"). As information, the sense of sound is conserved.

---

[20] Wang and Yan (1995, p. 224).

[21] Wang and Yan (1995, pp. 157–161).

[22] Wang and Yan (1995, p. 307).

Recently, I got a "case" of aphasia (it is a case in the eyes of a doctor but here it is a proof of the activation of the sense of sound transmitted from the foregone generations), which can act as a proof that **the sense of foreign sound (all the senses of sound) of the older generation can be inherited to the brains of the younger (consanguineous or non-consanguineous) one**.

According to the special dispatch of the Xinhua News Agency in the evening of January 29, 1998:

> A rare case of language mutation was reported in Lizhong Hospital of Taibei. The patient was a woman aged 40 or so. Originally, she could not speak any foreign language except for fluent Chinese. One morning, nevertheless, after a fairly tiring workday, she suddenly turned into a "foreigner" when she woke up, that is, she could no longer speak fluent Chinese but began to speak a foreign language. The hospital performed an overall examination of her but failed to find aphasia or language barrier. It was reported that a similar case emerged in Scotland before. The medical sphere of Taiwan says that aphasia is greatly related to the cortical lesions. The position of cortical lesions is usually at the cerebral cortex, but this case occurs at the lamina basalis. As to this, the medical sphere cannot explain much and will go on exploring.[23]

Primarily speaking, there are more than one case[24] (e.g., it also emerged in Scotland before) of aphasia (we tentatively call it a disease), which merits consideration.

There can be two explanations with respect to this rare aphasia. First, the sense of foreign sound of the older one or more (consanguineous) generations originally latent in her brain was abruptly activated. This is good news: going on the research, we might create a manifesting method of the sense of foreign sound in foregone generations. Secondly, if there is no one in her consanguineous older one or more generations who could speak a foreign language, it can be concluded that the sense of foreign sound of her older non-consanguineous generation or of another person is called out in her brain.

Now we go further into the second situation: why can a person's sense of foreign sound also hide in the brain of another non-consanguineous person (being contemporary or belonging to the younger generation)? The law of cosmos holography and the system theory can both explain this. Let us come to the law of cosmos holography first. The part is holographic with, and embraces all the information of, the whole. This is a most fundamental and important principle qua the foundation of the edifice of the theory of cosmos holography, which is stressed by me from the beginning to the end of the whole book. The individual person is holographic with and embraces all the information of the whole human beings. Therefore, the sense of sound of other people might be repeated in the individual brain of a non-consanguineous person. It is repetition rather than flying in from outside. When it is "repetition", the law of cosmos holography can offer a very acceptable explanation; when it is "flying in from

---

[23] See "A woman becomes a foreigner after one night's sleep". In *Yangcheng Evening News*, January 30, 1998, page 2.

[24] The latest news to my knowledge is, an English woman suddenly could speak four languages after suffering aphasia for three months (June 21, 2020).

outside", namely, flying in a person's brain from another one, it would become inconceivable. There is no need to fly in from outside. Anyone has already embraced all the information of the whole human beings. It is merely due to a particular serendipity and stimulation that the Taiwan woman's latent sense of sound was triggered and activated when she woke up from a sleep after a tiring day.

Now we come to the system theory for explanation. The organic connection of the system tells us that the factors of a system interact, and are interconnected, with one another. Insofar as any holistic system is concerned, the connection among its factors is organic. The principle of organic connection of the system covers the organic connections among the factors within a system (here it refers to a human being) on the one hand, and those between the system and the external environment (here it refers to other contemporaries or to others of the older one or more generations) on the other. The connection with the external environment is the open system in the ordinary sense, namely, its exchange with the external environment on material, energy, and information have corresponding input and output, and quantitive increase and decrease. This trait is very crucial for us to understand the gist of general system theory. Due to the fact that the open system makes information exchange with the external world, it has the tendency to resist the coming of death. **If it is not strange that the properties belonging to monkeys emerge on human bodies (there are a large quantity of facts to prove this) and cross the border as regards type and generation, it is all the less strange that the sense of foreign sound stored in a person's brain emerges in the brain of another one insomuch as it is the informational exchange between subsystems**.

This case of aphasia is encouraging. The reason is very clear: if the non-consanguineous individual can also inherit the sense of sound of the older generation or contemporaries, it would be more understandable that the consanguineous younger generation can store the sense of sound of the older one.

It can be said that **aphasia is not a disease but the activation in foregone generations or contemporary transference of the sense of sound**.

8. **Cognitive science admits that linguistic competence has biological heredity**. According to cognitive science, "The competence to grasp a language is related to hardwares, namely, it relies on the major center for language in the cerebral cortex and its motor center manipulating vocal organs; this notwithstanding, which kind of language is spoken is determined by the cultural environment. Therefore, linguistic competence is biologically genetic whereas specific language structure is produced during the cultural evolution."[25] Here there is an important proposition: "Linguistic competence is biologically genetic". The biological heritage of linguistic competence presupposes the latent possibility of the heritage of the sense of sound. After all, how could we talk about the biological heritage of linguistic competence if it were impossible for the speech sounds to be inherited? Language system cannot be abstract, inaudible, or uncatchable; rather, **it is embedded in speech sounds and syntax**. Moreover, syntax is ultimately corroborated via speech. **Given that the child can say something**

[25]Zhao (1994, p. 188).

without being taught by the adults, this proves that he/she has early had the sense of sound and has been brewing it, and it is just that the sense of sound will be activated at some time, by some condition.

This hardened constructive process, namely, the accumulation of the sense of sound and the crystallization of the heredity can be condensed and stored in a person's brain, is completely identical to the mechanism in which billions of years of biological evolutionary processes are condensed into the developing process of a biological individual.

It will be of extraordinary significance to induce the sense of sound transmitted in foregone generations. The successful inducement as such means that human beings' linguistic (to acquire native language and to learn foreign languages) and musical competences would be greatly advanced. The direct result would greatly advance the whole human beings' intelligence, promote human behaviors into the pioneering stage of career in advance, and greatly improve the civilizational progression of the whole humankind.

Nonetheless, this project goes beyond the reach of linguists. Linguists can act as a guide of it, say, to present some theories and presuppositions (e.g., as was noted in this book, **it stands to reason on theory that the sense of sound can be activated in foregone generations**), the direct tasks and the determinate work, nevertheless, would have to be accomplished by biologists and geneticists. Their assignment is to **reveal in toto the mechanism turning the implicit state of the sense of foreign sound into an explicit one**.

The trains of thought of this project might be as follows:

1. to clarify how the sense of sound is stored;
2. to explore the specific cerebral place in which the sense of sound is stored (the train of thought of the "ancestral brain" can be taken for reference);
3. to clarify how the sense of sound is inherited;
4. to seek the mechanism distilling and activating the sense of sound.

2 Robots Cannot Have Human-like Intelligence and Language

Many science fictions and films are trying to preach that the top robot would have human-like intelligence and language.

I argue that such a prediction cannot be reached from the perspective of the theory of holography.

Let us start from a famous argument——Chinese room argument.[26]

"Chinese room argument" refers to the debate relevant to strong artificial intelligence (Strong AI for short). Strong AI is such a presupposition: a digital computer

[26]Cf. Wilson and Keil (1999, p. 115); John R. Searle, *Computational Theory of Mind; Functionalism; Intentionality; Mental Representation (1980) Minds, Brains and Programs, Behavioral and Brain Sciences*, vol. 3 (together with 27 peer commentaries and author's reply).

properly programmed, rightly input and output, and having passed the Turing Test (a hypothetical test of computer that can evade from the constraint of the storage capacity) necessarily has a human-like mind. The thought of "Strong AI" is, **the implemented program by itself is constitutive of having a mind**. "Weak AI" is such a presupposition as to how the computer as such plays the same role in cognitive researches for example of any other sub-discipline. This is a useful device for the imitation and research of the intelligent process. Nevertheless, the programmed computer cannot automatically warrant the presentation of the intelligence state in the computer. "Weak AI" does not run counter to "Chinese room argument".

This argument is performed according to the following consideration. Suppose that an English native speaker who does not know Chinese is kept in a closed room in which there are a lot of boxes of Chinese signs (as the base of materials) and a guidebook telling how to operate these signs (programs); suppose again that a person outside the closed room hands in some other Chinese signs, viz., some questions designed with Chinese (input) strange to the person inside the room; and suppose still again that the person in the closed room can ultimately decode the Chinese signs via following the program guide hence can correctly answer those questions (output). **This program enables the person kept in the closed room to pass the Turing Test of understanding Chinese, but he does not know any Chinese character at all**.

The key point of this argument is, to understand Chinese, one must implement an appropriate program, which is the basis. If the man in the room does not understand Chinese on the basis of implementing the appropriate program for understanding it, neither will any other digital computer. The reason is: **the computer per se will not have that which human beings do not have**.

A bigger structure of the Chinese room argument can be stated into the derivative arguments of the following three presuppositions:

First, the implemented program is purely formal or syntactic insofar as it is defined. (An implemented program, say, that performed by the person in the Chinese room, is defined purely by formal or syntactic sign operation. "The same implemented program" definitely regulates a level of equivalence purely belonging to the syntactic operation and being independent of the implementation of the latter.)

Secondly, the human-like consideration has intelligent or semantic content. (For instance, to consider or understand a language, you have to have knowledge going beyond the syntax, and you have to connect some meanings, thoughts with words or signs.)

Thirdly, syntax is itself insufficient to semantics, and it cannot create the latter, either. (The sign operation purely defined by form or syntax is itself incapable of guaranteeing the co-presentation of any thought and sign operation.)

Conclusion: **the implemented program is incapable of creating and generating human-like intelligence. The "Strong AI" is false**.

May I ask: why did the person in the closed Chinese room pass the Turing Test of understanding Chinese but remain to know Chinese? The answer is, **he merely knew the formal syntax in the program but did not have the practical intelligent or semantic content connected with the vocabulary of a language (when a speaker knows it)**. So long as you compare the person in the closed Chinese room with the same person answering questions in English namely his native language, you will see it toto coelo. In either situation, he can pass the Truing Test. Observed from his perspective, nevertheless, there are great differences. That language which he knows is English rather than Chinese. **When answering the Chinese questions strange to him in the closed Chinese room, his behaviors were nothing but those of a digital computer**; when answering questions in his native language namely English, he behaved as an English speaker with normal capacity. This indicates that the Turing Test is incapable of differentiating between **real mental capacity and the simulation of it**. Simulation is no duplication, but the Turing Test cannot tell the difference between them.

According to Robert A. Wilson and Frank C. Keil, all the attempts to reply the Chinese room argument remain to be successful. Presumably, the most popular attempt is systematic: "While the man in the Chinese room does not understand Chinese, he is not the whole system. He is but the central processing unit, a simple cog in the large mechanism that includes room, books, etc. It is the whole room, the whole system, that understands Chinese, not the man."[27] The response to the systematic reply is, albeit the person cannot transfer from syntax to semantics, the whole closed room cannot, either. The whole closed room also cannot attach the thought or intelligent content to the formal signs. When you can imagine that the whole person is totally internalized into this closed room, you would see it. He remembers the rule guide and material base, the whole mental arithmetic process and, moreover, he works outside the room. At any rate, neither this person nor any subsystem within his body can attach meanings to the formal signs.

For a long time, the Chinese room has been misunderstood that it could explain many things beyond reach. The following three aspects are what it cannot explain:

1. The closed Chinese room cannot explain "The machine cannot think". Contrariwise, human brain is a machine, and it can think.
2. The closed Chinese room does not aim to explain "The computer cannot think". Contrariwise, a thing can be a computer that can think. If a computer is a machine capable of implementing calculation, all the normal people are computers that can think. The closed Chinese room indicates that **the calculation defined by Alan Turing and other formal-sign operations per se cannot produce thought**.
3. The closed Chinese room does not indicate that only human brain can think. As is known, **thinking is provoked by the biological process inside the brain**, so that there is no logical hinderance to make a machine capable of duplicating human brain's inferring capacity for the sake of producing the thinking process. The crux is, nevertheless, **to produce the biological process of thinking, the machine must be capable of duplicating the particular inferring capacity of human brain**. **Just as is shown by the closed Chinese room, merely moving the formal signs is insufficient to guarantee the inferring capacity as such**.

[27] Wilson and Keil (1999, p. 115).

The conclusion as regards the afore-mentioned "The computer can think" is correct. It also embraces this argument: the computer can only perform limited thinking. This argument is proved by cognitive linguistics. Cognitive linguistics is against the objectivist cognitive view, and its fundamental creeds are: (1) Thinking, i.e., cognitive or mental process, is the mechanic operation of the abstract signs, and it has the properties of algorithmic in the mathematical sense. (2) Mind is an abstract machine the sign-operating style of which essentially resembles that of the computer, to wit., the operation of calculation method. (3) It can be inferred from afore that the machine that can merely operate signs can also have the capacity for thinking and inference. Undoubtedly, the above three creeds support the robot's limited thinking capacity. These three creeds alone can lead to the computer, the robot, and the advanced robots. (4) Thinking is abstract and disembodied in that it is independent of any constraint of human body, and of human beings' perceptive and nervous systems. The computer thinking can make use of this cognitive creed, but there is the danger of abuse. This is because a slight carelessness in the previous parlance might lead to this absurd conclusion: human-like thinking (and language) is independent of human beings' perceptive and nervous systems.

Now let us come to the inspirations offered to us by the debates around the closed Chinese room.

The hypothesis of "Strong AI" is, the implemented program can create and generate human-like intelligence by itself. This train of thought is considerably attractive to many a people, particularly to cognitive scientists. In their views, the computer is more than a calculator; rather, it is analogized to human mind, and it is also a formal model capable of producing intelligent behaviors. Be that as it may, the behaviors of the subject in the closed Chinese room are no more than those of a digital computer. In other words, the person is equivalent to a computer. Facts have proved that albeit the subject knowing no Chinese passed the Turing Test and answered the questions designed with Chinese signs, he did not know any word or character of Chinese. Inferred from the experimental results on the human being to those on the computer, we can see that when a human being is faced with such results, it would be impossible for a digital computer to have human-like intelligence. **A fortiori, when the computer does not have human-like intelligence, it cannot produce linguistic competence solely founded on human intelligence**. What does this mean? **It means that the implemented program cannot produce human-like intelligence (and language) by itself**.

What are the problems?

One of the problems is, the implemented program of the digital computer is purely formal or syntactic in terms of definition. An implemented program, like that performed by the subject in the closed Chinese room, is purely defined by the formal or syntactic sign operation. Please note: human brain's thinking is supposed to have intelligent or semantic contents. For instance, to think about or understand a language, a human being is supposed to have knowledge going beyond syntax, namely, he/she must associate some meanings and thoughts with words or signs. The digital computer on the other hand cannot do this, namely, it cannot associate the contents or meanings of thought with signs, albeit its operation speed is considerably high. As is known, syntax alone is insufficient to semantics, and it cannot create the latter. This is because **the sign operation purely defined by form or syntax cannot guarantee the co-presentation of any content of thought or sign operation**. For instance, the string of signs of "$\because 3 + X = 8, \therefore X = 5$" cannot appear together with any content of thought, say, are 3, 8, 5 chicken or tigers or whatever? Is the concluded 5 the expenditure or whatever? No one knows. Seen in this vein, Dreyfus's strongest negation of the idea of mechanic equivalence between human brain and the computer is indeed reasonable.

The second problem is, there is another essential reason as to why the conclusion drawn from the experiment of closed Chinese room is "defined by Alan Turing and others as formal symbol manipulation, is not by itself constitutive of thinking"[28]: thinking is provoked by the neurobiological process inside human brain whereas **no computer can produce the neurobiological process**. "The point, however, is that any such machine would have to be able to duplicate the specific causal powers of the brain to produce the biological process of thinking. The mere shuffling of formal symbols is not sufficient to guarantee these causal powers, as the Chinese room shows."[29] The computer incapable of producing the neurobiological process loses the biological foundation of being completely holographic with human brain. To be sure, the computer imitating human nervous can produce partially holographic state with human brain (e.g., both of them can operate calculation); however, the holography in a system is hierarchic and is realized at different levels. A computer incapable of producing the neurobiological process is not at the same level with a flesh-and-blood human brain (just like the tadpoles are not at the same level with human beings), hence the mutual reflection and embracement of information cannot be realized in toto but only partially (the mutual reflection and embracement of information between human beings and the tadpoles is also partially realized). This is the reason why even the top computer (e.g., the hypothetical Strong AI machine) is incapable of obtaining human-like intelligence and, furthermore, linguistic competence. To corroborate this, I can also give the theories of cognitive linguistics for clarification. Directed upon the fact that the objectivist cognitive model is incapable of describing human mental activities and relevant human languages, Lakoff (1987) and Johnson (1987) presented "experientialist realism". It is primarily realism that denies pure solipsism and mentalism but attaches particular emphasis to experiences. Human cognitive process and activities described by experientialist cognitive theory are as follows: (1) The concept of basic-level and image schemas (the two most important concepts). (2) The mental process of imaginative projection, namely, the process whence the experiences perceived by the body are converted in the form of structure into the abstract cognitive models by virtue of mechanisms such as schematization, metaphor, metonymy, categorization, or something.[30] (3) The fundamental cognitive process is composed of focusing, scanning, putting upward, foreground-background

[28]Wilson and Keil (1999, p. 116).

[29]Wilson and Keil (1999, p. 116).

[30]Cf. Lakoff (1987).

transformation, view transform.[31] (4) Mental space. On the whole, this cognitive view attaches great importance to the body's position in human cognition. Albeit the computer has a body (the physical properties like hardwares and appearance, color, weight, etc.), it cannot produce experiences about itself. Its body is merely a carrier of calculating process and function (the softwares, i.e., programs or calculating methods) but cannot promote or decide the latter. So to speak, in terms of content, the calculating process and function is completely independent of the body. Apparently, this relationship differs from the body-mind relationship of human beings. It can be said that one of the essential differences between human brain and the computer is that the function of the former relies to a great extent on the body to which it is attached and on the interactional relationship between the body and the reality."[32] This is to say that the computer cannot sense its existence, as opposed to human body (its self-sense can be specifically manifested in the pain, itch, cold, hot, etc., of a very small spot). The computer's body can be completely separated from its softwares whereas a human being's body and mind cannot be separated: without the body, there would not be the human being, nor would there be his/her thinking and mental activities. What is human body? It is blood, flesh, and neurons. Does the computer (the so-called strong intelligent robot) have these constituents? What is the computer's body? It is a matter without blood, flesh, or neurons. Natural language is the product of human beings' blood, flesh, and neurons. On this account, I argue, **the top priority is that cognitive model attaches great importance to bodily experiences**.

In addition, the robot is not a natural product of the cosmos but an artificial "baby", namely, it is not originally embedded in the big Chinese box of the cosmos. To be sure, human beings make the robot imitate some of their functions according to their own structure, they however fail to, and it is impossible also, install human-like biological neurons on the computer. In Sect. 1 of Chapter 4, "The holographic relation between language and cognition", I mentioned the similar view. "The logic and cultural evolution mechanisms take shape in a new paradigm of artificial life. The emulation similar to life behavior is also a kind of artificial life. It is composed of many systems of semi-autonomous entities of human, and the partial communications between semi-autonomous entities are controlled by a set of simple rules.."[33] This situation however does not indicate that the semi-autonomous substantial human made via simulation is a human being with blood and flesh. What's more, cognitive scientists themselves also realize that the simulation as such is merely a "life-like behavior", a simulation, and is merely "semi-autonomous". The strong intelligent robot being strongly intelligent notwithstanding, the holography between it and human brain is several levels apart but not at one level.

It seems that this conclusion—the robot cannot have human-like intelligence and language—is merely relevant to the computer (say, whether or not the robot has human-like intelligence and language), it is however of significant inspirations to

[31]Cf. Langacker (1987).

[32]Cf. Zhang (1998, pp. 40–41).

[33]Langton (1988).

the direction as regards the civilization development of human society. In our age, scientists want to do everything, namely, they merely want to show, as quickly as possible, what they can do, but do not necessarily consider what they should do. More than moral and ethical factors, there are also some other aspects for consideration. For instance, after the animal cloning was successful, some scientists wanted to clone human beings as early as possible. Nevertheless, the heads of many big powers of the world successively issued the statement that they did not support the scientists to clone human beings lest there be social instability and moral as well as ethical troubles. Human beings only concern development without considering the sequels, which will promote the sharp sward of sciences to stab themselves. Any science and technology whatsoever is a double-edged sward that can bring both benefits and damages to human beings. The damages may be big enough to destroy human beings. This is because the robots with human-like intelligence and language will also fiercely conflict even battle with human beings for their own interests (e.g., subsistence and development), and the war as such would be unprecedentedly tragic (as is shown in scientific fictions or films). To this connection, when it comes to the developing direction of human civilization, the conclusion should be this: our civilization cannot be realized on the basis of scientism (science is beneficial but scientism is inadvisable). Our civilization is by no means the slave of science. The science without considering human spirit is inadvisable. We should take a cautious attitude toward the so-called strong intelligent robot. The point now is not whether or not we should develop robots with human-like intelligence. The experiment of the closed Chinese room has corroborated that the hypothesis of Strong AI cannot be realized. The essential reason lies in the fact that the holographic relationship between human beings and the so-called intelligent robots cannot be realized at the same level insomuch as the former has neurobiological cells while the latter has not. Be that as it may, in terms of information, human beings and intelligent robots can be embedded in and corroborate with one another at different levels.

References

Balandin, P. K., *Time, earth, and human brain.* Beijing: Science Press, 1982.

Chomsky, A. N., *Linguistic theory and language learning, aspects of the theory of syntax.* Cambridge: The Massachusetts Institute of Technology Press, 1965.

Chomsky, A. N., *Knowledge of language: Its nature, origin, and use.* New York: Praeger, 1986.

Foreign Language Research (Ed.), *Introduction to Chomsky's theory of language.* Harbin: Heilongjiang University, 1982.

Halle. Morris, Speculations about the representation of words in memory. In *Phonetic Linguistics: Essays in Honor of Pete Ladefoged.* Ed. Victoria A. Fromkin, Academic Press Inc., 1985.

Johnson, M., *The body in the mind: The bodily basis of meaning, imagination, and reason.* Chicago, University of Chicago Press, 1987.

Lakoff, G., *Women, fire, and dangerous things.* Chicago: University of Chicago Press, 1987.

Langacker, R., *Foundations of cognitive grammar*, Vol. 1. Palo Alto: Stanford University Press, 1987.

Langton, C. G., Artificial life, in Langton, C. G. (ed.), *Artificial life*, 1988.

Qian. Guanlian, Calling out the sense of sound. In *Foreign Language Research*, 1990 (5).
Wang. Cunzhen &Yan. Chunyou, *The theory of cosmic holographic unity*. Jinan: Shandong People's Publishing House, 1995.
Wilson, Robert A. & Frank. Keil, *The MIT encyclopedia of the cognitive science*, 1999.
Xu. Youyu, Zhou. Guoping, Chen. Jiaying & Shang. Jie, *Language and philosophy——Comparative studies between modern Anglo-American and traditional German-French ones*. Beijing: SDX Joint Publishing Company, 1996.
Yuan. Yulin, The comparison between the codings of linguistic information and biological information. In *Contemporary Linguistics*, 1998 (2).
Zhang. Min, *Cognitive linguistics and Chinese noun phrases*. Beijing: China Social Sciences Publishing House, 1998.
Zhang. Zengchang, Zhu. Yuanzhen, Zhu. Suping & Wang. Shouzhong, New theories of the function of the right and left hemispheres of human brain. In *Invention & Innovation*, 1988 (4).
Zhao. Nanyuan, *Cognitive science and the general theory of evolution*. Beijing: Tsing Hua University Press, 1994.

Part V
Conclusion

Chapter 10
From Science to Philosophy of Language

Abstract The theory of language holography and Western philosophy of language seems to be different but come to the same end: to observe the world structure from the linguistic one.

Keywords Natural sciences · Philosophy of language · Linguistic turn

1. The theory of language holography introduced from natural sciences

What on earth did this book do? From all the chapters—particularly the Introduction to Chapter 1, i.e., "The harmony of cosmos, human body, and language," Chapter 2 "The overall frame of the theory of language holography," Chapter 5 "The outer rootstock of the different characteristics of language," Chapter 6 "The outer rootstock of different theories of language," and Chapter 7 "Linguistic evidence for the law of cosmos holography," we can clearly see that this book only did one thing: to observe the cosmos in language, and to observe language in the cosmos; differently put: **to observe the world in language, and to observe language in the world**.

The assertion that the theory of language holography is a philosophy exactly starts from this recognition.

2. Western philosophy of language developing from ontology and epistemology

Is there a philosophy holding that the world can be seen in language? Yes, there is. The third historical phase of Western philosophy, namely, the philosophy of language, is a case in point. It developed from ontological recognition.

In Section 2 of Chapter 2, i.e., "Different linguistic directions of Chinese and Western philosophies," of my *Language: the Last Homestead of Human Beings*, I analyzed the reason why philosophy is attached to language in the West from the three aspects as follows:

To begin, philosophers after the linguistic turn believed that to analyze language was to study philosophy, namely, to study the ontology to which they showed special preference, the external world, or reality. This is a fundamental point as regards the interconnection between Western philosophy and linguistic analysis. As to this point,

G. Qian, *The Theory of Language Holography*,
https://doi.org/10.1007/978-981-16-2039-3_10

I have discussed it in detail,[1] so I will not repeat the discussions here. In this respect, Dummett's assertion can be used as a typical model: the two beliefs distinguishing analytic philosophy and other philosophical schools are: first, the philosophical interpretations of thought can be obtained via the linguistic ones; secondly, the overall and in-depth interpretations of thought can only be obtained via the philosophical interpretations of language.[2]

In the second place, Western philosophy was constrained by formal logic hence accepted the guidance from mathematics and scientific knowledge; on the other hand, logics, mathematics, etc., could not but be helped by signs, and, a fortiori, they headed for language analysis. **Western philosophy is characterized by the highly symbolized, logicalized, and rigorous formal demonstration, which sowed the seed of its heading for language analysis. Thus was caused linguistic turn**. Given that there are so many examples in this regard, I merely give one more here: Frege is considered as the founder of analytic philosophy, the person having comprehensive influences on philosophy of language. To analyze his work is representative in terms of answering why Western philosophy headed for language analysis. Frege tried to reduce the calculating method to logic, which provided the fundamental contributions to formal logic and the philosophy of mathematics. His concept of logic guided him to study some concepts (e.g., the concept of meaning) which were the foundation of language study. As to meaning, he distinguished sense and reference. Sense is the semantic content relevant to the sign; reference is the object (thing) designated by the sign. He was also the first man who employed such concepts as "the force of language," presupposition, and so on, and who dealt with the analysis of the sentences expressing the propositional attitude. That which is based on the analytic linguistic turn is a basic concept, i.e., the concept called by Dummett "the extrusion of thoughts from the mind." In the context of this concept, a thought is the meaning of a sentence and is grasped by a mental act; nevertheless, it itself is not a mental content in that the sense (as opposed to subjective expression) can enter into communicative process hence is objective. This belief bestows a non-psychological direction on the conceptual and propositional analyses. **This direction soon turned into the linguistic trend among analytic philosophers. To parse a sentence, one must correspondingly parse the thought it expresses. In this line, to understand a structure of thought means to understand the semantic interrelations between corresponding sentence components**. This passage is virtually a key to the clear understanding of analytic philosophy, even of the philosophy of language.

Thirdly, **the main "problem" of Western philosophical studies is manifested in "be, beings, what it is, being" that are gradually generated from Western languages**. In my *Language: the Last Homestead of Human Beings*, I used a large quantity of facts (see Chapters 1 and 2) to show that the first phase of Western philosophy being called "ontology" is due to the fact that its foundation of gradual generation is Western languages, and the most intuitive examples are the Greek *on* (ontology came from it), the English t*o be, being, Being*, and the German *sein, Sein,*

[1] Cf. Qian (1999a, 2000, 1999b).

[2] Cf. Dummett (1975, pp. 97–138; 1976, pp. 67–137).

seiend, das Seiendes. The Greek *on* (equivalent to *being* in English) corresponds to the English *being* (participle), *Being* (gerund), and to the German *sein* (infinitive), *Sein* (gerund), *seiend* (participle), *das Seiendes* (the noun converted from the participle).

From the previous three aspects, we can get an overall clue: Western philosophers of language show particular preference to language analysis merely because they can find the world's structure therein. In other words, Western philosophers are so devoted to language analysis merely because **language (its structure, reference, meaning, etc.) enables them to see the world, and the structure of linguistic substances can reveal the structure of the reality**, and hence the age-old philosophical problems left by ontology and epistemology can be settled, e.g., What is there?

Is the view as such, namely, language enables them to see the world, held and confirmed by Western philosophers of language?

In the introduction to *Modern Philosophy of Language*, Maria Baghramian the editor thus notes, "Philosophy of language is an attempt to understand the nature of language and its **relationship with speakers, their thoughts, and the world,**" "Philosophers of language are also concerned with questions about **the relationship between language and the world,**" and "Their concern was with language as an abstract entity that expresses thought and **whose structure**, if analyzed correctly, **can reveal the structure of reality** and they had no, or very little, interest in the actual use of language in its social context."[3] That which merits explanation here is, in the eyes of Western philosophers, "reality" is identical to "world" on meaning.

In *Oxford Dictionary of Philosophy*, S. Blackblum points out in the item "philosophy of language," "Philosophy of language is the general attempt to understand the components of a working language, the relationship the understanding speaker has to its elements, and the relationship they bear to the world."[4]

The discussions afore corroborate two points: first, Western philosophy of language tries to observe in language structure the world's structure and the relationship between language and the world. Secondly, Western philosophy of language developed from ontology and epistemology.

3. The idea of Heaven–human integration upheld by Chinese philosophy will necessarily lead to "Heaven-language integration"

Chinese philosophy upholds the idea of Heaven–human integration, which is a universally accepted assertion. De facto, in the introduction to Chapter 1 ("The harmony of cosmos, human body, and language"), Section 4 of Chapter 2 ("The law of the cosmos holography: the first theory of foundation-stone"), and Section 1 of Chapter 3 ("Some key terms of the law of cosmos holography"), **the trinity of Heaven, human beings, and language** was already clearly demonstrated.

In *Daodejing*道德经, Laozi thus says, "*Dao* is primal, Heaven primal, Earth primal, and human primal." The four are interconnected. How to prove this? He again says, "Human follows Earth, Earth follows Heaven, Heaven follows *Dao*, and *Dao* follows Nature." The four are integrated by means of the successive "follow"s.

---

[3]Baghramian (1999).

[4]*Oxford Dictionary of Philosophy* (1994, p. 211).

According to Feng Youlan, "The top accomplishment of the sage is to be individually identical to the cosmos," and "That which a person should do is to cultivate him/herself and maintain the selfless pure experiences continuously and constantly so as to be integrated with the cosmos."[5]

Chinese philosophy failing to take the approach of language analysis[6] notwithstanding, in the illumination of the philosophical spirit of Heaven–human integration, when human beings are integral with Heaven, it is merely a one-click matter that language is integrated with Heaven.

Conclusion

Seen from the spirit of either Western or Chinese philosophy, the theory of language holography can be said a philosophical idea, a fulfilling philosophy of language.

It is after tramping through the long journey of ontological and epistemological phases that Western philosophy carried out the linguistic turn and headed for the philosophy of language; the theory of language holography on the other hand comes directly from sciences (the law of biology holography, the law of cosmos holography, and the system theory), and hence it is also a philosophy of language.

If we compare "Heaven" to the world, the cosmos, or the reality, then the theory of language holography is the theory of "Heaven-language integration" in the true sense of the word.

References

Baghramian, Maria, *Modern philosophy of language*. Washington D. C.: Counterpoint, 1999.

Dummett, M., What is a theory of meaning? (part1). In S. Guttenplan (ed.) *Mind and language*. Oxford: Oxford University Press, 1975, pp. 97–138.

Dummett, M., What is a theory of meaning? (part2). In G. Evans & J. McDowell (eds.) *Truth and meaning*. Oxford: Oxford University Press, 1976, pp. 67–137.

Feng, Youlan, *A short history of chinese philosophy*. Beijing: Peking University Press, 1985, pp. 6, 9.

Oxford Dictionary of Philosophy. Oxford: Oxford University Press, 1994, p. 211.

Qian, Guanlian, Language researches in orbit round philosophy of the West. In J*ournal of Foreign Languages*, 1999a (6).

Qian, Guanlian, The philosophical origins of pragmatics. In *Foreign languages and their teaching*, 1999b (6).

Qian, Guanlian, Language researches in orbit round philosophy of the West. In J*ournal of PLA Foreign Languages University*, 2000 (1).

[5]Youlan (1985, pp. 6, 9).

[6]For the details, cf. section 2 of Chapter 2, "Different linguistic directions of Chinese and Western philosophies", in my *Language: The last homestead of human beings*.

Postscript

When I Wake Up

When I finished *Pragmatics in Chinese Culture* in 1997, I began to think about and develop *Language: the Last Homestead of Human Beings* (*Homestead* for short hereafter), taking for reference the essays as regards the third phase of Western philosophy, namely, analytical philosophy and the philosophy of language. After I started, I found that a chapter, i.e., "The theory of language holography", was not coincident with the main idea of *Homestead*, which, in the terminology of cognitive linguistics, meant that something went wrong at the level of categorization or conceptualization. I then confirmed that "the theory of language holography" based on the law of biological holography, the law of cosmos holography, and the system theory were totally different on nature from *Homestead* discussing language and the being of human beings. Therefore, I singled out "the theory of language holography" and developed it into another system, and started such an attempt: to write at the same time two books completely different on nature, to read at the same time two literatures completely different on nature, and to consider at the same time two problems completely different on nature. At first, I worried that in doing so, intertwining difficulties might occur; later, nevertheless, I found that it was exactly these two considerations completely different on nature that guaranteed themselves from interfering and intertwining with one another, and produced an effect of mutual promotion.

In the following days, I continuously took two different literatures for reference, generated new considerations, supplemented the results of the considerations into the two different books, and finally determined them as two different categories of thought. The relevant convenience on obtaining references and writing via the computer enabled my writing speed and efficiency to go far beyond the laborious situation in which I wrote *Aesthetic Linguistics* word after word, paragraph after paragraph, and chapter after chapter.

G. Qian, *The Theory of Language Holography*,
https://doi.org/10.1007/978-981-16-2039-3

The Theory of Language Holography presented to the readers today belongs to the philosophy of language, whereas the *Homestead* finished virtually at the same time is the result of the interdisciplinary study between language and philosophy.

As a matter of fact, from 1997 till now, I have been reading at the same time three completely different types of books. I say so because the book I read before sleep belongs in another type: British and American novels and stories. Almost every night, as I read the book for one or two pages, my eyelids became heavy and I fell asleep shortly afterwards. During some nights, of course, I could not lay down the book and hence there were usually some sleepless nights. These situations are still vivid in my mind, and I write this merely for the sake of telling the experiences in which *The Theory of Language Holography* was written, so I don't think it is nonsense.

At the beginning of the writing, I planned to say something when I reached the postscript; at present when it is finished, nevertheless, I can recall nothing. The passion at the beginning of the trek already converted into the tranquility in the end. It seems that this does not conform to the verse of Mikhail Lermontov, to wit., "…in storm lucked clam and peace", they are however of the same meaning. One's peaceful mind when one reaches the other side is exactly converted, little by little, from the passion at the beginning of the trek.

Trekked, reached, pitched the camp, and settled down. Waking up, one will start a new journey. What is new for the seeking? All the people, from the travelers with definite purposes to those who are fond of thinking, might not have the feeling of belonging to nowhere. That which they do is nothing but turning illusion into reality, nothing into being. ——Interesting as it is, it is very hard; hard as it is, it is very interesting.

QIAN Guanlian

in Dongshou Zhai at the foot of Mt. Baiyun, Guangzhou, April 7, 2001.

Lightning Source UK Ltd.
Milton Keynes UK
UKHW020641050722
405403UK00006B/536

9 789811 620416